The Model as Performance

Performance + Design is a series of monographs and essay collections that explore understandings of performance design and scenography, examining the potential of the visual, spatial, material and environmental to shape performative encounters and to offer sites for imaginative exchange. This series focuses on design both for and as performance in a variety of contexts, including theatre, art installations, museum displays, mega-events, site-specific and community-based performance, street theatre, design of public space, festivals, protests and state-sanctioned spectacle.

Performance + Design takes as its starting point the growth of scenography and the expansion from theatre or stage design to a wider notion of scenography as a spatial practice. As such, it recognizes the recent accompanying interest from a number of converging scholarly disciplines (theatre, performance, art, architecture, design) and examines twenty-first-century practices of performance design in the context of debates about post-dramatic theatre, aesthetic representation, visual and material culture, spectatorship, participation and co-authorship.

SERIES EDITORS

Stephen Di Benedetto
Joslin McKinney
Scott Palmer

Scenography Expanded: An Introduction to Contemporary Performance and Design
Edited by Joslin McKinney and Scott Palmer
978-1-4742-4439-8

The History and Theory of Environmental Scenography: Second Edition
Arnold Aronson
978-1-4742-8396-0

The Model as Performance

Staging Space in Theatre and Architecture

**THEA BREJZEK
AND LAWRENCE WALLEN**

methuen | drama

LONDON · NEW YORK · OXFORD · NEW DELHI · SYDNEY

METHUEN DRAMA
Bloomsbury Publishing Plc
50 Bedford Square, London, WC1B 3DP, UK
1385 Broadway, New York, NY 10018, USA

BLOOMSBURY, METHUEN DRAMA and the Methuen Drama logo
are trademarks of Bloomsbury Publishing Plc

First published in Great Britain 2018
This paperback edition published 2019

Series design: Burge Agency
Cover image: *Digitally Fabricated House for New Orleans in Home Delivery:
Fabricating the Modern Dwelling* at the Museum of Modern Art, New York 2008.
Courtesy Lawrence Sass. Photo © Suzi Camarata Ball.

A catalogue record for this book is available from the British Library.

A catalog record for this book is available from the Library of Congress.

ISBN: HB: 978-1-4742-7138-7
         PB: 978-1-350-09590-8
         ePDF: 978-1-4742-7140-0
         eBook: 978-1-4742-7139-4

Series: Performance and Design

Typeset by Integra Software Services Pvt. Ltd.
Printed and bound in Great Britain

To find out more about our authors and books visit www.bloomsbury.com
and sign up for our newsletters.

Contents

List of Figures

Introduction

Filling a critical research gap, *The Model as Performance* charts new territory by examining the history and development of the physical scale model across theatre and architecture practice from the Renaissance to the present. This constitutes a seminal undertaking whose aim it is to establish the model as an active agent in the making of space within an extended theatre and performance studies and architectural discourse.

There are two associated elements to this project that draws from theory and practice in both disciplines. The first rallies against the prevailing assumption of the model as a second-order object awaiting its realization as a future 'real' building or a 'real' set design, and argues instead for the model to be inherently performative and epistemic. The second originates from a scenographic perspective that focuses on the creation of space through the material artefact, and from a performative paradigm that looks upon cultural practice as performance and argues the architectural and set design model's potential for *cosmopoiesis*, or world-making.

Employing an ontological view, we ask, what the model is, and whether and how knowledge is produced through the model, and we conclude, through our case studies, that models are epistemic tools.

As a result, *The Model as Performance* theorizes the model in theatre and architecture, contextualizing it historically while unfolding a dialogue in relation to it. From theatre, we bring the antithetical notion of the performative to the traditional understanding of the architectural model as fixed and stable. We introduce architecture's established discourse on the model's history, use and terminology to theatre and performance design. In this, we not only articulate the fact that the model and its material and verbal language straddles both disciplines, but also reveal that divisions between architecture's durability and theatre's ephemerality are artificial in terms of drawing out the model's performative potential. This project is positioned within the overall territory of an expanded scenography (Brejzek 2011; McKinney and Palmer 2017) that acknowledges the agency of material and extends this to an articulation of the agency of the model.

Overall, what is proposed here is a new writing of the model's history as a history of agency and performativity that frees the model from its professional pragmatism yet acknowledges its central importance in the design process, and that enables the model in theatre and architecture to be read anew – as an authored, staged and performative space.

We identify as a catalyst for the development and proliferation of the scale model the exploration of one-point perspective in the Italian Renaissance by Filippo Brunelleschi and Leon Battista Alberti and its subsequent codified application. From there on, the model became common practice in architecture and is discussed in the contemporary treatises as both the materialization of an idea and a method of communicating with builders and artisans. At the same time, the scale model is first mentioned in relation to theatre by Sebastiano Serlio as an instrument for testing new perspectival scenery within the dimensions of stage and theatre building.

In design terms, architectural and stage set models emerge through iterations, material experiments and explorations that are elliptical and nonlinear, with most models being displayed as representative, final objects.

Our close examination of the model, however, reveals instances in theatre and architecture where the model defies traditional definition and instead possesses an autonomous status. In this project, we define the autonomous model as an object unto itself that sees no further artefact produced from it. We argue that this type of model is simultaneously referential and self-referential and is neither process-driven nor representational but rather conceptualized and built to be autonomous. The autonomous model no longer represents progress from 'model to reality but from model to model' (Eliasson 2007: 19). It is framed in our project against the background of expanded practices in theatre and architecture and aligned with the disciplines' desire to reflect on conventional modes of making and representation. In the history of theatre, this development is linked to the interpretive mirroring of the world in the confined space of the stage. This project seeks not only to establish the existence of the autonomous model but also to explore its significance to scenography and architecture.

Not every case study discussed in this project fits neatly into the model categories of 'iterative', 'representative' or 'autonomous', and in fact, most of the models discussed belong to more than one category. The overall purpose of this project lies not in a rigid categorical classification of the architectural and scenographical model throughout history, but rather in a pointing towards key models that occupy the blurred territories between the genres and that unfold their performative potentials towards becoming performances in and out of themselves in the immediate interaction with the viewer or participant.

The Model as Performance analyses, in particular, the scenographic strategies of scale, materiality and narrative employed by the autonomous model and its hybrids, and links the specific treatment of these concerns to scenographers' and architects' desire to disrupt and extend conventional modes of function, making, representation and reading.

Critical to the model is the perceptual effect of size rather than scale, and we argue that scale itself is less relevant than the dimensional relationship of the viewer to object or space, and the level of immersion achieved. Material choices depend on the future artefact's programme and function, along with questions of how to reach particular levels of similarity and approximation while at the same time the designer or model-maker not only is aware of but also requires the materials' specific properties and resistances to advance the design during the modelling process. Meanwhile, material choices express design intentions and are a testament of artistic expression. Finally, the embedding of narratives in the model affirms its status as a space of action that may or may not require activation by the viewer.

This project results from the convergence of our working relationship as director and designer with strong interests in the performative rather than representative aspects of models, developed through artistic projects in coalescence with studio-based teaching and scholarly research. Our wish to interrogate not only what the model is but also its performative and discursive potential stems from a long engagement with the model in architectural, theatrical and curatorial practice and in conceptualizing and teaching design studios where the physical scale model continues to be a core discursive component.

The journey towards theoretical engagement with the model began with our exploration of 'double spaces', that is, spaces that exist more than once and that are positioned opposite each other, a category of spaces that are both 'same' and 'other'. The twin churches Santa Maria di Miracoli (from 1675) and Santa Maria di Montesanto (completed in 1681) on Rome's Piazza del Popolo serve as a striking instance for the 'doubling' of an architectural object. Extending our argument, we proposed that 'double spaces' can also exist far apart in time and location, such as van de Beek's *Maison Dom-ino* from 2014 and St John Caruso and Thomas Demand's *Nail House* from 2010, which have become case studies in *The Model as Performance*. In each, the two buildings are visually similar, yet their *doppelgänger* status is realized only with the viewer's simultaneous gaze to both objects, thus opening up a performative field between the two objects and the observing eye. In this case, the double is removed from questions of original versus copy, and instead, it takes on a role where each building claims equal status. Both 'same' and 'other', the double is thus highly referential yet autonomous. Similarly, the autonomous model transcends the model's traditional representational function, collapsing the categories of original and copy, past and present.

Understood as yet another manifestation of the spatial double, the virtual model and its physical manifestation provoke and enable new and complex relationships between the material and non-material worlds, whereby the concepts of time, location, distance and authenticity require new definitions. The increasingly porous edge between physical and virtual spaces – that is, the ubiquity of digital space and its various interfaces with the material world – is accelerating at a speed that from a typological point of view remains too fluid to be central to the arguments set out in *The Model as Performance*. These considerations have therefore been reserved for another publication that will build on the current project in a discussion of the digital model's relationship to the production of reality, its performative potential as distinct from the physical model, material aesthetics and its fabrication methods. Despite the rise of the use and application of digital and virtual models in architecture and scenography, the last decades have seen the rapid development of physical autonomous models made specifically for architecture and scenography exhibitions, evident in contemporary exhibitions and international survey shows such as the Prague Quadrennial of Performance Design and Space and the International Architecture Exhibition of the Venice Biennale. Scenographers and architects are embracing the potential of the autonomous model and its hybrids, in particular for the production and communication of individual and disciplinary knowledge and the testing of materials, atmospheres and ideas.

In a merging of sculpture and installation, scenography and architecture, and realized in a myriad of scales, materialities and embodied narratives, the predominantly large-scale autonomous model in exhibition not only comprises cosmopoiesis but allows the visitor to experience the model-maker's subjective creation first-hand. Often enterable, atmospheric and discursive overall, these performative spatial environments question long-held assumptions about the role and function of the discipline beyond its genre-specific context, showing the autonomous model to possess agency in commenting on social and cultural realities.

While the scale model is central to all spatial practice, there has to date been no study focusing on the history and development of the model across theatre and architecture, nor a study of the context and conditions that enabled the autonomous model to emerge. Existing literature includes practical model-making guides for theatre and architecture,[1] and a small number of specialized publications offer histories of the architectural model and introduce current analogue and digital model-making processes and applications in architecture with detailed case studies,[2] with Patrick Healy's 2008 *The Model and Its Architecture* presenting an extended essay on theories and concepts of the model in architecture, science, and platonic and Deleuzian philosophy. Notably, it also discusses pre-Islamic cosmological and metaphysical considerations relating to architecture, geometry and the body.

In five, loosely chronological chapters, *The Model as Performance* develops and performs a new reading of physical models in theatre and architecture. It establishes the autonomous and performative model and its hybrids in the context of this series as a cross-disciplinary global practice of spatial production that has operated from the Renaissance until today at the intersection of theatre and architecture, fuelled by the designer's desire for technological innovation and artistic expression.

The opening chapter unfolds the models' implicit dual character as both material object and immaterial idea by firstly carefully tracing its physical and conceptual emergence in architecture and theatre throughout history on the (sometimes scarce) foundation of extant objects and contemporary descriptions. Secondly, the model's significance as the designer's central tool for ideation and communication is articulated across the disciplines and then differentiated for each. This is necessary as the interdisciplinary language of the model suggests a high degree of similarity between the architectural and the scenographic model, yet models of buildings and models of stage design typically differ in terms of the design and representation of stable, durable spaces in architecture against transformative, temporary spaces on the stage. Where, however, in both historic and contemporary models, the categorical boundaries between 'stable' and 'transformative' become porous, untidy and mangled, the model's inherent performativity comes to the fore, and as performative instruments, these models take on and produce a reality far beyond their sheer material presence and genre. They are autonomous and able to stage space and enable performance as well as produce, communicate and store knowledge. The first chapter closes with the thesis that the autonomous model has the capacity to redefine the relationship between model, viewer and environment, and it is this notion that forms the departure point of the following chapter but also comprises the overall arc of this project, namely in its focus not only on what the model is but also on what the model does.

The second chapter, 'Staging Politics and Knowledge through the Model', presents a detailed historical study and clarification of these concerns and seeks to establish the model in the Italian Renaissance as closely linked to the 'invention' of central perspective in introducing the 1588–1590 Teatro all'Antica in Sabbioneta as a programmatic convergence of scenography and architecture. In a careful reading of material elements and conceptual origin, we show how Scamozzi's scaled city model on the stage enables and strengthens the staging and performance of political power, namely through the construction of a single central perspective that links the urban exterior and the scenographic interior. A staging not of absolutist power as in Duke Vespasiano's Sabbioneta, but rather the performance of all possible knowledge in a scaled-down wooden model theatre was presented by the Italian hermeticist Giulio Camillo in 1550, and through the construction of a collection room with a large model box in its centre in the scenographer and architect Furttenbach's 1641 publication of *Architectura Privata*, a detailed description of art chamber and the residential floors of his own home complete with ground plans. In the eighteenth century, the tradition of the cabinet of curiosities that influenced Furttenbach's inhabitable models of the universe reappears in a kinetic theatre, in Servandoni's 1737 *Spectacles d'optique*, showing the theatre set itself to be a machine that operates from the inside out, an autonomous model of the world complete with volcanoes, storms, thunder and lightning. Where Servandoni's Tuilleries spectacles operated as mute tableaux, Loutherbourg's 1781 *Eidophusikon*, a 2 × 3 metre mechanical theatre performed natural phenomena through scenic effects, complex mirror and pulley systems. Neither representation nor experimental tool, the Eidophusikon as a scale model of the natural world enabled performance through scenographic innovation. The models discussed in this chapter progress our project in two ways: firstly, in the positioning of the autonomous model as emerging in parallel with the exploration of perspective in the Italian Renaissance and, secondly, in attributing what we call a 'semantic surplus' to the model in Chapter 1. Our readings of the models by Scamozzi, Furttenbach, Camillo, Servandoni and Loutherbourg show that the model, beyond its pragmatic use, has in different ways served to convey diverse knowledge sets or sets of meanings that are much more than the sum of the model's individual components or parts.

The trajectory of the third chapter, titled 'Performing Architecture: Edward Gordon Craig and the Model Stage', continues to discuss the central role of the stage set model as an epistemic tool in the history of scenography and outlines the discipline's shift towards abstraction at the turn of the century through the systematic, rigorous and obsessively iterative model practices of English symbolist director, actor and scenographer Edward Gordon Craig (1872–1966). Inspired by the eighteenth-century immersive mechanical theatre of Philip James de Loutherbourg and by Richard Wagner's concept of a synthesis of all arts, Craig set out to systematically reform and re-theatricalize the theatre. Between 1907 and 1921, through rigorous iterative modelling, he developed a system of mobile screens for expressing basic architectural elements (beginning with floor and ceiling) from which he could conceptualize and design a stage to mobilize them all. At the core of Craig's scenic innovations lay the construction of small-scale iterative models and large- to full-scale model stages complete with figurines. Using mobility and lighting as key expressive media in performance, he steered the modernist stage towards abstraction. Inherently performative, Craig's full-size 1911 London model, that is, the prototype that demonstrated the workings of the screen system to a studio audience, constituted a model that comprised a live performance when operated.

The discussion of the 1:1 model as enabling and comprising performance is taken up in the fourth chapter, titled 'Staging the Future: The Model as Performance of Inhabitation', in tracing an arc of the development of the enterable full-scale architectural model in exhibition from the mid-nineteenth-century post-industrial revolution through twentieth-century modernism and into the present day.

Focusing on the designers of these representational models, the institutions that commissioned them and the artefact itself, a case unfolds arguing that this form of the model is located within a highly politicized sphere and presents as a discursive object and agent of socio-economic change regardless of where it appears on our defined timeline. The architects' intention, through the model, to develop new typologies and propositional solutions to issues surrounding the built environment, including housing, sustainability, urban landscapes and domestic futures, emerges as a significant and persistent theme.

The performative nature of the enterable, and in some cases the inhabited, model is argued as a critical quality in the success of this formats' widespread influence and appeal to a broad and highly diverse audience. The case studies in this chapter concentrate on developments in the United States and Germany, analysing scenographic and performative space-making strategies including scale, materiality and narrative in exhibited full-scale architectural and urban models.

A point of departure for our discussion is identified as the *Prince Albert's Model Lodging House*, a social housing project shown at the 1851 Great Exhibition in London. Against this precedent, we look at two pivotal projects by highly influential modernist architects Mies van der Rohe and Lilly Reich. The Deutscher Werkbund exhibition *The Dwelling* (Stuttgart 1927) showed modernist full-scale inhabitable building fragments and fully furnished interiors, and in *The Dwelling of Our Time* (Berlin 1931) actors performed in full-scale interiors that visitors were invited to enter and 'test' the future of residential housing. In both cases, new typologies were proposed through the model in exhibition, and the format of the enterable model was established as a vehicle to deliver early twentieth-century modernist ideas around form and socio-political positions. Moving from Germany to America, we introduce designer and scenographer Norman Bel Geddes' *Futurama* (New York 1939), an immersive environment where visitors, seated in a mobile cabin, circled a large-scale model of their city. Using the model as a seductive and propositional vehicle for a utopic automobile-centred future, *Futurama* used the miniature as a device for the audience to project themselves into a near-future urban environment. Simultaneous developments in Germany saw the post-war period's focus on reconstruction, as well as social equity with strong financial and ideological support from America that delivered many post-war reconstruction exhibitions including *We're Building a Better Life* (West Berlin

1952) and the American National Exhibition (Moscow 1959). In both, actors portraying wife, husband and children inhabited a model home in two shifts. In Berlin, a white-coated narrator directed events from a central viewing tower turning the exhibition into a performance, and in Moscow, the stage was set for the notorious televised 'kitchen debate' between US Vice President Richard Nixon and Soviet Premier Nikita Khrushchev who traded opinions on their political systems through the quality and affordability of their consumer products.

Institutions, including the Museum of Modern Art in New York and the Deutscher Werkbund, emerge as key players in the commissioning, curating and exhibiting of full-scale models, while tracing the model's development in the twentieth and twenty-first centuries and consequently providing a context for this chapter's most contemporary case study, the 2013 project *Mies in Krefeld*. With a close reading of *Mies in Krefeld*, the enquiry is concluded by developing a cohesive argument around the nature of performative space in an occupiable model. Rather than proposing a new architectural typology, *Mies in Krefeld* recreates, performatively, an unbuilt modernist prototype that affirms McKinney's and Palmer's proposition that such projects 'reflect wider trends in hybrid practices in theatre, performance, art and architecture as well as a tendency towards the blurring of boundaries between performance and audience' (McKinney and Palmer 2017: 1).

The fifth chapter, 'Performing the Past: The Full-Scale Model and Mock-Up', confirms that the model or mock-up at full scale is integral to twentieth-century theatre and architecture, both as hybrids such as the reconstructed and reinvented Mies club house discussed previously and as purely teleological future referents but also, significantly, as carrier of memories and past narratives. Urban propositions in the form of 1:1 models and façade mock-ups discussed in this chapter range from the manipulative power of the architectural model in 1930s Germany in its disturbing combination of neoclassicism and invented National Socialist symbols that sought to deceptively construct a glorious national past and future to Aldo Rossi's architecture of memory in the form of the 1980 *Teatro del Mondo*, a full-scale model that recalls Venice's traditional floating theatres yet remains conceptually autonomous. Bert Neumann's full-scale mock-ups of past architectures, both real and imagined, as in the 'non-places' of the former German Democratic Republic (GDR) and in B-grade Hollywood-style film sets, show the model's critical faculty in the complex reference system of the stage.

Our project closes with the chapter 'Staging the White Cube: The Autonomous Model as a Performance of Space' where, while still concerned with the performative and ideological potential of the full-scale model, we shift our focus of observation from the stage and urban space to the contemporary exhibition space and its expansion towards multi-site exhibitions. We show

how curators aim to redefine their respective disciplines through performative model environments, and we trace in this chapter the emergence of the autonomous model in the large international survey shows of the Venice Architecture Biennale and the Prague Quadrennial of Performance Design and Space (PQ).

The Model as Performance builds on current theories of performative space in theatre (Fischer-Lichte 2008) and relational art (Bourriaud 2002). It argues the model's reality-producing capacity and pivotal role in the 'making of space' (Brejzek 2011) and in scenography as a practice that gives meaning to space (Collins and Nisbet 2010). This project complements contemporary research on spaces between architecture and art (Rendell 2009), expanded scenographic practices (Aronson 2008, 2012; Hannah and Harsløf 2008) and expanded architectural practices (Perren and Lovett 2013, Perren and Lovett 2016), and it makes use of aspects of classical mathematical and philosophical modelling theory posited by Stachowiak (1973), and by Wartofsky (1979), in particular to the latter's theory of the scientific model as creative and future-oriented, and by Mahr (2008), who proposes that the model carries an innate semantic surplus or cargo.

Exhibition catalogues, websites with archived material and collateral publications from the Museum of Modern Art in New York, the Victoria and Albert Museum in London, the Venice Biennale and the Prague Quadrennial became key sources along with our personal impressions from these exhibitions and museums. Repeat visits to Sabbioneta confirmed the importance of Scamozzi's unique Teatro all'Antica in our research as comprising a convergence of scenography and architecture: a model theatre in a model town. Observing Patrick Le Boeuf, Library Curator in the Performing Arts department at the Bibliothèque nationale de France in Paris, as he carefully unpacked some of Edward Gordon Craig's 'Model A' components and screens for us to photograph (they had lain untouched since he deposited them in archival boxes fifteen years earlier), was an exceptional experience that reminded us of the value of the material archive to the researcher.

Due to the vast field of historical and contemporary models and their corresponding paucity of literature, it became apparent early in our research that we needed to work across primary and secondary sources in more than one language. Subsequently, German, Italian and (to a lesser extent) French sources in our translation stand next to those in English. Parts of Chapters 5 and 6 were previously published as Brejzek, T. (2007), 'A Theatre of Ghosts: Some Thoughts Relating to the Representation of Art and Scenography', in Aronson, A. (ed), *Exhibition on the Stage: Reflections on the 2007 Prague Quadrennial*, Prague: The Theatre Institute, 17–26; and in Brejzek, T. and Wallen, L. P. (2014), 'The 1:1 Architectural Model as Performance and Double', *PROCEEDINGS*, [in]arch international conference 2014, Universitas Indonesia,

Universitas Indonesia, Jakarta, 95–105. We gratefully acknowledge permission to use them here.

This project was completed during a research residency undertaken at the Ligurian Study Centre in Bogliasco, Italy, as fellows of the New York-based Bogliasco Foundation in the spring of 2017. We would like to thank the Foundation's President, Laura Harrison, and its Vice President and Director of the Study Centre, Ivana Folle, for their generous support and hospitality.

1

The Model as Object and Idea

The model as object and idea plays a prime role in the design processes of architecture and theatre. In professional practice as much as in design studio education, the model is essential to the generation and representation of ideas. Numerous models are typically produced during a design process, many of them discarded immediately, others kept, and the ideas expressed within them integrated at a later stage. Models are discussed here as epistemic tools or instruments that consistently produce and communicate knowledge as concept and form progress incrementally and converge in the final product. It will be shown that model-making and modelling processes comprise fundamental research practices to explore form, extend material properties or speculate on future developments and uses in the disciplines. But there is also another dimension to the model, linked to invention and imagination more than to the pragmatic needs of the scenographer and architect in that models are physical and conceptual instruments of the *cosmopoietic* (world-making) act – they are able to comprise entire worlds. This ultimately performative and reality-constructing dimension of the model, and with it the observation of architectural and scenographic models throughout history that have been conceptualized as singular artefacts, demands the development and introduction of a new taxonomy of the model at this stage of the project. Beyond the categories of the developmental (iterative) and the final (representative) model, this project proposes the autonomous model beyond original and copy. Before close readings of the model in all its aspects in the following fully help to unfold its significance in the advancement of technologies and the questioning of conventionalized modes of what a building can be and what a stage can be throughout the histories of theatre and architecture, the model's emergence and its general history must be traced and its diverse manifestations contextualized. The model's history is sketchy and extant models are scarce, in theatre even more so than in architecture. In architecture, the model came to prominence with the exploration of perspective and its canonized use in the Renaissance, and its first use in theatre dates from the same era when it became necessary to construct a scaled model to test the size, construction and perspective of the actual set.

The vast majority of models discussed in the brief historical overview that closes this chapter are final, representative models. Iterative models are rarely collected and preserved, and if, they will typically be shown in a designer personalities retrospective to illustrate their design process in detail. The representative and autonomous models, often appearing as hybrids between the two, are the subjects of close readings in the following chapters and are only mentioned in passing here with the exception of the emergence of the singular, revolutionary object in architecture, theatre and sculpture in the 1920s in a prefiguration of contemporary autonomous models that operate both in and between the genres.

Staging space: The autonomous model

Alongside plans and drawings, models are principal instruments in the design and communication processes of theatre and architecture. Design models clarify and explain spatial configurations and relations, placing the building or set design in its scalar and topographical context. Thus, models of built structures and set designs alike always lay a claim to something, in that they propose a reality by their sheer object status. In turn, they typically refer to something prior – to another model, plan, drawing, idea or another artefact to be constructed in the future at a congruent or differing scale. Different types have specific functions, and no one model can aspire to a complete representation of any conceptual design process. Models can be speculative, projective or retrospective, as well as realistic, experimental or pragmatic. They might possess a material analogy to their future artefact, or may be constructed to test structural, textual and haptic properties of materials.

In the design processes of scenography and architecture, the physical scale model appears in two distinct phases: first, in conceptual development, where it is used to generate form, resolve issues of materiality and physically manifest theoretical and programmatic ideas, and second, in model-making where a non-linear dialogue between emerging artefact and emerging idea in an iterative and incremental method of continual refinement takes place. The result of this latter phase is referred to as an iterative model. In a later, more stable phase, the model is constructed and used to represent a finalized design, either to communicate a proposed scheme or to exhibit an existing structure. Here, a dialogue occurs between the model and what it represents in the past or future. This is referred to as a representative model. In both cases, the scale model constructs and projects its reality while anticipating a reality beyond. While iterative models might not be constructed to scale and will primarily serve material and formal exploration, representative models are usually constructed at scale. Different scales allow for different levels of reduction or detail, and models are thus built in various scales to test a wide range of phenomena and conditions. Modelling not only carves out possibilities and predicts spatial outcomes relating to the site and its context, but makes them visible.

However, visual models are not 'truthful' representations of present or future states but are subject to ideology and intent, so that their reading is dependent on visual trends, histories, cultures and diverse perceptual conventions. Ideologies and intents are inscribed into the model and determine its scale, its aesthetics, materials and construction. They are responsible for the model's emphasis on specific aspects and the reduction or omission of others. As physical communication media, models are highly context-dependent, and this extends to the object's live performance in any final design presentation to colleagues or clients. The model presentation may well determine whether a project will be built, and presentations today are typically rehearsed and scripted[1] with the careful staging of setting and lighting in the presentation space. Diverse narratives that describe the model to different audiences are crucial, and the 'performance' of the model must be seamless to engender confidence in the design's future workability. Here then is a performative act in which the presenter brings the model's semantic complexities ('model of' and 'model for') into live relation with audience and environment. In the performative space that emerges from the interaction between environment (model), presenter and audience, time is extended from the present towards a future of construction, realization and inhabitation of the set or building. During design and presentation, figurines are typically used to simulate movement and behaviour in the scaled-down model-world, and for that exquisite moment, it exists in its space and time, presenting an alternate reality: the reality of the model.

The core difference between theatre and architecture models lies not in their construction but the reality of their practices. While set design models must allow for lighting and set changes in working towards a live performance that happens in time, architectural models are static representations for presentation, or else have been built specifically for exhibition. The architectural model may not be an interior or spatial model and may focus exclusively on the architectural object. The theatre model in contrast always includes space and time as central, whereas in architecture it is the physical object that is of primary concern.

The word 'model', first used in the Italian Renaissance as *modello*, from the Latin *modulus*, an architectural 'measure', is highly equivocal in its use in architecture, theatre, philosophy and science. This is because the model is always both idea and object, and is seen in all these contexts as the physical, virtual or theoretical representation of an object, behaviour or a set of relations. The general function of models is to link theoretical concepts with practical applications by providing a tactile environment and specific semantic context to develop theories, extend hypotheses or predict developments. Model theory, as a sub-discipline of mathematical logic and philosophy, offers definitions and frameworks that help to explain functions and attributes of models in a way that is valid not only for mathematical models, and by extension for scientific models, but also for stage set and architectural models in view of their performativity and agency, as proposed in this study.

Marx W. Wartofsky, philosopher and model theorist, posits that the primary task of models is to enable the future. For Wartofsky, models are purposeful 'modes of action' and 'experimental probes' that require being 'performed' rather than merely devised (Wartofsky 1979: 148). As teleological instruments, they are creative rather than conservative and able to communicate beyond what they comprise.

The argument here is that models are more than abstract ideas. They are technological means for conceptual exploration leading to experimentation. But an experiment is something that has to be performed and not merely conceived to be useful. In this sense, models are experimental probes, essential parts of the human technique for confronting the future – but not as a passive encounter with something already formed. Rather, in a unique way in which human action is creative, such an encounter shapes the future. Thus, we may suggest, that models constitute the distinctive technology of purpose. (Wartofsky 1979: 148)

Herbert Stachowiak, in his basic research into graphic, technical and semantic models, argues in his classic study *Allgemeine Modelltheorie* (*Basic Model Theory*) from 1973 that the model is a necessarily abstracted representation of reality. Primarily, it denotes an intended reduction in complexity and a focus on specific elements and attributes to be visualized and interrogated for the sake of understanding distinct phenomena. Stachowiak maintains that there is no singular relation between model and original, but that its representative function occurs for specific subjects within specific time periods and limited to precise operations. This implies there are no right or wrong models, and that there may be diverse models for the same original. In addition, the original may also be a model, in the form of an idea or future plan (Wartofsky 1979: 131–133). Considerations of the model typically revolve around its usefulness for proof, visualization, future-testing and prototyping. However, in terms that exceed its functional properties, the model also operates to express material experiments, utopian ideals and speculative construction. It thus occupies a critical role in developing spatial ideas, in that it develops a material identity in parallel with the conceptual. Any model, be it theoretical, mathematical, architectural or of a stage set, comes into being through complex processes of modelling marked by corrections and optimizations, inclusions and rejections. The model thus has a dual epistemic function: it produces knowledge through distinct modelling processes, and it communicates knowledge through its final form.

'Models are carriers of a cargo', writes Bernd Mahr in his study on the relation between model and image. For Mahr, the model acts as a mediator and communicator of complex issues. When looking at it, we rather look beyond it to understand the workings of a system, the function of a machine, the structural design of a building or transformation of a theatre stage. This 'look beyond' equates with 'cargo', Mahr's succinct term, by relating the substance and function for which the object or idea is a model (Mahr 2008: 32).[2]

Beyond their pragmatic value, architecture and theatre models carry cargo or semantic surplus that does not sit in strictly analogous relation to reality, scale or purpose but that might be best described as an atmosphere, a distinct aesthetics, and a set of meanings or symbolic representations. The sum of these immaterial qualities in coalescence with the material reality of the model comprises the world or the reality of the model and is testament to its cosmopoietic capacity. The origin of cosmopoiesis as aligned with the model rests with Plato's notion of the world as a *paradeigma* (model) of an eternal cosmos. In the *Timaeus* dialogue, Plato develops a cosmology based on the idea of the creation of a unified cosmos from chaos after an eternal model by a divine creator, the demiurge (see *Timaeus* 28A).

Now, anything created is necessarily created by some cause, because nothing can possibly come to be without there being something that is responsible for its coming to be. Also, whenever a craftsman takes something consistent as his model and reproduces its form and properties, the result is bound in every case to be a thing of beauty, but if he takes as his model something that has been created, the product is bound to be imperfect. (Plato 2008: 16)

A model, to Plato, is a rational construct that is reproduced from an eternal original, and it is teleological in that it strives for an ordered and harmonious outcome yet all depends on the original (model) the craftsman chooses.

So what we have to ask is, again, which of those two kinds of model the creator was using as he constructed the universe. Was he looking at what is consistent and permanent or at what has been created? Well, if this universe of ours is beautiful and if its craftsman was good, it evidently follows that he was looking at an eternal model, while he was looking at a created model if the opposite is the case – though it's blasphemous even to think it. It's perfectly clear, then, that he used an eternal model, because nothing in creation is more beautiful than the world and no cause is better than its maker. The craftsman of this universe, then, took as his model that which is grasped by reason and intelligence and is consistent, and it necessarily follows from these premises that this world of ours is an image of something. It is, of course, crucial to begin any subject at its natural starting-point. Where an image and its original are concerned, we had better appreciate that statements about them are similar to the objects they explicate, in the sense that statements about that which is stable, secure, and manifest to intellect are themselves stable and reliable (and it's important for statements about such things to be just as irrefutable). (Plato 2008: 17)

The eternal model must be understood as a rational and intellectual ideal rather than an existing perfect model. The universe thus created by the demiurge or divine craftsman, according to Plato, is 'an image of something' yet it is not a copy but rather the materialization of an immaterial idea. The model is thus unique and always an original. It is 'stable and reliable' and, in other words, 'real' and by the process of its creation has collapsed the boundaries between original and copy, idea, intention and realization. The significance of Plato's concept of the created model as reality lies in exactly the refusal to classify the model as a second-order product. Posited as both real and reality-producing, Plato's notion of the *paradeigma* strongly resonates with the concept of the autonomous model developed in this project.

Equally relevant for the expanded taxonomy of the model is Olafur Eliasson's notion of models as 'co-producers of reality' in that they create their own reality:

What we are witnessing is a shift in the traditional relationship between reality and representation. We no longer progress from model to reality, but from model to model while acknowledging that both models are, in fact, real. As a result, we may work in a very productive manner with reality experienced as a conglomeration of models. Rather than seeing model and reality as polarized modes, they now function on the same level. Models have become co-producers of reality. (Eliasson 2007:17)

Eliasson's radical redefinition of the model as an active agent in the (co-) production of reality further supports the extension of the traditional model typology: rather than operating within the defined action sequence of being a model of and for something, the model can exist instead as a singular object without past or future. This new type of model sits outside the binary relationship between iteration and representation and is newly defined in *The Model as Performance* as the *autonomous model*. This is particularly potent in contexts outside traditional theatre and architecture practice, where key parameters of theatre (transformation) and architecture (structure) merge, and where the autonomous model not only affords performative agency but also blurs the disciplinary boundaries between theatre, architecture and the fine arts.

A contemporary instance of the model in performance makes tangible this notion of autonomy. At the 2016 Edinburgh Fringe Festival, spectators were presented with a unique live event. On the open stage of the Summerhall Old Lab, photographer Charlotte Bouckaert and architect Steve Salembier staged *Bildraum* (Image Space), a performance installation with the architectural scale model at its centre. For forty minutes, architect and photographer engaged in the creation of a narrative that emerged from the live production and interplay of an object (the scale model), a technical apparatus (the photographic camera), a soundscape and the performers' actions and words. With spectators as witnesses, Salembier worked with nine architectural models of differing sizes – each a blurred[3] representation of a former residence, and assembled and reassembled them during the event. Bouckaert meanwhile photographed the models and their interiors and projected them onto a large screen behind. For the artists,

> *Bildraum* intertwines image, memory and reality into a new liminal environment which recalls the moment our perception of space was formed. (Bouckaert and Salembier n.d.)

The architectural model on the stage was thus instrumental in the construction of this liminal, threshold space, proposing an indistinct space of inhabitation while operating as an active agent in the co-production of collective and individual memories.

In elevating the physical scale model as principal protagonist, *Bildraum* embodies the notion of the model as an active agent in the making and performing of space. By proposing myriad imagined narratives complemented by those of the viewer, the model's relationship to representation, reality and temporality comes distinctly to the fore. Stage director and playwright Robert Lepage's 2015 production *887*, a staged monological exploration of his childhood in 1960s Quebec City that operates through the catalyst of several physical models on the stage is another instance where the model is a carrier of symbolic meaning and, while also representative, acts as a co-actor and agent. In contrast to *Bildraum*, however, *887* requires the human actor to activate the model and contextualize the spaces the viewer observes. In a sophisticated dramaturgical twist, Lepage's models are at different scales, at small scale for an apartment building and at full scale for a kitchen and living space that the protagonist can inhabit and thus act and speak from the inside of a model. Lepage's dramaturgical concept is reminiscent of the structure of Giulio Camillo's Memory Theatre from 1550,[4] where the orator was able to elicit memories (fragments of past speeches) physically and assemble those spatially and in real time in a scaled-down wooden model theatre.

In both productions, *Bildraum* and *887*, the model in performance develops its reality and presentness in a dialogue with the viewer-participant and its setting, thus supporting this projects' central argument that the traditional terminological and functional divisions into iterative and representative models must be extended to a third category, namely to a model that exists autonomously to either future construction or past precedent. The autonomous model thus carries many references but is not the representation of any. It is complete in what it is and comprises its world; its maker has no intention to construct another world or artefact from it. The autonomous model is always an original, always conceived as a singular experiential and performative space. It redefines the relationship between model, viewer and environment, from a focus on what the model *is* towards what it *does*.

Performing research: The processes of modelling

The notion (rarely articulated) of scenographer and architect as researchers, who develop specific strategies and methods to translate an idea into three-dimensional form, is the central motivation behind the making of models and is strongly linked to man's desire for mimesis. Benjamin understands this to encompass both representation and expression and aid in the dissolution of subject and object (Benjamin 1968: 218–220). Michael Taussig, in describing Benjamin's mimesis as a process of constructing 'same and other' in *Mimesis and Alterity*, designates models as mimetic tools in addition to their imitative functions and qualities:

> I call it the mimetic faculty, the nature that culture uses to create second nature, the faculty to copy, imitate, make models, explore difference, yield into and become Other. The wonder of mimesis lies in the copy drawing of the character and power of the original to the point whereby the representation may even assume that character and that power. (Taussig 1993: xiii)

To the anthropologist Taussig, mimetic processes can produce more than a copy if they take on – through a kind of mimetic alchemy and animistic transformative act – the power of the original. In this, while always mediating between idea and reality, present and future, the model ultimately results from mimetic processes and may become Other. In the case where there is no original or future artefact, the model transcends mimesis and becomes its own original and takes on autonomous status. Whether 'same and other' as Benjamin has stated or whether the workings of mimesis further an ideology that results in the (architectural) 'production of models rather than copies and of the production of architecture itself as a model' (see Hayes 1998: 194), mimesis is at work throughout the modelling processes of the designer as iterative and explorative conceptual, material and structural research.

Scenographer Thomas Dreissigacker defines his work with the model as artistic research into space, with all its material and immaterial properties. Modelling, to Dreissigacker, comprises non-linear and non-schematic acts of thinking and doing while attuning one's awareness to the (stage and theatre) space's potential architectural, acoustic and logistic configurations. Its atmospheric conditions, its possibilities and limitations, come to be explored in the modelling process, where the model is no mere pragmatic tool but a three-dimensional laboratory for spatial ideas and original solutions (see Dreissigacker 2015: 183). The iterative model is thus a meeting point or forum for negotiation between the qualities of existing theatre space and the scenographer's yet-to-be-articulated spatial interventions and insertions on a small scale. Continuous and contradictory rather than linear, simulating and testing spatial situations, materials, colours, acoustics and lighting, the model communicates a growing body of knowledge. During this time of exploration, the model operates as a physical communication platform between director and designer, where a concept is negotiated not in words but spatial operations. These often act as provocations to both parties, in that potential failure is necessarily inscribed. As the designer manipulates the model during intense working sessions, instrumental decisions are being made in it and with it. Materially, the model increases in spatial logic and detail. Scene transitions are worked into the model, and a full spatial narrative emerges. Ideally, the lighting designer joins the working sessions around the physical model and extrapolates their lighting concept. Once the major design decisions have been made, and a functioning model exists, usually at a metric scale of 1:50, 1:25, 1:20 or 1:15, the theatre's technical team typically enters the process to analyse material, structural and logistical aspects of the set design as well as to cost the scenography.

In some instances in theatre, dance and opera, a full-scale model is then constructed for the so-called *Bauprobe* ('building rehearsal'). Long established in the German-speaking world, this term denotes the full-sized construction of the set design in temporary materials and its exact placement on the stage. The *Bauprobe* (see Figure 1.1) signifies a central event in the design

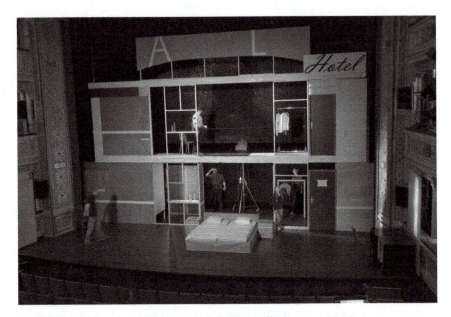

FIGURE 1.1 Bauprobe Cactus-Land, *Schauspielhaus Graz, 2015.*

development and the built structure and allows the creative and technical teams to test the design for practicability, aesthetics and cost. All entrances and exits, heights, proportions and joinery are examined for optimization in subsequent iterations of the design. Viewing axes and sight lines (areas of reduced visibility) are tested from various auditorium positions, and potential lighting issues concerning height, perspective or scene changes are identified. Precisely timed to precede set construction, and ideally, months before rehearsal, a successful *Bauprobe* constitutes the designer's official 'sign off'. If issues are detected, a partial or complete reworking of the set can be done. Regarding a model typology, the *Bauprobe* can be considered a full-scale enterable iterative model.

In architecture, it is common practice to build full-scale models of a building, or its fragments and details. Set up in either temporary materials or the actual materials and colour scheme, this model may be a prototype, that is, the first construction of its type. In both disciplines, the expensive development of the large or full-scale model or mock-up is reserved for instances where only the direct interaction between building, site and viewer can help determine the design's success or failure.

Digital models of set, scene changes and lighting are constructed in tandem, and their task is now both technical and design-oriented. Dreissigacker reflects that in his scenographic research the design process starts with analogue sketches and drawings followed by the physical handling of iterative models before the possibilities of digital modelling are explored. In architecture, historically, the design process similarly followed an iterative path, from analogue idea generation in different media, and spatial experiments without limitation of scale and architectural programme in the process of form-finding, to digital models that can calculate and simulate the user's experience in navigating the building.[5]

In architectural terms, the equivalent of the *Bauprobe* is referred to as a mock-up and comes in two identifiable forms. The first is a fragment or component of the proposed building that is built using the same materials and specifications as the final product, and ranges in size from a small detail built and tested in the studio to large external modules assembled from hundreds of custom-built components that are placed on-site. These check the design and operate as a marketing tool, and are often later deployed as full-scale examples for the contractors. Open-air mock-up fragments commonly include 'facades, balconies, and exoskeletons' (McCaughan 2016), and as Deyan Sudjic, director of London's Design Museum, points out:

> For the architect, these are not toys or sales aids but working tools. They are the means to explore the impact of design decisions, at the scale of both the smallest detail, and at the level of the master plan. (Sudjic 2010: 260)

As customized prototyping and construction, systems have evolved to allow the design of highly complex geometries, prototyping and manufacturing, this type of mock-up has become prevalent (McCaughan 2016). Cost, quality and accuracy are positively impacted by computer numerical control (CNC) routers, 3D printers and other additive manufacturing technologies that allow rapid construction of the mock-up and design modifications to be iterated and implemented in very short timeframes.

The second form of mock-up, closer in physical resemblance to the *Bauprobe*, is the full-scale building created in alternate materials to approximate the volume or look of the finished building. This strategy prevails throughout history, and 'perhaps the most astonishing known ancient mock up is the so-called trial passage made for the construction of the great pyramids at Giza' (Jones 2003: 232) in 2580 BCE. While the mock-up is a persuasive tool, it does not always convince the client to the architect's advantage. In the case of seminal modernist architect Mies van der Rohe's mock-up of his first commission, the mock-up was to be the end of the project for him as

> his client decided that the house he was working on wasn't quite what he wanted on the basis of what he saw from the full-size elevations that were painted on canvas screens and positioned on the site. (Sudjic 2010: 261)

The full-scale model or mock-up allows the user or the client to project themselves fully into the scheme and envision the aesthetics, spatiality and functionality of a proposed project in an immersive way. The experience of being inside the mock-up is more immediate than reading a set of drawings that usually requires highly advanced abilities in abstraction and three-dimensional visualization. In the case of Mies' client, the mock-up made it clear to him that the architect's vision did not align with his own, and he consequently backed out of the project.

Besides client or investor interest in the in situ full-scale representation of a proposed building, the mock-up has been used to test the wind, overshadowing and impact on the urban fabric to the satisfaction of regulatory bodies, clients and architects. Within our typology of the model, the architectural mock-up can be seen primarily as a representational model, while from the architects' point of view it has been used as an iterative model, albeit a laborious and expensive one to modify. Richard Pommer writes on the fine-scale model in the catalogue of the pivotal 1976 New York exhibition *Idea as Model:*

Previously the model was used as a representation of an idea which had been very clearly defined before the model was started. Now both the model and the idea develop simultaneously. The models are as precise as before but more experimental; no longer cased in glass, the potential of the model is greater. (Pommer et al. 1981: 116)

The notion of the architectural scale model to not only represent but be an active agent in ideation, as proposed by the discourse surrounding the exhibition *Idea as Model* at Peter Eisenman's New York Institute for Architecture and Urban Studies, has belatedly occurred with the 1:1 mock-up. Driven by prototyping technologies that now rapidly produce components in response to design changes, the role of the mock-up has shifted from near-static representational object (both expensive and time-consuming to adjust) to a dynamic tool for design development.

In *Idea as Model*, models and installations including the New York Five (Peter Eisenman, Michael Graves, Charles Gwathmey, John Hejduk and Richard Meier) spoke of architecture through the material discourse of the model. The exhibition showed the model as a unique object that encourages the testing of ideas and provokes a redefinition of architecture. *Idea as Model* sought to foreground the model not as a small-scale future building but as a construction of difference that investigated the discipline itself (see Pommer et al. 1981: 3).

The exhibition included the ultimately censored contribution *Window Blow-Out*, staged as a real-life experience by Gordon Matta-Clark. His original proposal was to show a photographic 1:1 mock-up of vandalized windows in the South Bronx as a critique of New York's socio-economic problems and the city's decay in the 1970s. Instead of displaying black-and-white photographs of monotonous Bronx brick façades and windows, Matta-Clark shot out the gallery windows with an air rifle, thus doubling the photographic exhibit. Significantly, the architect was turning publicly against the modernist tradition in which he had been taught, while performing the very violence local politics and architecture did nothing to address. While the curator had agreed to a small number of damaged windows, Matta-Clark continued to shoot out every single window of the floor of the Institute, from the inside out. *Window Blow-Out* exemplifies the creation of a 1:1 model through the performative processes of destruction and (re-) enactment. While its violent gesture and context make it a temporary and unstable anti-architecture, it simultaneously presents as a material object and an architectural *doppelgänger* of the Bronx façades. It was far removed from Matta-Clark's much less spectacular original idea to exhibit a small model of his seminar room at Cornell where he had studied architecture. The latter would have been understood as a model of a particular architectural education and thus perceived as institutional critique. *Window Blow-Out*, however, promoted the model as a performance of political, urban and architectural analysis.

In 1981, five years after *The Idea as Model*, Pommer concludes that the exhibition as a whole could not be staged again, mainly for the reason that the artefacts of architectural process had now joined the fine arts (see Pommer 1981: 10) and been subsumed into the art market. To Pommer this is a double loss, weakening Eisenman's modernist position that models hold value over drawings since they can represent more than mere materiality by communicating an idea (of architecture). Pommer concludes that drawings have once again become the dominant medium of architectural communication. However, he admits that models have not altogether disappeared as they continue, together with sketches and drawings, to be a principal medium for idea generation and communication.

Viewed from the first decades of the twenty-first century, it is hard to share Pommer's dystopian 1981 evaluation of the architectural model and drawing becoming marketable artefacts and architecture. Neither the architecture nor set design model has 'sold out', and their critical currency continues in architecture and scenography exhibitions internationally from the Prague Quadrennial for Performance Design and Space (PQ) and the bi-annual Venice International Exhibition for Architecture to the recent World Stage Design Exhibitions held since 2005 in Toronto, Seoul, Cardiff and Taiwan, as well as thematic exhibitions in museums and collections worldwide.

Making worlds: The emergence of the model

Any attempt to trace the history of the model in theatre and architecture is necessarily limited to the analysis of extant artefacts and written documents, be it the actual model or a later reconstruction, original comments by the architect, the scenographer or contemporaries, or accounts of model-making, painting and photography of models. Compared to the plethora of plans and drawings for buildings and performances, the number of surviving stage set and architectural models is worryingly small, and even where they exist, or their fabrication is mentioned by contemporaries, it is often unknown whether they represent others unaccounted for or are singular occurrences. When comparing the quantity of available information on stage set models to that on architectural models, the imbalance is even greater. Reasons for this disparity (while historically unsupported) may be found in the materiality of the set model, usually originating from paper, and its vulnerability regarding storage and preservation compared to more sturdy architectural models made from wood. Architectural models of future buildings, made for the client's approval and with substantial costs,[6] may have been found more worthy of inclusion in permanent collections than the more ephemeral set models. Further, the dissemination of drawings and etchings in print publications promised to reach a wider public than that of set models housed in theatre workshops or private collections.

The first extant models are small-scale representations of objects dating from the Egyptian Pre-dynastic Period (c. 6000 to 3150 BCE) and the Han Period in China (206 BCE to 220 CE). As votive representations and objects of transition to ease the 'rite of passage' (van Gennep 1960) between life, death and the afterlife, models of shops, houses, gardens or boats were placed in graves, sometimes accompanied by small figurines. These operated as mediating objects to ensure the deceased person would be provided with essentials for continuing their social standing and cultural practices in the afterlife. In some cultures of the Middle Bronze Age, models of tools, weapons and household objects were found in graves. The small scale of the votive offerings meant that large and precious objects could be symbolically represented, often in clay, wood or metal, in an economic way within the confined burial site.[7]

In Ancient Greece, the term *paradeigma* denoted architectural detail models that served as tactile guides for builders and decorative painters, particularly regarding columns and other three-dimensional constructions. The relationship between the architect's design intention and the resulting drawings and models remains unclear. Coulton (1983) states in his research on the transmission of architectural design in Ancient Greece that no extant documents offer insight into the architects' concepts, developments and decisions. He looks instead at different formats by which they communicated ideas to contractors, builders, masons, sculptors and (to a lesser extent) patrons and clients. Informed by Bundgaard's 1957 study on the Greek architect Mnesicles and his findings, Coulton suggests that the so-called *syngraphe*, a technical specification document written by the architect that listed the dimensions, materials and required workmanship, was central to the transmission of design intentions. According to Coulton, drawings were of much lesser importance than the written documents:

> To my mind the classical Greeks developed a system of planning, based on calculation rather than drawing, which well suited their particular type of architecture. (Coulton 1983: 468)

Through the construction of the *paradeigmata*, presumably under the architect's supervision, the design of architectural elements and decorations could then be specified.[8] Full-scale detail models could then be built to ensure uniformity in realizing the whole building. Finished *paradeigmata* in stone, beyond possible earlier iterations in wood, were usually incorporated into the building, whereas full-scale models, as suggested by Benndorf (cited in Coulton 1983: 458), were used not on-site but rather as representative tools to secure the building's approval by the *Boule*, the Ancient Greek council of town citizens.

Roman architects also understood the persuasive quality of the small-scale model as well as the complex relationship and possible dilemma between scale and realization. Vitruvius (c. 90 to c. 20 BCE), in *Ten Books on Architecture*, tells of a Greek architects deceit made possible by demonstrating a scale model of a city wall and war machine that promised certain victory over the attacking enemy. The seduction of this miniature vanished when it was found that at full scale the wondrous machine ceased to operate as promised:

> There are some things that achieve large-scale results like those achieved with small models. And then there are other things for which models cannot be made at all, and they must be built to scale in the first place. And some things that seem perfectly realistic in a model vanish when their scale begins to be enlarged … in some models things that seem to happen on a tiny scale might seem to occur on a larger scale as well, and that is how the Rhodians, deceived along the same lines, inflicted injury and insult upon Diognetus. (Vitruvius, Book 10, Ch. 16.4)

The architect Callias's deceitful miniature was pure persuasion, and Vitruvius's account highlights the model's potential failure as scaled-down architecture.

The architectural model in diverse scales, including the 1:1 detail model, came to prominence in the Italian Renaissance and greatly furthered its project. Andres Lepik (1994) points in his early history of the architecture model in Italy to the correlation between the emergence of the model and the discovery of perspectival theory. For him, the model captures the architect's need to visualize and apply a new understanding of space through the model's three-dimensional form, its immediate tactility and the perspectival consequences of a single vanishing point. To Lefebvre, in *The Production of Space*, perspective theory both privileges and prescribes visuality and leads to a logical system of visual representation:

The vanishing-point and the meeting of parallel lines 'at infinity' were the determinants of a representation, at once intellectual and visual, which promoted the primacy of the gaze in a kind of 'logic of visualization'. This representation, which had been in the making for centuries, now became enshrined in architectural and urbanistic practice as the *code* of linear perspective. (Lefebvre 1991 [1974]: 41)

This code meant that the model – used to communicate, discuss and test a project before and during design and building – also became a subject of theoretical discussion amongst architect's, artists and scholars of the time. Thought of as more accessible than drawings or plans, Renaissance models (most of which have not survived) point to often complex and contradictory building histories and design decisions. The continuous construction and deconstruction of St Peter's Basilica in Rome or Santa Maria del Fiore in Florence come to mind, both accompanied by numerous models created by successive architects.

In *De Re Aedificatoria* (On the Art of Building in Ten Books) written between 1443 and 1452, Leon Battista Alberti, the Renaissance humanist, art theorist, mathematician and architect, argues for the model's significance as a tool for design and technical optimization, in describing what is now called an iterative model:

Having constructed these models, it will be possible to examine clearly and consider thoroughly the relationship between the site and the surrounding district, the shape of the area, the number and order of the parts of a building, the appearance of the walls, the strength of the covering, and in short the design and construction of all the elements discussed in the previous book. It will also allow one to increase or decrease the size of those elements freely, to exchange them, and to make new proposals and alterations until everything fits together well and meets with approval. (Alberti 1988: 34)

Alberti's vision of the model as creative tool is extended by architect and scenographer Vincenzo Scamozzi, whose 1588 *Teatro all'Antica* in the Renaissance model city of Sabbioneta is central to this study as one of the first autonomous models (besides Giulio Camillo's *Theatro* from 1550) in the merging of architecture and scenography.[9] Scamozzi describes the model as a mute object and, stressing the manipulative value of the model, emphasizes the need for skilled and showman like presentations to the client:

We are accustomed to say, and rightly so, that Inventions, and drawings traced on paper, and for the most part also the Models in relief, no matter how they are made, the ones, and the others are only Inanimate, soulless bodies, therefore they need the voice of the Architect or of other person of science and value to express in words and to demonstrate in reasoning what they really are, to give them soul and speech. Because in this way people become excited and inflamed and decisions are reached concerning Important and great ventures. (Scamozzi as cited in Frascari 2011: 188–189)

For Scamozzi, the architectural model is a 'messenger' and an 'art which is a sensorial and acting demonstration' (Scamozzi as cited in Frascari 2011: 188–189). Despite his own theatre projects such as built streetscapes for the *Teatro all'Antica*'s single-perspective stage, there is no mention in his writings of the stage set model. A possible explanation for such lack of theoretical engagement lies in the strictly architectural character of the stage design (modelled as it is after Vitruvius) for which he had provided illustrations in the 1511 Venice edition of *De Architectura Libri Decem*. Further, Scamozzi's original drawings for the *Teatro all'Antica* (held at Florence's Uffizi Gallery) show ground plans and side elevations for both theatre building and stage, thus attesting to their conceptual unity. Scamozzi's plans for Sabbioneta show that the set was drawn not as a separate element or addition but as part of the original architectural plan, elevation and section.

The small-scale set model is first mentioned by the Italian Renaissance architect, painter and theorist Sebastiano Serlio (1475 to c.1554) in the second book of his treatise *Tutte l'opere d'architettura et prospettiva*, published between 1537 and 1584. In this highly influential work, Serlio sets out the rules of perspective for architecture and theatre and establishes the aesthetics and design principles of the Renaissance city to be the 'model' for the stage design of the time.[10] Renaissance stage design thus scales down the city and brings it onto the stage in the form of a permanent, built set (see Figure 1.2). In the third chapter of Book 2 under the heading 'A Treatise of Scenes, or Places to Play In', Serlio writes:

… and for that men should break the wall, if they should use all this horizon in grosse, which may not bee done, therefore I have always made a small

FIGURE 1.2 *Scene setting for tragedy, Book II of* Tutte l'opere d'architettura et prospettiva *by Sebastiano Serlio, 1611.*

modell of wood and Paper, just of the same bignes, and by the same modell set it downe in grosse, from piece to piece. But this wall will fall out hard for some men to understand, neverthelesse, it will be necessary to make by models and experiments, and by study a man shall find the way, and for that a man can hardly finde any Halls how great soever, wherin he can place a Theater without imperfection and impediment; therefore to follow Antiequities, according to my power and abilitie, I have made all such parts of these Theaters, as may stand in a Hall. (Serlio 1611: Book 2, Chapter 3, Fol. 24)

The practice of making set models 'in the Italian fashion' (Reid 1976: xiv) was taken up and administered by the Revels Office, a courtly institution set up to construct, stage and produce the elaborate masks of the English Elizabethan court theatre. Akin to Serlio's aim of testing a design's stability and dimensions, the Revels Office supplied working models to the painters, plasterers and carpenters who built and decorated the scenery. W. R. Streitberger mentions in his study *The Masters of the Revels and Elizabeth I's Court Theatre*, a so-called 'device' or written description of the overall concept (Streitberger 2016: 20) that left details of construction and decoration to the masons and painters, not unlike the (earlier mentioned) Greek *syngraphe*. It can be assumed that models were made on the basis of the written descriptions in the device and were possibly specified during the process. Costs for models were set out in detailed account books of the Revels Office throughout Elizabeth's reign (1558–1603) and under James I until 1625:

> Necessaries for the clerk: The Clerk of the office for his ordinary Greene cloth, Paper, Ink, Cownters Tooles and Necessary Implementes for the Making & conserving of Bills Bookes Plottes & Models. (1574/5, Feuillerat 1908: 247. 22–4, as cited in Turner 2006: 131)

From the 1619 record of payment to scenographer, costume designer and architect Inigo Jones (1573–1652) for at least two models, it is clear that the production of not only set models but also architectural models was administered by the Revels Office:

> To Inigo Jones upon the Councells Warr dated 27 June 1619 for making two several models the one for the Star Chamber, the other for the Banquetting House. xxxvij. (Cunningham 1842: xiv)

Inigo Jones introduced the proportions and orders of classical Greek and Roman Architecture to England and was chiefly responsible for designing the spectacular sets, machines and costumes for masques at the English court between 1604 and 1640. Like many architect-scenographers of the time, Jones, who had been to Italy several times and had studied Palladio's 1585 *Teatro Olimpico* in Vicenza, moved seamlessly between architectural and theatre practice. Peacock looks especially to Jones's 1638 stage design for *Britannia Triumphans* as embodying his architectural and stage reform:

> The houses in the foreground recall the King's efforts to regulate building in London (in which Jones was involved as an administrator) and the architect's efforts to promote a more regular, classical style of urban housing. The centrepiece of the background, St Paul's Cathedral in the course of restoration, symbolises both Charles I's reforms of the Anglican Church and Jones' austere revision of Italian classical architecture. (Peacock 1995: 326)

In seventeenth-century architecture, the making and exhibition of models grew in prominence, and small-scale models were collected and exhibited in private and public art chambers.[11] Historical sources and scholarly literature enter a silent phase in regard to the stage set model, where neither artefacts nor written descriptions are conveyed. It can be assumed that scenographers such as Jones continued to test their full-scale designs in small versions, yet the extent of stage set model-making between the seventeenth and mid-eighteenth centuries is largely unknown. One explanation is that by the mid-eighteenth century the model had become a technical necessity due to multiple scene changes, and it had become an aesthetic pleasure in its painterly mastery and detail. In the wake of Nicola Sabbatini's improvements in devices enabling scene changes (Sabbatini 1638) and the ever-increasing attraction of contraptions like wave machines and flying *apparati* (apparatuses) to enable a performer's apotheosis in full sight, the stage was increasingly freed from the constraints of the single set in the manner of Vitruvius and Serlio. From the mid-eighteenth century on, scenographers embraced the small-scale representative set model[12] as a way to display various locations for the opera or play, and for the first time it was placed in a model box for viewing. The number of contemporary models produced is unknown since few have survived, in stark contrast to the profusion of set and performance drawings and engravings produced and disseminated. This situation differs greatly from the increasing model-making practices and numbers preserved in architecture at the time.

The few extant models, such as the twenty set models for the Opéra de Paris designed by painters and scenographers between 1757 and 1761, were made from paper or cardboard and painted with gouache. Some examples comprehensively show that not only the set but also the elaborate proscenium arches that framed the designs were deemed worthy of representation and subsequent collection. With median dimensions of 44.5 cm high and 55 cm wide in roughly 1:25 scale,[13] these designs for operas by Jean-Philippe Rameau, Jean-Baptiste Lully, a ballet-héroïque by Francois Rebel and Francois Francoeur and an opéra-ballet by Antoine Dauvergne were executed in the formal symmetric and angular French style of the period while showing Italian influence, notably in multi-perspectival painted backdrops and allusions to several building levels and connecting staircases (see Figure 1.3).[14]

Jerome de la Gorce's research as to provenance and authorship of the models at the Château de Chambord, where the complete set is being housed, clarifies that rather than being the work of Italian painter and scenographer Jean-Nicolas Servandoni (as was long thought), the models were designed by his students. Amongst them were the painter Pietro Algieri and the team of painters Guillet and de Leuse (de la Gorce 1983: 439) who had worked at the Opéra de Paris under Servandoni from 1735.[15] Despite Servandoni's innovations in projecting onstage depth of field and giving the illusion of enormous height in perspective scenery,[16] French scenography until the latter part of the eighteenth century appears to have been characterized by

FIGURE 1.3 *Set design model of the finale of* Dardanus *(Jean-Philippe Rameau) by Piero Bonifazio Algieri (1760), Château de Champs-sur-Marne.*

a 'shocking symmetry' and 'the most boring uniformity' (Cochin 1781, as cited in Howarth 1997: 502, and Cochin 1793 in Howarth 1997: 512–513). With the European-wide Romantic movement and the artistic movement of neoclassicism, individual expression was privileged over formal language, and nature became a topos for the artist's desire to articulate atmosphere through colour, light and shadow. A significant artefact in this respect is one of the oldest-surviving set models in London's Victoria and Albert Museum, by landscape painter and scenographer Philip James de Loutherbourg, creator of the spectacular 1781 *Eidophusikon*.[17]

Beyond the generic eighteenth-century scenic settings of wing flats and painted backcloths, Loutherbourg's model from his 1779 pantomime *The Wonders of Derbyshire* (premiered at London's Drury Lane) shows the Peak's Hole, a Derbyshire cave and one of its seven scenic 'wonders', in a perspectival treatment (see Figure 1.4). Loutherbourg achieved this by the irregular horizontal layering of five cut-outs whose spatial configuration allowed for subtle lighting states and pronounced depth of field. Combining the diversely coloured cut-outs with freestanding boulders, Loutherbourg

FIGURE 1.4 *Set design model of* The Wonders of Derbyshire *by Philip James de Loutherbourg, 1799.*

created a specific site in which the actors could move freely from traditional front-of-stage positions to mid-stage and beyond.

Loutherbourg's strongly articulated and individual design language prefigured departures in the nineteenth century from wing stage arrangements and backcloths painted in perspective towards atmospheric stage environments that comprised lighting, scenery, furnishings and props. With the emergence of Wagner's concept of theatre as *Gesamtkunstwerk* in 1849[18] and Naturalism's and Realism's desire for accurate representations of reality in the late nineteenth century,[19] the set model gained currency as a design, communication and representational tool that began to be systematically collected. A prominent example was the 1881–1882 group of models by painter-scenographers Max and Gotthold Brückner for the first staging of Wagner's *Parsifal* at Bayreuth. These followed the original highly detailed yet atmospheric and romantic design drawings by Brückner and Paul von Joubowsky (see Figure 1.5).

Such attention to detail is also found in late nineteenth-century architectural models, at a time when the discipline re-created and reinterpreted historical precedents in classical architecture from the Greek and Roman to the Egyptian and Byzantine. Desire for historical accuracy and an abundance of decorative architectural elements help to explain not only the continued building and

FIGURE 1.5 *Set design model of* Parsifal *(Richard Wagner) by Max Brückner, 1882.*

increased collecting of small-scale models[20] but also the emergence of the 1:1 architecture model or prototype. The making of façade parts and corner elements for the dual purpose of testing and client persuasion became common practice, and a condition for several competition entries in the early twentieth century,[21] continuing to this day.

After the 1917 Russian Revolution, Russian artists and architects sought to visualize and disseminate the utopian ideals of a new society ruled by the proletariat. Much of what they designed remained as paper architecture, drawings and sketches. The model, however, became a means to give physical form to a desired social, cultural and political future. The presentation of models in exhibitions and public space visualized a future that, as in the case of workers carrying a model of *Tatlin's Tower* in the 1925 Petrograd May Day Parade, was fuelled by Socialism's promise of equality and the abolition of private property and worker exploitation. Constructivist small-scale set models, such as Ljubov Popova's 1922 design for Meyerhold's production of *The Magnanimous Cuckold*, took on a semantic role beyond their material status. Popova's model pointed to a future where seemingly disparate functional elements such as blades of a watermill, a wheel and a scaffold worked in ideal socialist harmony. In the context of the constructivist stage, Georgii Kovolenko describes the constructivist set model as an 'autonomous installation' rather than a painted set, asserting:

Essentially it was a spatial formula, whose components, as well as their interactions and correlations, were abstracted and reduced to a minimal level of expression. (Kovolenko 1991: 145)

The energy expressed in the spiralling structure of Tatlin's unrealized *Tower* and the machine-like construction of Popova's set (that seemed to await the actor to bring it to life through action) resounds in Austro-American architect and scenographer Frederick (Friedrich) Kiesler's *Railway Theatre* (see Figure 1.6). Here, model and machine come together in that the model is the stage set itself, no longer its small-scale precursor. First exhibited at the Vienna International Exhibition of Theatre Technology in 1924, the *Railway Theatre*, as one of the manifestations of Kiesler's overall concept of the Space Theatre, visualizes a theatre without a proscenium, defined by the immersion of actors and audience in a single, dynamic mechanical environment:

The first attempt to design electro-mechanical scenery. The fixed scenery has become alive, an active part in the play. De la nature morte vivante. The means to fill the stage with life are: movement of lines, sharp contrasts of

FIGURE 1.6 *Model and stage of* Railway Theatre *by Frederick (Friedrich) Kiesler, Vienna 1924.*

colours, the transformation of surfaces towards relief and curved human forms (actors). There is the interplay of moving lights of various colours on the scenery, in rhythm according to speech intonation and the movement of the actors.... (Kiesler 1924: n.p.)

In the performative, autonomous models of Russian constructivism, in *Tatlin's Tower* (see Figure 1.7) and Popova's model machines that stood for an idealized socialism, and in Kiesler's 'correalist'[22] vision of theatre as a self-regulating machine built as an autonomous 1:1 model, the future manifested in the form of the singular object deeply coded with meaning, not unlike the utopian theatre models of the *Bauhaus* era that envisaged theatre's future as a single encompassing immersive organism.

In 1926–1927, *Bauhaus* founder and architect Walter Gropius was invited by director Erwin Piscator to design the *Totaltheater* (total theatre) whose aim was to immerse the spectator and all architectural elements in a kinetic architecture underlined by film projections throughout the space. In 1927, Hungarian artist Andor Weininger designed the *Kugeltheater* (spheric theatre) for the opening of the Dessau *Bauhaus* Architecture Department. Seated on the inside wall of the sphere, the audience would follow the action to be shown simultaneously on several steep ramps that rose vertically in the centre of the globe. The belief of scenographers, artists and architects of Constructivism and Modernism, in the singular revolutionary object that (whether realized or not) sought to radically redefine and transgress social, political and cultural conventions and boundaries once and for all, explains the emergence of the utopian, forward-pointing model in the 1920s.

From the mid-nineteenth century onwards, architecture exhibitions had added to the visibility of the utopian and representative models in the public eye. They grew in range and ambition to the use of full-size models in exhibitions dedicated to the future of living and emerging in the commercial world as new typologies, *Show Homes* and *Display Apartments*, for the purpose of selling real estate prior to construction. Beyond the commercial use of the model home, housing exhibitions have emerged across the world as an opportunity to propose new typologies of domestic space and contemporary living.

The examples detailed in this volume that begin with the *Prince Albert's Model Lodging House* in the 1851 Great Exhibition in London and move to the 2008 exhibition at the Museum of Modern Art (MoMA) in New York, entitled *Home Delivery: Fabricating the Modern Dwelling*, are a small representative sample of hundreds of housing exhibitions that have been staged across the world.

A glance at the geographic and temporal range of this format will consider the 1883 Art and Industry Exhibition at Tullinløkka, the ongoing Internationale Bauausstellung (IBA) in Germany, in Darmstadt in 1901 (and continued in

FIGURE 1.7 *Model of the* Monument to the Third International *by Vladimir Tatlin, 1919–1920.*

Leipzig in 1913, Stuttgart in 1927, and Berlin in 1957 and 1984), the 1908 Franco-British Exhibition in London, the 1924 Form and Colour exhibition in Oslo, the 1930 Stockholm Exhibition, the 1932 International Style Exhibition at MoMA, the 1939 New Zealand Centennial Exhibition, the 1947 Exhibition Internationale de l'habitation et de l'urbanisme in Paris and many others that contributed to a conceptual framework and discourse around the staging of the domestic that has made the housing exhibition a uniquely influential authority in the shaping of the built environment worldwide.

Similarly, theatre exhibitions that emerged in the early twentieth century had been internationally oriented in their presentation of set designs in the form of model boxes and drawings, costumes and drawings, etchings and photographs of performances and actors in costume, influencing future staging practices immensely. The 1914 Zurich Theaterkunst Exhibition in the Swiss National Museum deserves mention as, while only fourteen exhibits and no stage set models were shown, this exhibition was the site of the only encounter between the two great modernist theatre reformers Adolphe Appia and Edward Gordon Craig. Peter Eversmann (2007) examines the International Theatre Exhibition at Amsterdam's Stedelijk Theatre from 1922, which subsequently travelled to London, Manchester and Bradford and on to New York. Designs, sets, models and costumes by ninety-five scenographers and architects of the international avant-garde, amongst them Adolphe Appia, Léon Bakst, Edward Gordon Craig and Hendrik Berlage, were displayed. Eversmann identifies a critique of present Dutch theatre practices and aesthetics as the conceptual and programmatic point of departure of this seminal exhibition. In the central figure of the Dutch architect and set designer H. T. Wijdeveldt, a member of the Amsterdamse School of architecture and editor of the art and architecture journal *Wendingen*, the exhibition had found a vocal and active proponent (Wijdeveldt was responsible for the invitation to Craig) of abstraction and focus on what he perceived as the essential elements in theatre architecture and scenography. Another highly influential, large-scale exhibition, the International Theatre Exhibition at MoMA, New York, in 1934, curated by the architect and set designer Lee Simonson, presented set designs, costume drawings and treatises from the sixteenth to the twentieth centuries and occupied all four floors of the museum with the lighted stage set models positioned in designated rooms. MoMA's first press release, almost three months prior to the opening in January 1934, states that

> [f]our centuries of progress in the art of the theatre will be shown by period and by country, with models and drawings of stage sets and costumed from Sweden, Germany, France, England, Austria, Italy and Switzerland. (MoMA Press Release 7 October 1933)

Due to the late arrival of material from the Soviet Union, the opening had to be postponed by one week, and the museum remained closed to the public for that time to mount the exhibition that comprised more than 700 exhibits. The final press release from 13 or 14 January 1934, announcing the opening of the exhibition on 16 January, lists all artists and their exhibits with an explanatory commentary of the significance of the exhibiting artists and their works. Appia and Craig, exhibited in the section 'Pioneers of modern theatre art', are singled out in the document, and it seems the writer is particularly eager to make the press understand their standing in the history, present and future of theatre.

> Adolphe Appia, the great Swiss artist, anticipated as early as 1895 the principles of simple forms and subtly controlled lighting which were later developed and popularized by Gordon Craig abroad and by Robert Edmond Jones in this country. The executors of the Appia estate has lent twenty-two of his original drawings, almost the entire body of his work, none of which has ever been seen in this country. In addition, six authentic models will be shown of settings he designed for *The Valkyrie* and *The Rheingold*, stage pictures created 'out of the music's spirit' for the Wagner operas. The models, which will be lighted, have been lent by the Cologne Theatre Museum. Like Appia, Gordon Craig was a prophet who went almost unrecognized in his own country, England. He is represented in the Exhibition by twelve etchings of settings for an Ideal Theatre. (MoMA Press Release undated, for release on 13 or 14 January 1934)

The press release mentions six models by Adolphe Appia, on loan from the then Theatre Collection at Castle Wahn in Cologne, Germany.[23] These were part of the Niessen collection; however, they never returned to Cologne, and while it is known that parts of the collection landed at the Swiss Theatre Collection in Berne, the precious Appia models were not among them, and they appear to be lost. Regrettably, no photographic documentation exists of the models that would have been particularly atmospheric when, as the press release states, lit for exhibition. A success story for Lee Simonson who had travelled across Europe for two months in 1933 to secure the exhibits, and MoMA, the International Theatre Exhibition was seen by 10,000 people in the first week alone, and in recognition of the 'great interest that the Exhibition holds for people of the theatre' (MoMA Press Release 30 January 1934), the museum extended an invitation for members of Actor's Equity and Chorus Equity Associations.

In Zurich, Amsterdam and New York, the exhibited scenographic model remained at small scale, and the dimensions of the original stage set model box equalled that of the exhibit until the mid to end of the twentieth century. Only once new exhibition formats and curatorial concepts allowed for the model to have autonomous presence in the exhibition space, be it in a group show, solo exhibition or experimental modes of representation, as in the development of the Prague Quadrennial and the inaugural Venice Architecture Biennale, could the model's emancipation from a second-order status be observed and its autonomy confirmed. One of the earliest exhibitions of autonomous models was Czech scenographer Josef Svoboda's *Polyekran*, a multi-channel interactive projection system, set up in the black box of the Czech Brutalist pavilion designed by Miroslav Řepa and Vladimír Pýcha for the 1967 Montreal Expo where the presentation of state-of-the-art scenographic, immersive technology was shown at full scale for the visitor to experience, not unlike Kiesler's autonomous model of the *Railway Stage* exhibited in Vienna in 1924.

To the designer and the scenographer, formal, material and technological experimentation through the model present infinite research approaches into the generation of form and the exploration of materials, thus futuring present practices and past conventions, and in this, the autonomous model not only enables the performance of space but becomes a performance.

2

Staging Politics
and Knowledge through
the Model

The unique capacity of the model to embody a world in a single object has led architects and scenographers to exploit this potential since the Italian Renaissance, when the model became a central tool not only for design development and communication but also for the staging of political ideas and abstract concepts. At different scales, from the full-scale urban space to the miniature theatre, the model was explored as a site to communicate and celebrate intellectual, artistic and technological knowledge and progress. In the following, close readings of four scenographic and architectural models across Renaissance, Baroque and the eighteenth century, all of which this project defines as autonomous in that they are the one and final artefact rather than an iterative or representative manifestation of future realizations, seek to establish how the contained worlds of these model environments enable seemingly universal concepts such as the representation of all of mankind's knowledge in one or the essence of absolutist governance in another came to be staged as a direct and immediate experience.

Understood in the context of this project as a physical medium able to stage and thus to externalize the singular hierarchical principle of Baroque rulership, Vincenzo Scamozzi's 1588–1590 *Teatro all'Antica* is introduced to this project as the programmatic convergence of scenography and architecture in a scaled city model on the stage that enabled the staging and performance of absolutist political power through the construction of a single central perspective. The utopian thought not of a staging of power but rather of knowledge, and in particular that all prior, current and future knowledge of man could be stored, represented and retrieved through performance, propelled Giulio Camillo around 1550 to design and build a scaled-down, inhabitable model of a *teatro memoria*, a memory theatre. The *teatro*'s singular interior, in plan not dissimilar to the anatomical theatres in Leiden (1593), Padua (1594) and Bologna (1637), which staged in their centre both the corpse as exhibit and the dissector as performer, comprised both model, stage and auditorium in a unique understanding of memory and knowledge as precisely sited yet dynamic and interrelated entities. Against the singular, autonomous model that is capable of staging all knowledge, scenographer and architect Joseph Furttenbach posited in the mid-sixteenth century the art chamber as comprised of a subjective collection of models, paintings and text documents. In his 1641 *Architectura Privata*, the world itself, with its natural and technical wonders, could be comprehended and understood through the exhibited miniatures, and by prescribing the visitors' parcours, knowledge was to be explored in dialogue with the models and thematically as well as in time. In a school theatre for an audience of ultimately 1,000, that he built in his hometown of Ulm in the same year, 1641, Furttenbach conducted detailed experiments with scene changes, stage machinery and lighting on what was effectively a model stage in a model theatre for experimentation and demonstration (staging) of knowledge.

The large-scale model environment of Jean-Nicolas Servandoni's 1737 *spectacles d'optique* housed on the immense stage of the Tuileries' Salle des Machines and Philip James de Loutherbourg's 1781 miniature theatre *Eidophusikon* show the theatre set itself to be a knowledge machine that operates from the inside out, comprising an autonomous and dramatically configured model of the world, testament to the discipline's technological advancement. Neither representation nor experimental tool, the *Eidophusikon* as a scale model of the natural world enabled performance through scenographic innovation.

The models introduced in this part of the project that speaks of the Renaissance and Baroque model's epistemic capacity in the staging and the performance of abstract concepts and ideologies are linked in that they are creative, purposeful and future-oriented. As autonomous models, they are affirmative of the creative potential and dramatic power of scenography as the art of giving meaning to space.

Model and system: Staging the city

Vincenzo Scamozzi: *Teatro all'Antica*, Sabbioneta 1588

During the Italian Renaissance, models became the architect's central instrument in communication and negotiation with patrons, clients, craftspeople and builders. Architectural material and perspectival knowledge sets were produced and communicated through elaborate, predominantly wooden models and these contributed significantly to the epistemes of the discipline at the time. In coalescence with extant drawings and plans, these models are still studied today to further our detailed understanding of Renaissance architecture. By the mid-fifteenth century, the traditional making of full-scale models and *paradeigmata* denoted general practice, allowing the architect to significantly extend his control over aesthetic and formal aspects of a future building. As early as the fourteenth century, the use of models is documented in the construction of cathedrals in Northern Italy, and in the work of prominent Renaissance architects and artists Filippo Brunelleschi, Leon Battista Alberti, Vincenzo Scamozzi and Michelangelo. Brunelleschi's biographer Antonio Manetti mentions a fourteenth-century model of the Florentine dome Santa Maria del Fiore (see Millon 1994: 19), confirming that the Florentine architect had, in fact, won the competition for the dome by presenting a large-scale model made from brick and wood (1994). Brunelleschi's models were deliberately unfinished, substituting (as in his dome and apse iterations of the Florence dome) structural detail for decorative detail. This bias indicates their primary use as a visual control and testing tool for designer and builders (1994).

For Brunelleschi's contemporary Alberti, the model presented above all the material externalization of an idea and a tactile opportunity for design optimization. It was to be constructed simply and without any distracting or persuasive decoration, supporting Brunelleschi's process of selective presentation of architectural and decorative detail:

> There is a particularly relevant consideration that I feel should be mentioned here: the presentation of models that have been coloured and lewdly dressed with the allurement of painting is the mark of no architect intent on conveying the facts; rather it is that of a conceited one, striving to attract and seduce the eye of the beholder, and to divert his attention from a proper examination of the parts to be considered, toward admiration of himself. (Alberti 1988: 34)

Despite the large number of more or less detailed contemporary Renaissance models, few gained similar prominence to those of St Peter's Cathedral in Rome, where the making of a succession of architectural models accompanied not only its initial 100-year construction but numerous subsequent reconstructions and alterations. Of the models by Bramante, Raphael, Peruzzi, Sangallo the Younger, Michelangelo, Giacomo della Porta and Maderno, only Sangallo's large-scale wooden model (built between 1539 and 1546 in four iterations) survived. Designed to facilitate communication with the builders, at a scale of 1:30 and situated on a plinth just over one metre high, the model is partially enterable, allowing the viewer to study both exterior and interior elements close-up and at eye level. At a height of 155 centimetres and with an interior width of 80 centimetres, the Sangallo model presents a counterpoint to Alberti's and Brunelleschi's deliberately incomplete models. Highly detailed, and painted in different shades to suggest the stucco treatment of the interior, the Sangallo model exhibits both persuasion and performance in that it demands the viewer physically enter its very body (see Millon 1994).

In the purpose-built theatres of the Cinquecento that came to replace the earlier temporary stages in courtly halls, courtyards and gardens, the architecture model reconfigured itself as a scaled, ideal city on the stage. Here, newly formalized laws of perspective were eagerly exploited for visual persuasion and immersion. The stage architectures of Andrea Palladio's and Vincenzo Scamozzi's theatres in Vicenza (*Teatro Olimpico*, built between 1580 and 1585) and Sabbioneta (built between 1588 and 1590) embodied the Renaissance notion of the master-planned, unified and harmonious *città ideale* (ideal city). Rows of houses were built in foreshortened perspective with a central corridor that appeared to converge at the central vanishing point beyond the back of the stage. Inspired by Serlio's drawings of a generic setting for tragedy, namely a central street flanked by Renaissance-style buildings of differing heights and dimensions, the architect-scenographers set out to realize the representation of the ideal contemporary city in terms of scaled architectural models on the stage, and thus have the city enter the stage, visibly linking urban reality and ephemeral performance.

The small town of Sabbioneta (situated between the cities of Parma and Mantua in the North of Italy) comprises, with Pienza and Palmanova, one of only three Italian Renaissance ideal cities ever built. For the architects of the fifteenth and sixteenth centuries, who saw themselves as humanists in the tradition of Ancient Greece, the new notion of an 'ideal city' represented a much-desired departure from the feudal structures evident in the layout of medieval cities with a religious centre and labyrinthic surrounds that defined and segregated all sites according to social class. According to humanist principles, the city was to be conceived as one unified urban fabric in which, however, social segregation was still generally upheld. The town hall rather than the church became the city's centre, and surrounding streets were designed to form either a chessboard structure or grid or concentric circles with streets radiating outwards. The influence of Alberti's first theoretical architectural treatise of the Renaissance, *De Re Aedificatoria* (On the Art of Building), published in 1485 but already circulated in manuscript from 1452, is clearly visible in these design schemata. Drawing predominantly on Vitruvius, Alberti developed mathematical ratios as a valid foundation for the creation of harmony, unity and beauty in architecture and the arts. And while *De Re Aedificatoria* was largely based on Vitruvius' (rediscovered) seminal *De Architectura* (1414), Alberti brought to the discourse a new focus on geometry and perspective. Further, he suggested different design solutions for different conditions rather than prescribing one rigid city model. Eaton rightly argues that for the first time in the Italian Renaissance, the city is viewed as an object that can be planned and designed in its entirety (Eaton 2002: 44). As a result, town planning became a new methodological tool for the design and realization of new urban principles. In this context, architectural drawing techniques flourished, with *Ichnographia* (ground plan) allowing for an immediate overview of an often schematic city design, and *Scenographiae* (perspective) letting the viewer inhabit diverse points of view.[1]

The Renaissance ideal city, as documented in writings, drawings and built form, comprised a distinct model for living according to the architectural expression of civic pride and an ideal political system. And in the same way that Plato's and Aristotle's visions of the ideal city-state always included a ruler or law-maker to guide a stratified society, the ideal city of the Renaissance provided for places of political decision-making and administration in the form of aristocratic residences, ducal palaces and town halls.[2]

The roofed court theatre at Sabbioneta was commissioned by Duke Vespasiano Gonzaga as the completion of his master-planned ideal city. The theatre, freestanding on three sides, was designed by architect and scenographer Vincenzo Scamozzi (a collaborator of the late Andrea Palladio) and, due to the designer's complex perspectival treatment of interior and stage, has been the subject of several art-historical, scenographic and architectural studies.[3] Following the Renaissance treatises on perspective, the first raked stages in Vicenza, Sabbioneta and Ferrara had been built to exploit the vanishing point and illusion of depth through the use of perspectival fixed sets. In contrast to Palladio's *Teatro Olimpico* in Vicenza, where the proscenium and Roman-type *frons scenae* (stage wall) clearly divide auditorium, stage and background into three distinct spaces, Scamozzi in Sabbioneta abolished proscenium and stage wall (and thus the framed separation between stage and auditorium) in favour of a unified interior. In effect, he extended the single-point perspective through and beyond the central axis of the entire building. This design decision led Kurt W. Forster, in his study 'Stagecraft and Statecraft: Architectural Integration of Public Life and Theatrical Spectacle in Scamozzi's Theatre at Sabbioneta', to analyse the relationship between the Duke's feudal rulership and the auditorium's perspectival treatment and seating order.

In simple terms, the stage signified 'city square', and the ducal loggia indicated 'urban palace'. They were held in balance, but reality was on the side of the princely spectator, who stood among real columns against a representation of Roman emperors, while the fake architecture of the stage was entirely conditioned in its perspective dislocation by the princely point of view. (Forster 1977: 81)

The central position of the theatre, imperceptibly to one side of Sabbioneta's main axis, the Via Imperatore (*sic*), is a testament to the importance Duke Vespasiano gave to this new type of building in the context of his master-planned city. Where earlier theatres had been nothing more than temporary constructions in courtyards, halls or gardens, the typology of the permanent theatre building, initiated with Palladio's *Teatro Olimpico*, was embedded by Scamozzi's just five years later. Differences between the two theatres can be largely explained by political divergences in the cities of Vicenza and Sabbioneta and thus the theatres' sponsors, and are expressed in the respective interiors, stage set-up and spatial organization. The *Teatro Olimpico* had been commissioned in 1580 by Vicenza's *Accademia Olimpica* (Olympic Academy), a small and private humanist organization of which the theatre's architect Palladio was a member. By contrast to Sabbioneta, the theatre's site in Vicenza was a pre-existing rectangular building and the interior needed to fit inside. The site's condition resulted in an almost square space denoting the non-hierarchical Greek model of 'democratic seating' (Carlson 1989: 135). Sabbioneta's theatre, on the other hand, had been a princely commission, and while it can be assumed that Vespasiano knew Palladio's theatre in Vicenza (completed after his death by Scamozzi), its singular spatial organization stands in sharp contrast to the sense of social equality found in Vicenza.

By combining three single-point perspectival schemes in the theatre's interior, the model character of the town is extended into the theatre space, serving to cement the Duke's absolutist vision of power. Social stratification and segregation, as articulated through architectural form, begins with access to the theatre. The Duke and noble ladies would enter unseen through a covered walkway directly to the loggia on the second floor, while the aristocratic men would enter by means of the north portal and proceed to the curved, tiered seating underneath the Duke's colonnade. Meanwhile, the general audience, that is, the Duke's political subjects, entered through the ground-floor western entrance door to be seated in the level zone of the orchestra. A separate entrance for the performers is to be found behind the stage on the south side of the building. Between the stage at one end and the tiered seating at the other sits the open and neutral orchestra space.

With interior-space proportions in length-to-width ratio of 3:1 and a total length of around 27 metres, the theatre at Sabbioneta is a small and intimate space, made immersive through its use of perspective (see Figure 2.1). The permanent built and painted single-vista scenography denotes a *strada nobile*, a grand street with representative buildings of differing heights on either side (see Figure 2.1). Recalling Serlio's set for the *scena tragica*, Scamozzi uses the perspectival architectural scene on the raked stage for an enhanced effect of depth. The frescoed sidewalls depict triumphal arches reaching up to the balustraded colonnade and the seats of Duke and aristocracy. The eye is led,

FIGURE 2.1 *View onto stage,* Teatro all'Antica *by Vincenzo Scamozzi, Sabbioneta 1588.*

through single-point perspective painting, to collaged Roman monuments amid an idyllic landscape. The limits of the physical space thereby extend towards an ideal exterior, providing a visual link between the past grandeur of Rome and the present rulership of the Duke. Additional *trompe l'oeil* depicting generic peoples links the meeting point of the sidewall with the colonnade and its inhabitants, again strengthening the bond between decorative elements, perspective and audience (see Figure 2.2).

In her monograph on Scamozzi's works, viewed as a 'choreography of early modern architecture', Ann Marie Borys suggests convincingly that Sabbioneta in its entirety constitutes an 'instrument for looking' (Borys 2014: 38) with the theatre forming a 'camera obscura' whereby the ideal city is projected into the theatre, and where the performance space extends from stage to theatre, to street and to city. Borys' analogy is enhanced by the camera obscura's functional dependency on the bundling of light into a single beam so that the image may be projected completely yet with its perspective preserved. The camera obscura's singular beam of light, able to project an exterior image onto an interior surface and vice versa, corresponds to Scamozzi's precise use of perspective in the theatre's interior and stage in order to spatialize the singular rulership of the Duke. To achieve such a correlation, Scamozzi's idealized city on the stage is constructed, following Alberti's perspectival theory and viewing pyramid, with an idealized and elevated spectator in mind. Alberti suggests that such a spectator occupy a fixed and standing position as visualized from the top of a pyramid through a disembodied eye. Only at

FIGURE 2.2 *View onto Duke's box and entrance,* Teatro all'Antica *by Vincenzo Scamozzi, Sabbioneta 1588.*

this point is the perspectival painting visible without distortion (Alberti 2011: 125). The elevated spectator, in the case of Sabbioneta, is the Duke, seated in the centre of the balustrade directly above the north portal and acting as a 'visual anchor' (Forster 1977: 74) within the theatre's central axis, linking the scenographic construction on the stage to the elevated box of the permanent building. With the Duke as the sole spectator of the intact and undistorted perspective, the stage with its simulated central street leading to the horizon and vanishing point becomes a contained model of the Duke's political realm and combines architecture and performers within an idealized city architecture. During performances, when stage and auditorium came alive with people, movement, lights and sound, a second model is seen to emerge, namely the theatre's entire interior as a model for the Duke's social position in the daily reality of Sabbioneta. Not only was the Duke's idealized territory permanently displayed on the stage but the spatial organization of the interior mirrored the contemporary social stratification of Sabbioneta. Centrally seated and flanked by the members of his court and aristocracy, the Duke in his box was raised above the lower classes. At any juncture, the Duke presided over the stage area and over every person in the theatre. Thereby, the theatre's interior, in the spatial relationship between stage and auditorium, and by means of an inversion of interior and exterior spaces, constitutes a model of an extended Sabbioneta whereby the city's political hierarchy is expressed.

If the theatre's interior is extended out into the urban master plan of Sabbioneta, a third model can be identified (after the stage and theatre-interior models) that relates to the placement of the theatre between the Duke's private and political residences. These three buildings form the spatial narrative of an absolutist ruler in his city, and the model comprises (in conjunction with the streetscapes leading to and from) a representation of the Duke's presence in the ideal Renaissance city. Incongruously, this is a model for an absolutist rather than a humanist rulership. Thus, in the three models of Sabbioneta, scenography and architecture are inextricably joined, according to the Renaissance technique of single-point perspective, to affirm and strengthen the absolutist political hierarchies of the city. The stage model, the model of the interior and the model of the city, conjoin to create, both individually and as an interrelated body, a distinct mise-en-scène that is concerned with scenographic and architectural advancement as much as with the performance of politics. This performance is enabled and strengthened in the theatre's programmatic convergence of architecture and scenography with the construction of a single central perspective that links the ducal presence with the architectural construction and scenographic interior. In an overall scenographic reading of Sabbioneta's architectonic and symbolic relationships, according to the placement of its buildings and streets and the theatre's interior and permanent scene, the planned and constructed model properties of city, theatre and stage become evident. The performative qualities of model city, model theatre building and model stage demonstrate a unified and collective capacity to stage political power.

Model and cosmos: Performing the theatres of knowledge

Giulio Camillo: *L'Idea del Theatro*, Venice/Florence 1550

Samuel Quiccheberg: *Inscriptiones vel Tituli Theatri Amplissimi*, Munich 1565

Marino Auriti: *Palazzo Enciclopedico*, Venice Biennale 2013

Between the sixteenth and eighteenth centuries, the term 'theatrum' ('theatre', 'theater', 'teatro') was used widely beyond the immediate discipline of theatre in the context of encyclopaedic collections and exhibitions in the form of 'art chambers' or enterable 'cabinets of curiosities' as well as for printed treatises aiming at a systematized representation of nature, art, architecture and science.[4] Collections and exhibitions are here discussed in the framework of the performative potential of the model according to both autonomous and teleological models of the universe. The use of the term 'theatre' by scholars of the time, while on the surface primarily metonymical, relates in fact to central parameters of theatre such as the act of looking and gestures of showing and demonstrating, and to spatial appropriations and variations of the Vitruvian theatre model.

The Mantuan apothecary Filippo Costa's natural history *studiolino*, was described in 1586 as 'indeed a *genteel* theater of the rarest simples that our age has discovered' (Findlen 1994: 105). The *teatro della natura* (1551–1554) by the Bolognese scholar Ulisse Aldrovandi comprised an ever-expanding collection of plant and herb specimens, illustrations and commentaries on natural history, also including depictions of imaginary monsters and dragons.[5] The list of publications in the 'theatrum' genre is extensive and includes monumental works such as Theodor Zwinger the Elder's *Theatrum Vitae Humane* (Basel 1565), an encyclopaedic account and astounding topographic representation of knowledge, with a scope of 1,500 pages in the first edition and more than 8,000 pages in the last edition from 1707.[6]

While the term 'theatrum' was used metonymically,[7] and thus did not relate to an actual theatre or theatre performance, the term rapidly became a central metaphor, and universal perspective for an individual in a world likened to that of an actor on a stage. Representing worldly transience, ephemerality and illusion, the late Renaissance and Baroque theatre metaphor served to enrich and validate art chambers and publications with a cosmological dimension. In a bold departure from the medieval religious emphasis on the afterlife, it supported a new focus on living in the present.[8] In this, the exhibitions and large volumes titled *theatrum* related both to the direct meaning of theatre as a site for producing and viewing performance and, more widely, to theatre as a mirror of society.

A close look at the model theatres and staged environments of knowledge by Giulio Camillo from 1550 and by Joseph Furttenbach from 1628 and 1641, respectively, reveals a scenographic and theatrical impetus in the constructions of their *theatri mundi* (theatres of the world). These *theatri* operated as speculative, enterable models of the universe and aimed to represent all possible knowledge within their collection of objects, models, drawings, specimens and texts. They were, in today's terms, designed to be at once models and participative sites of knowledge.

A view of models such as Wartofsky's, who argues for a performative reading of models due to their teleological, creative and experiential capacities, rings particularly true for the forward-looking theatres of knowledge. Camillo's theatre and Furttenbach's collections and exhibitions, in particular, presented the current state of knowledge in model form and at the same time provided a visionary outlook for a future world that would make use of it. As purposeful models for the future, the universal collections of the sixteenth and seventeenth centuries operated at once as contemplative art chamber, participatory environment and interactive laboratory in the service of knowledge production, its exhibition and its documentation. To comprehend and enjoy the theatres of knowledge, the visitor had to engage in an intense act of looking not dissimilar to viewing a performance. In contrast to the classical theatre experience, however, the theatres of knowledge invited direct participation in both the demonstration of the workings of diverse instruments and machines and the performance of scientific experiments. In today's terms, it can be said that the theatres of knowledge were characterized by an inherent performativity, tactility and immersion. Objects might be taken up off the tables, handled, scrutinized from all sides, compared with other exemplars, and read about in the accompanying theoretical treatises. The objects' variations in scale, materiality and perspective supported the visitor's absorption into the concept and physicality of the theatre. The use of different media, from printed matter to paintings, to sculpture to diverse kinetic constructions, offered a rich and tangible experience of the wonders of the world.

Belgian scholar Samuel Quiccheberg, in the first-ever theoretical treatise on how to order, plan and exhibit a collection that would succeed in representing all knowledge and aiding its future advancement, titled his 1565 Munich treatise, *Inscriptiones vel Tituli Theatri Amplissimi* (titles of the most ample theatre) with the term 'theatre', carrying both conceptual and actual architectonic meaning. Quiccheberg's design envisaged four collection rooms around a central courtyard that he described as resembling an amphitheatre:

> Also, the term 'theater' is not unsuitably, but rather properly employed here for a grand building that is in the form of an arc, or oval, or in the shape of an ambulatory, of a kind which in basilicas or cloisters are called 'circuits' by those who reside in them, and that is constructed with high storeys on four sides, in the middle of which a garden or interior courtyard might be left (as, for example, the Bavarian theater of artefacts appears), so that four enormous halls open out in very broad fashion towards the four directions of the sky. For this reason, it would also be possible in some way to apply the term 'amphitheatre' to it. (Quiccheberg *Inscriptiones* [at the beginning of the *Digressiones*] in Meadow and Robertson 2003)

In extrapolating Wartofsky's notion of the purposeful model to Quiccheberg's theatre, it is evident that the *Inscriptiones* describe an autonomous, teleological model, one that presents the current world in model form while extending an invitation to the future. In this paradigm, the deliberate staging of what

Quiccheberg assumed to be the totality of knowledge allowed the model's performative potential to be realized in the visitor's acts of participation.

While Quiccheberg's ideal theatre was only partially built during his lifetime, he was critically aware of other scholars of the time who employed the 'theatrum' metaphor in print publications, namely the Italian rhetorician and hermeticist Giulio Camillo (1480–1544) who had proposed and built a model theatre that was dedicated to the art of memory and rhetorics:

> Here it is necessary to mention that the museum of Giulio Camillo, on account of its semi-circular construction, could also properly be called a theater. On the other hand, others have used this term figuratively, as did Christoph Mylaeus, Conrad Lycosthenes, Theodorus Zwinger and Guilelme de la Perriere, and perhaps others as well, when they, nonetheless beautifully, so titled certain books on, for example, the conditions of human life, the science of writing history and remaining matters of exposition and narrative, though not on the importance of situating a building and the objects displayed or presented within it. (Meadow and Robertson 2003)

In contrast to Quiccheberg's propositional theatre-art chamber, Camillo's memory theatre was a scaled-down actual construction that operated both as a representative model of a theatre and as an autonomous model for the production of knowledge through a performative act.

First built in Venice and later rebuilt in Paris at the urgent request of Francis I, King of France, the theatre aimed at representing all knowledge accessible to man through text and image. In a curious entanglement of encyclopaedia and magic, the theatre would also contain man's yet unknown inner knowledge and enable its articulation. Camillo's description of the theatre and the complex ideas behind it are collected in the manuscript L'Idea del Theatro from 1550, published posthumously in Venice and Florence.[9] The wooden miniature theatre promised to turn the single spectator into an accomplished orator on all possible topics in the tradition of Cicero.[10]

The mnemotechnical techniques of the antique ars memoriae thus revived by Camillo were based on linking images and words in specific locations within an overall physical environment; that is, a shelf, room, house, street or even an entire city. The orator placed the words and phrases to be remembered into exact locations, as well as choosing and delivering imagery that would evoke a specific term. During the mental operation of navigating the complete spatial narrative from object to object and between words and imagery, the speech in its totality would be retrieved from the loci. It could thus be remembered chronologically, linked and enriched with the orator's subjective associations, ensuring a masterful delivery. Far from denoting a purely rhetorical and literary exercise, Lina Bolzoni, in *The Play of Memory between Words and Images*, points out the theatrical dimension of these antique mnemotechnical spatial constructions, and particularly of the images, the so-called *imagines agentes* (agent images) themselves.

> Animated by mnemonic images, they [the locations] became scenes in a theatre where every element was disguised and transformed so that it could be used in a performance of *ars memoriae*. (Bolzoni 1999: 13)

Following the antique rhetorical tradition, Camillo's memory theatre offered an abundance of mythological, magical and historical *imagines agentes*. These would provide a single verbal association to the orator as well as written material. Written and visual material was stored in the tiered seating areas of the theatre, thereby leaving no space for a potential audience to sit.

Camillo based the spatial organization of his theatre of memory on Vitruvius' model of the Roman theatre,[11] but intriguingly reversed the audience–stage relationship. Instead of the action occurring on the stage with audience positioned in the orchestra and tiered ascending seating, the single orator-protagonist situated himself on the stage facing the semi-circular-tiered seating area where the eternal knowledge, in images and written documents, was deposited for his retrieval. Camillo's reversed theatre for one with the auditorium operating as an analogous yet interactive scenography, required to be accessed and activated both mentally and physically. The individual act of linking the exhibited knowledge together to compose the perfect speech carried explicit performative character. There are no extant models or illustrations, and Camillo's fragmentary text does not fully explicate the design and workings of his theatre. Yet there is an identifiable order to his memory system, based, as Frances Yates has meticulously reconstructed in her classic study, *The Art of Memory*,[12] on the Hebrew *Sefiroth* (the ten divine emanations or spheres in the Cabbalistic Tree of Life) as locations of eternity, and on the seven columns of the Temple of Salomon. Angels and planets are grouped with each of the *Sefiroth*, and each of the seven horizontally ascending segments of the auditorium is linked with one planet. The seven planets (moon, sun, mercury, venus, mars, jupiter and saturn) are placed on the lowest tiers, similar to the hierarchical seating of the Greek theatre where the highest-ranked spectators were seated in the first row. Each planet defines the imagery in its ascending vertical segment according to its planetary properties. Seven horizontal tiers cut across the seven vertical ones, thus creating a total of forty-nine smaller divisions. From the first horizontal tier to the seventh, Camillo devised a topological and hierarchical order, from the first order of the *Sefiroth* to the pure elements on the second rank, the mixed elements on the third, the creation of soul and mind on the fourth, the unity of soul and body on the fifth, human activities on the sixth, and the arts, sciences and law on the highest and seventh rank (see Yates 1996: 144–145 and Laube 2009: 6–7)

The description of Camillo's original Venice theatre by Vigilius in a letter to Erasmus of Rotterdam[13] proves that the theatre had indeed been built as a miniature or scale model into which two people could enter at the same time:

> The work is of wood … marked with many images, and full of little boxes; there are various orders and grades in it. He gives a place to each individual figure and ornament, and he showed me such a mass of papers, that though I always heard that Cicero was the fountain of richest eloquence, scarcely would I have thought that one author could contain so much or that so many volumes could be pieced together out of his writings.... (Erasmus, *Epistolae*, ed. P. S. Allen and others, IX, p. 479, as cited in Yates 1996: 136)

Vigilius thus confirms that Camillo's memory theatre was no passive construction, but one in which the orator on the stage must choose and link imagery and texts to their fullest potential. In his letter to Erasmus, he describes Camillo's operating of the many little boxes containing excerpts from famous speeches (mostly Cicero's, it can be assumed). This implies that for the orator to access the collected knowledge, he would need either an assistant to move between the tiered segments to open boxes and select excerpts to hand to the orator or the actor-orator himself would be moving on and off the stage to do so. The necessity for the orator to physically and mentally activate the repository to create ever-new and different productions of knowledge through the live linking of concept, image and word shows Camillo's model theatre to be a highly performative and immersive space. The scaled-down memory theatre comprises a model that enables the intimate performance of scenes of knowledge by and for the orator, whose stage, in fact, extends to the auditorium, thereby performing the theatre's entire interior. In sum, Camillo presents a theatre able to contain and produce all of man's present and future knowledge: a creative, teleological, physical and conceptual model operating now but directed to the future. While not influential at the time, Camillo's strategies for the ordering of knowledge and the theatricalization of its production saw a resurgence from the 1990s onwards. Artists and scholars, analogizing the World Wide Web and its locational, associative and near-infinite network structure, in effect digitally reinterpreted his memory theatre. Departing from Yates' earlier focus on the theatre's cabbalistic and hermetic symbolism, these new works sought to distil a kind of embryonic, iconographic 'programming' language from Camillo's sixteenth-century model. Peter Matussek argues for a contemporary resurgence of the theatre of memory, stating recent neuropsychological findings in relation to the organization, storage and retrieval of memory:

> Memories no longer seem to us to constitute a passive inventory for deposit and withdrawal; rather, they seem far more like actors in a succession of changing stage settings. A telling metaphor shift in the neuro-sciences goes hand in hand with corresponding changes in the ways we speak about computers. In the wake of advances in interactive applications, the function of digital technology is no longer described merely in terms of 'storage and retrieval', but rather in terms of the performativeness of images in motion. (Matussek 2001: 3)

Media installations as diverse as Agnes Hegedues' interactive *Memory Theatre VR* and Flavia Sparacina's digital 'architecture machine', both from 1997, to name a few, show digital artists' desire to devise networks of imagery and information that can combine infinitely to extend memory and produce new knowledge. Camillo's teleological model theatre is reinvented as a production of immaterial yet performative knowledge, according to a 1990s media art intrigued by the seemingly limitless World Wide Web and its epistemological implication that knowledge is ever in process. Further, in each contemporary re-appropriation of Camillo's *Memory Theatre*, artists created their own associative systems with distinct spatialized and theatricalized relationships between memory and recall. Hegedues and Sparacina reconfigured Camillo's theatre as a purposive model for the representation, recall and actualization of all past, present and future knowledge as programmed by digital, immaterial memory architectures. The 2011 Performance Studies International conference in Utrecht, *Camillo 2.0: Technology, Memory, Experience*, and the subsequent 2012 issue of *Performance Research,* titled *On Technology & Memory*, examined the 'coevolution of technology and memory from the vantage point of performance as artistic practice, as embodiment of culturally specific symbolic systems and as functional technology' (Bleeker 2012). In particular, Peter Matussek, in building on his 2001 work on Camillo cited earlier, and William Uricchio proposed an understanding of Camillo's memory theatre as an active system rather than as a fixed method of retrieval and recall in this issue, and Stephen di Benedetto argues convincingly the contemporary phenomenon of the theme park as a four-dimensional memory theatre after Camillo where stored architectural and sensory simulations combine to an overall virtual narrative and environment.[14]

In contrast to singular digital or performative appropriations of the memory theatre, a contemporary physical and image-oriented manifestation and 'application' of Camillo's associative system of knowledge is found in curator Massimiliano Gioni's 2013 exhibition, 'Encyclopedic Palace' in the Arsenale[15] at the Venice Biennale. To Gioni, Camillo was primarily a philosopher whose iconographic and hermetic ordering of knowledge forms the conceptual basis for his curatorial concept:

> Like the theatres of memory devised in the sixteenth century by Venetian philosopher Giulio Camillo – mental cathedrals invented to order knowledge through pictures and magical associations – the exhibition 'Encyclopaedic Palace' will compile a cartography of our image-world, composing a bestiary of the imagination. (Gioni 2013)

Gioni's exhibition took its title from a work by self-taught Italian-American artist Marino Auriti who over many years had constructed a model for a 136-storey building that sought to contain all human knowledge, dubbed the *Palazzo Enciclopedico*. Gioni exhibited Auriti's obsessive project at the entrance to the Arsenale in the form of the original 1:200 model. This he saw as a tangible and iconic marker for what he identifies as both the necessity and desperation of today's global information society to represent universal knowledge:

> The personal cosmologies [i.e. that eccentrics like Auriti share with many other artists], with their delusions of omniscience, shed light on the constant challenge of reconciling the self with the universe, the subjective with the collective, the specific with the general, and the individual with the culture of her time. Today, as we grapple with a constant flood of information, such attempts seem even more necessary and even more desperate. (Gioni 2013)

Auriti's model in exhibition operated in a very different way from the model as originally intended by its maker. Placed in the Biennale's artistic context, Auriti's utopian yet scaled and representational model became a symbolic referent for both the desire and necessary failure to represent universal knowledge. What Gioni calls a 'cartography of the image-world' and a 'bestiary of the imagination' (Gioni 2013) became a contemporary mixed media 'theatrum' in its explicit staging of diverse physical and conceptual cosmological models unified in their effort to represent universal knowledge.

Amongst the many 'theatrum' metaphors of the late Renaissance and Baroque, Camillo's model theatre remains conceptually the most abstract yet physically concrete, in that seemingly endless narrative strands could be simultaneously constructed and performed in a purpose-built architecture.

Model theatre and model stage: Architecture as laboratory and exhibit

Joseph Furttenbach: *Architectura Civilis*, Ulm 1628

Joseph Furttenbach: *Architectura Privata*, Ulm 1641

Joseph Furttenbach: *Mannhafter Kunst-Spiegel*, Ulm 1663

Some seventy years after *L'Idea del Theatro* was published, the German architect, scenographer and universal engineer Joseph Furttenbach (1591–1667) presented the integration of the theatrum's object-oriented and relational aspects in a surprising spatial synthesis of theatre, art chamber and encyclopaedic publication. Furttenbach, better known for his innovations in theatre lighting than for his architecture, had returned to Ulm after ten influential years in Italy where he gained extensive knowledge and experience in stage practice and the universal arts and sciences of the time. In his 1628 treatise *Architectura Civilis*, Furttenbach developed for the first time a detailed ground plan and description of an exhibition hall and theatre in one, placed on the ground floor of a private residence. It remained, however, propositional and was never built:

C is the entrance to the *Theatro*. This theatre is a large hall wherein an architect or some other amateur may put on display things which please. ... At P P are two stairways leading to the gallery. Between the grotto and the stage at the two sides, nine little rooms or cabinets are built of strong wood and finished with columns and cornices in the best architectural style. Above them, the gallery or passageway is finished with *pallaustrelli* of little columns and pedestals. In these compartments are prepared the following designs and instruments: in I, mechanical displays of mills, wind machines, etc., set in motion by pulleys; in H, an exhibition of naval architecture with galleys and ships and instruments of navigation; in G, military architecture; ... In E, civil architecture with plans and houses and models of wood built to scale; ... in F, astronomy; ... in G, geography ... (Furttenbach, as cited in Hewitt 1958: 187–188).[16]

The theatre itself was to be a standard stage with three side wings or *telari* after the Italian model, with capacity for quick scene changes. Intriguing, though, in the context of the 'theatrum' as a model for representing universal knowledge, was Furttenbach's spatial organization of the *Theatro*. The theatre was also a thematically ordered exhibition hall, in which the displayed objects were predominantly scaled architectural models and models of scientific instruments. The interplay between miniature physical objects and ephemeral performance on a perspectival stage (skilfully lit with oil lamps mounted on pivots and complete with mechanical provisions for the descent of the gods) undoubtedly aimed at a unified and heightened realm of knowledge, wonder and surprise. In a conceptual extension of the synthesis between theatrical experience and architectural representation, nine small cabinets on either side of the open space operated as miniature stages, complete with curtains that could be moved to reveal the architectural model or scientific instrument behind. The experiential layout of Furttenbach's propositional theatre was completed by a mobile library with reading benches. This fluid transformation from theatre to information space would enable Furttenbach to simultaneously examine tactile models, drawings and scientific writings in his 'studiolo', thereby furthering his speculative and innovative talents.

In Furttenbach's realized private residence in Ulm, as described in minute detail in the last volume of the *Architectura* series titled *Architectura Privata* (1641), the architectural scale model was for the first time positioned at the centre of an art chamber (see Figure 2.3). Located on the fourth floor, and open to the public, the art chamber housed the architect and scenographer's extensive collection of architectural models, curious natural history objects

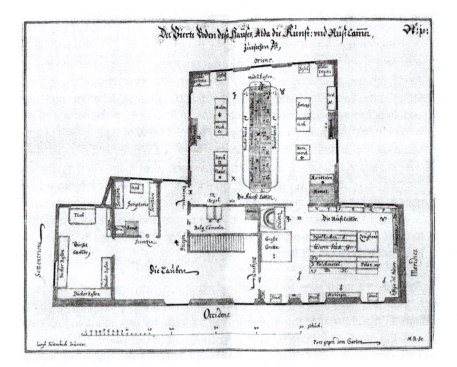

FIGURE 2.3 *Groundplan of the art and weapons chamber in* Architectura Privata *by Joseph Furttenbach, Ulm 1641 [engraving by Matthias Rembold].*

and instruments, maps and books. For the centre of the chamber, Furttenbach designed a large wooden *Modellkasten* (model box) that was flanked on either side by book benches. The model box itself was a table-like construction on which architectural models were placed, divided into twelve separate thematic 'quartiers' and covered with glass flaps that visitors could open. Spatially anchoring the exhibition space at its centre, the model box acted as a container for diverse genres of architecture: civil buildings, military and naval, churches and palaces. Positioned along the sides of the space and in the four corners, as if radiating from the central table's miniature models, were objects such as paintings, drawings, books and scientific instruments.

Furttenbach's spatial organization should be seen, therefore, not as a collection of accidentally placed displayed objects that in their totality assume universality, but as a representation of the universe through architectural and scenographic strategies of scale, perspective and narrative.

Lévi-Strauss argues in *The Savage Mind* that a model's diminished scale allows for more immediate understanding and control, in that the miniature gives a better view of the whole object than a detailed study of its parts. He links the reduction in scale and simplification of detail to greater power over the object:

What is the virtue of reduction either of scale or in the number of properties? It seems to result from a sort of reversal in the process of understanding. To understand a real object in its totality, we always tend to work from its parts. The resistance it offers us is overcome by dividing it. Reduction in scale reverses this situation. Being smaller, the object as a whole seems less formidable. By being quantitatively diminished, it seems to us qualitatively simplified. More exactly, this quantitative transposition extends and diversifies our power over a homologue of the thing, and by means of it the latter can be grasped, assessed and apprehended at a glance. (Lévi-Strauss 1962: 16)

By placing his real-sized objects in perspectival relation to the centrally located miniature models, Furttenbach, as collector, curator and exhibition architect in unison, performed what Lévi-Strauss calls the 'reversal in the process of understanding'. For the visitor, Furttenbach's miniature architecture models, as singular and necessarily simplified structures in the centre, encompassed the world of the built environment at a glance. From there, the individual real-sized paintings, sculptures and books placed in thematic and perspectival relation to the models, as well as the comfortable chairs placed strategically throughout the space, allowed for diverse viewing axes onto his knowledge universe. This was not unlike the spectators' experience of the perspectival theatre stages and sets of the time.

And whereas the proposed theatre in *Architectura Civilis* denoted a participatory theatre of architecture where miniature models represented entire scenographies on nine separate stages within the theatre's side walls in no particular order, Furttenbach's realized art chamber showed a distinct dramaturgical concept that interlocked the visitor's movements with a particular order of objects and experiences. Furttenbach for the first time expanded the traditional art chamber, in both its spatial and conceptual configurations, to a universal theatre of knowledge with a perspectival, inherently scenographic paradigm at its centre. Further, Furttenbach's detailed instructions to the visitor to remove models from their glass casings or mini-stages, allowing for detailed observation of all their physical aspects, recall Vitruvius' classical definition of scenography as 'perspective'.[17]

The traditional theatre expanded in Furttenbach's vision to a multi-stage experiential space of several miniature architectures within an overall architecture. His only built theatre architecture was a *theatrum* in the Florentine fashion, built in 1641 into an existing building, a former granary next to the Dominican monastery in Ulm that was to be the school theatre of the academic gymnasium as well as a venue for travelling theatre troupes. Described in Furttenbach's typical detailed manner in the chapter *Prospettiva* in the *Mannhafter Kunst-Spiegel* from 1663, this *theatrum* with a raked stage for initially 800, and from 1650 onwards for an audience of 1,000, seated on benches and standing in the aisles of an auditorium that rose up on a raked platform. The Ulm school theatre provided Furttenbach with the playing field he desired in order to test and extend his practical knowledge in stage machinery, scenic design, decoration, lighting, seating and ventilation, and he designed the lighting and scenery for the two school dramas of 1641, namely the opening performance *Tragico-Comoedia von dem Leben und Geschichten Moysis* and in 1650 a dramatic collage of Christian martyr legends, both performed by the schools' students. In the context of discussing lighting techniques in the *Prospettiva* chapter, Furttenbach indicates that he had previously tested the strategic use of wax candles instead of oil lamps in a purpose-built *Theatrino* or *Comoedi Sceneli* (Furttenbach 1663: 229–230) in his private residence where ten- to twelve-year-old children performed diverse comedies that could be lit with as few as ten wax candles (see Kernodle in Hewitt 1958: 236, and Palmer 2013). In contrast to such a small-scale lighting laboratory, Furttenbach's Ulm *theatrum* comprised an experimental stage and full-scale testing facility that supported several of his lighting innovations such as the use of reflectors with oil lamps and wax candles, portable lamps and footlights, and in its inception, his 'model theatre as laboratory' prefigured the technological and light experiments by Servandoni and Loutherbourg in the mid- to late seventeenth century (see the next section) and by von Herkomer in the early twentieth century. The notion of the model stage as innovative testing ground culminated in the elaborate model stage settings by symbolist actor, director and scenographer Edward Gordon Craig in the first decades of the twentieth century where the actor, for the first time, denoted nothing more than an equal element within an overall architectural and highly abstracted landscape of a mobile scenography understood as an autonomous art of form and rhythm. (See Chapter 3 for a detailed discussion of Craig's performative stage architectures.)

Model, miniature and machine: Staging the theatre of nature

Jean-Nicolas Servandoni: *La Representation de l'église Saint Pierre de Rome,* **Paris 1738**

Jean-Nicolas Servandoni: *Spectacles d'optique,* **Paris 1739**

Philip James de Loutherbourg: *Eidophusikon,* **London 1781**

The eighteenth century, framed at one end by the neoclassical notion of the divine nature of art with man at its centre, and at the other by a romanticism that deifies landscape, colour, light and atmosphere as its central topoi, saw the tradition of the cabinet of curiosities that had influenced Quiccheberg's, Camillo's and Furttenbach's inhabitable models and theatres of knowledge extended to both large-scale staged presentations and small-scale mechanical theatres.[18] Nature, landscape and architecture became for the first time protagonists of a theatre that, in contrast to the Italian and French machine operas of the Baroque, could now do entirely without the performer. In the intimate experience of large, silent architectural tableaux or vivid miniature representations of natural catastrophes, the visitor was immersed in the action through perspective and lighting techniques rather than identification with the actor. Thus, and in contrast to the chamber of curiosities whose exhibits were primarily static and whose spatial narratives of the wonders of *naturalia* and *artificialia* came to life with the visitor's movements and actions alone, the new spectacles, both large and small, not only dynamized the representation of nature and technology but were highly inventive in the creation of stage atmosphere.

In this unique development that in many ways anticipated mediatized presentational forms such as panoramas and dioramas,[19] two names stand out: Italian architect, painter and scenographer Jean-Nicolas Servandoni (1695–1766) and Alsatian landscape painter and scenographer Philip James de Loutherbourg (1740–1812). Servandoni's large-scale spectacles proved to be a direct influence on Loutherbourg, who was to appropriate and advance Servandoni's scenographic techniques in his enormously popular small-scale model theatre, *Eidophusikon* (1781).

Extending the scope and functions of their elaborate stage machines, and mobilizing Renaissance and Baroque-era perspective scenery according to both the formal, dignified language of neoclassicism and the painterly subjective expressions of romanticism, Servandoni and (later) Loutherbourg transformed theatre itself into a machine capable of the rapid scene changes and optical illusions that would define that era's design. The small-scale machine models – key exhibits in the Renaissance and Baroque art chamber as actors in the theatres of knowledge – now served to reframe that chamber's representation of the world's artificial and natural wonders into direct experience of a fully staged, unified dramatic narrative. The cosmopoietic (world-making) aspect of the art chamber continued its evolution into a technological spectacle and miniature theatre, while the model's performative aspect (as discussed in regard to de Quiccheberg's and especially Furttenbach's participative exhibitions)[20] was now fully realized in that the teleological or action aspect of the theatre as a model of the universe was exploited in all its technical possibilities. Such a focus on the visual and kinetic properties of the theatre and thus the elevation of scenography to a scenic actor in its own right may also account for the emergence of the representative stage set model in France from around 1750 onwards and denoted the interrelationship between technological and scenic knowledge.[21]

Servandoni, from 1738 onwards in Paris, had developed the new genre of the *spectacle d'optique* at the Theatre des Tuileries, also named the Salle des Machines[22] after its extensive built-in stage machinery. Servandoni established this enormous theatre with the unique stage to auditorium ratio in depth of 3:1 as a 'vision machine' (Virilio 1994) capable of eliciting the spectator's emotions without the manipulative quality of the dramatic text.[23] Equally, in demand for his design of ephemeral structures, his temporary architectures, use of pyrotechnics, lighting, perspective, painting, scenography and technology, Servandoni served up his illusionist spectacles.

Described by Diderot as 'a great stage designer, great architect, good painter and sublime decorator' (Diderot 1765 as cited in Pelletier 2006: 26), Servandoni exploited the grand dimensions and enormous depth of the Tuileries stage in his immense multi-perspectival architectural fragments and landscape configurations. His perfection of Galli-Bibiena's *scena per angolo*, the so-called corner stage, featured complex diagonal architectural compositions constructed with two or three vanishing points that (since geometrically they could never meet) evoked the infinite continuation of buildings and streets. To the baroque sensibility, the architectural fragment of columns, buildings and façades that reached beyond the proscenium frame into the infinite, seemed to connect the spectator to the inexplicable vastness of a divine cosmos, while the perspectival treatment afforded him the illusion of being part of it all. In his extensive study on Galli-Bibiena's architectural and perspective designs, A. Hyatt Mayor vividly describes the effect of Galli-Bibiena's limitless perspectives as 'restless flights of architecture running diagonally offstage toward undetermined distances' (1964: vi).

By contrast, Servandoni's more than sixty scenographies for the Paris Opéra (the Royal Theatres in Paris), and presumably also those of the spectacles d'optique, rarely featured Galli-Bibiena's typically confusing staircases and his 'dissolution of bodies and forms' (Zucker 1917: 66, trans. by the authors). Rather, they showed the signature symmetry and uniformity of neoclassicism's restrained formal language. As Paul Zucker (1917) points out in his article on the history on the classicist set design, Servandoni's set designs could easily have been converted into 'real' architecture whereas Galli-Bibiena's architectural fantasies were ever to remain paper architecture.

There are no extant stage models[24] depicting the gigantic architectures and exotic landscapes of Servandoni's spectacles d'optique, and it is only the printed programmes given out to the audience, outlining the scenic locations and dramatic action of the customary five-act spectacles, with or without music, that offer some inkling of the technology that transported the spectator by means of scene changes and effects[25] to a rapid succession of far-away worlds and mythic plots.[26]

The 1739 spectacle d'optique Pandora belonged to the 'mute' spectacles, that is, staged entirely without performers. In their stead, the illusion of pantomime actors was conjured by several thousand painted figures. During the hour-long performance, the stage was in constant movement – so the French architecture historian Quatremère de Quincy describes – ending with Pandora's opening of the fatal box and the dramatic enactment of the spreading of all evil previously contained (see Quatremère de Quincy 1830: 289). By the time of the staging of La Forêt Enchantée in 1754, orchestral music had come to play a central part in the visual spectacles with up to 160 instrumentalists in one performance and with Servandoni adding actual pantomime actors to the scene.

Nonetheless, Servandoni's first representation, La Representation de l'église de Saint Pierre de Rome from 1738 comprised a single architectural setting. Based on Giovanni Paolo Panini's perspectival and highly detailed 1730 painting of the interior of the Basilica of St Peter in Rome, Servandoni produced a perspectival, drawn representation of Panini's painting by scaling it up.[27] [28] Erika Huhtamo, in Illusions in Motions: Media Archaeology of the Moving Panorama and Related Spectacles, points to Servandoni's importance in the history of pre-cinema and calls the Saint Pierre installation his 'most radical' work (Huhtamo 2013: 95). He notes that its installation in the Salle des Machines relied entirely on both the immersive character of the massive perspectival drawing and the atmospheric lighting, in order to bring certain lines forward and have others appear to move back. Servandoni understood the visual to be at the centre of theatrical perception, and between the restrained 'architecture as scenography' of the Saint Pierre *representation* and the visual opulence of the staged *spectacles d'optique*, he developed a theatre-as-machine that presented the world and its wonders in constant movement as a kinetic scaled-up re-articulation of the art chamber. As such, Servandoni's spectacles operate as both representative models of nature and autonomous, self-referring models that consciously exhibit their artificial and constructed nature.

Servandoni's technological innovations in live performance, ever in pursuit of greater immersion by means of scenography in conjunction with light and sound, were taken even further by the painter Philip James de Loutherbourg, who in 1771 presented himself (undoubtedly as Servandoni's successor) to the actor and theatre producer David Garrick at London's Drury Lane in 1771.[29] In his first letter to Garrick, Loutherbourg succinctly presented his wish to reinvent scenery and stage machinery in the service of the audience's emotive response:

I must invent scenery, which will have the effect of creating a new sensation upon the public. To this end, I must change the manner of lighting the stage so as to serve the effects of the painting. I must also change the method of pulling off simultaneously an entire scene (set of scenes) – and generally, alter such machinery as might be necessary to the aspiration of my talents, such as I have. ... Furthermore, I must make a small model of the settings and everything which is required, to scale, painted and detailed so as to put the working painters and machinists and others on the right track by being able to faithfully copy my models, and, if I deem it necessary to retouch something in the final display to enhance the effect then I must do so. I shall draw in colour the costumes for the actors and the dancers. I must discuss (*ressonne* in the French original, see Baugh 127) my work with the composer and the ballet master. (Loutherbourg 1772, as cited in Baugh 1987: 127)

Loutherbourg's explication to Garrick is remarkable in many ways. Not only is this the voice of a self-confident artist demanding full control over all aesthetic and technical performance aspects who at that point had not designed a single set,[30] but it is one of the first extant direct accounts of the relevance of the scaled set model to the creative team, and the set model is articulated as a communication tool between technical and artistic departments, that is, of equal importance to each team member.

In a surprisingly modern articulation of the theatrical *Gesamtkunstwerk avant la lettre*, the scenographer Loutherbourg assumes authority over the realization of his ideas, seeking the integration of set, costumes, lighting, machinery, music and choreography, and portraying himself as the single author of the visuality of a performance. The model, so Loutherbourg declares, serves as the central representative and mediating tool in the creation of the performance.

In the seventeenth century, architectural and topographical models had already been key exhibits in the chamber of curiosities and the subsequent art chamber (as earlier discussed). Yet from the mid-eighteenth century, fascination with the miniature object led the London public to attend numerous exhibitions of models and of curious natural and artificial miniatures – from flea circuses to architectural and landscape copies. Richard Altick lists, in *The Shows of London* in the first half of the century, exhibitions of models of scriptural sites, and in the latter part a topographical model of the Alps and city models of London, Paris, Rome and Venice (Altick 1978: 114–115). When Loutherbourg opened his model theatre at his residence in Leicester Square, he was already renowned for his scenic and lighting innovations. His atmospheric set designs amounted to a radical rethinking of three-dimensional and perspectival scenery. Using a series of two-dimensional cut-outs positioned in a vertical sequence in such a way that light cast no shadow from one plane to the next, and working with transparencies, coloured glass and strategically positioned lighting to produce subtle transitions, Loutherbourg linked lighting and scene transition into what would evolve into a display of imagery in motion.

This model theatre, set up for 130 people and situated in a panelled room on the first floor of Loutherbourg's residence, was an immediate success as it took up two streams resonant in the cultural context of the time. For one, this wooden box of dimensions three metres wide, two metres high and three metres deep – called *Eidophusikon* after the Greek words *eidos* for form or figure and *physis* for natural – intensified the late eighteenth-century romantic discourse on the spiritual properties of nature and landscape by staging natural dramatic phenomena in a realistic and recognizable way (see Figure 2.4). Second, Loutherbourg's mechanical theatre, like Servandoni in his time, linked nature and technology to evoke wonder, fear and amazement in his audience, bringing to mind Burke's description of the effects of the sublime:

> The passion caused by the great and sublime in nature ... is Astonishment; and astonishment is that state of the soul, in which all its motions are suspended, with some degree of horror. In this case the mind is so entirely filled with its object, that it cannot entertain any other. (Burke 1756: 58)

The miniature, in forbidding the presence of the living performer, allowed for the scenographer's complete authorship over all performance elements. Instead, machines – thunder and rain machines, mechanical actors, a wave-machine with three-dimensional wooden waves, three-dimensional scenic elements and objects together with lighting – authored narratives of sea battles, of city views, of day turning into night. According to the sole extant

FIGURE 2.4 Eidophusikon *by Philip James de Loutherbourg, London 1781 [drawing by Edward Frances Burney 1782].*

contemporary visualization, Edward Francis Burney's watercolour from 1782, the construction seems to have comprised a large proscenium frame on which a curtain rose, with a smaller proscenium frame behind it and a painted backcloth with a harpsichord between the two frames. In its miniaturization of both theatre and nature, the *Eidophusikon* was indeed a representative model, yet by skilfully displaying its artifice, also an autonomous, self-referential one.

The theatrical environments created by Servandoni and Loutherbourg operated very differently, yet were related in their common understanding of the theatre as a unique, dynamic space where the scenographer claims complete aesthetic and technological ownership over the production, radically privileging the visual over the verbal. Within Servandoni's neoclassical scenographies of exotic yet symmetrically ordered nature and Loutherbourg's wildly romantic, atmospherically lit tales of catastrophe and destruction lies an early history of mediatization that was to be fully realized in the moving panoramas of the 1790s and the dioramas of the early nineteenth century. In their works, scenery, lighting, sound effects and music coalesced to fabricate a singular theatrical machine whose sole aim it was to generate the utmost illusion and immersion. Broadly, and distinct from the cabinet of curiosities and the art chamber's static representations of the universe, Servandoni's *Spectacles d'optique* and Loutherbourg's *Eidophusikon* presented as kinetic models of nature. In continually underscoring their machine character through the relentless workings of the stage machinery, both exposed their artificiality as created works of theatre. To the audience, this meant that while being immersed in illusionary worlds, they were alive to the scenographer's methods, techniques and skill in representing architecture and nature.

Servandoni's and Loutherbourg's models, in their representations of natural catastrophes and wonders, and heightened by the displacement of the actor, constituted both models of nature and models for the future of media and significantly contributed to the epistemes of scenography. The knowledge staged in the *spectacles* and the miniature theatre was at the same time material and immaterial in that technological advancement and conceptual and artistic rigour in coalescence allowed for the creation of distinct atmospheres, architectures and scenic transformations hitherto unseen on the stage.

The autonomous, performative models realized with the *Spectacles d'optique* and the *Eidophusikon* turned the stage into a knowledge machine that over the duration of the performance displayed its wonders and affirmed its dramatic power. These theatrical constructions, contained by scale, elevated the scenographic art to the complete performative integration of stage technology, lighting, mobile perspectival scenery and sound in the service of a complex spatial narrative and must be judged as predecessors not only to the analogue pre-cinematic forms of nineteenth-century panorama and diorama but also to future digital, multimedia and virtual creations.

3

Performing Architecture: Edward Gordon Craig and the Model Stage

Model and screen: Abstraction on the stage

Edward Gordon Craig: *The Actor and the Uber-Marionette,* 1908

Inspired by Loutherbourg's eighteenth-century immersive mechanical theatre, *Eidophusikon,* and by Richard Wagner's concept of a synthesis of all arts, the English symbolist director, actor and scenographer Edward Gordon Craig (1872–1966) set out to systematically reform and re-theatricalize the theatre. This chapter reveals Craig's work with stage set models and model elements to be the core, iterative method with which he was able to redefine and expand the notion of set design from operating as mere decoration to a fully integrated scenographic concept with the stage as an autonomous space. In conjunction with his architectural, compositional talent, the symbolist notion of the fluidity of emotion and the emphasis symbolist artists gave to the creation of atmosphere in their works, Craig aimed to uncover the essence of theatre. Symbolism emerged in the late decades of the nineteenth century in literature, painting, music and the theatre as an artistic gesture that embraced notions of inner consciousness and symbolic imagery rather than the detached observation of behaviour and the mimetic representation of daily life as advocated and practised by realism and naturalism. Nietzsche's scepticism of the existence of universal cognition, and his attacks on the conventions of contemporary theatre, strongly influenced the European symbolist movement. In repudiating the sentiment of the romantic period and the nineteenth century's excessive realism and psychologism, the symbolists demanded the renewal of theatre's art character along with freedom from the dominance of literature and the word as the primary carrier of dramatic action. Congruent with the 1872 publication and enthusiastic reception of Nietzsche's first book, *The Birth of Tragedy: Out of the Spirit of Music*, the distinct questioning of the word as arbiter of theatrical experience, allied to discontent with the perceived gap between theatre's truth and autonomy and its institutionalized reality, awoke a desire in many artists to return to the antique, cultic roots of theatre and to arrive at the Wagnerian concept of the *Gesamtkunstwerk* as a synthesis of all arts:

> Words are but symbols for the relations of things to one another and to us; nowhere do they touch upon absolute truth... Through words and concepts we shall never reach beyond the wall of relations, to some sort of fabulous primal ground of things. (Nietzsche 1998: 83)

At the same time, theatre was required to transcend the actor, now increasingly regarded as imperfect, unable to shed individuality and subjectivity in his bodily movement and interpretation of character. In 1890, the French dramatist Maurice Maeterlinck wrote in an article for *La Jeune Belgique*:

> Maybe, one has wholly to eliminate man on the stage ... Will man be replaced by a shadow, a reflex, a projection of symbolic forms, or by a being which seems to be alive without being alive? I don't know but the absence of man appears absolutely necessary to me. (Maeterlinck 1890: 331)

Symbolist concepts now extended from dramatic texts to the rethinking of both stage and theatre architecture and the elevation of the director as the sole creator of the performance in a communally experienced rite.

In this exciting period of the re-theatricalization of theatre, Craig began to think of the stage as a unified non-hierarchical composition of movement, architecture and light. Contrasting with his contemporary, Swiss scenographer Adolphe Appia, whose rhythmic spaces and abstracted stage elements were always in the service of the actor, Craig did not see the actor as the dramatic anchor of a performance but rather as one of its elements.[1]

Throughout his numerous (unsystematic and often contradictory) writings,[2] and in his etchings, woodcuts, drawings and models, Craig developed a scenic system of abstracted and mobile stage elements that comprised a performative mobile stage architecture and mobile proscenium. Many of his core ideas and methods were prefigured in his knowledge of Loutherbourg's mechanical model theatre from 1781, the *Eidophusikon*, which created optimal immersion through the intricate interplay of changing scenery, light and sound – yet without the actor's presence.

Tellingly, Craig twice referred to the *Eidophusikon*, once in relation to the autonomous stage and once to a theatre without actors. In an article on stage scenery for London's *Morning Post*, he wrote of the miniature theatre as an 'entertainment where actors were dispensed with', adding: 'Why should the actors and actresses spoil the view by standing between the scene and the audience?' (Craig 1903: 13.10). Craig also acknowledged (in an unpublished draft manuscript) the *Eidophusikon* as a 'precursor of the mobile stage that he [Craig] came to call Scene' (Innes 1998: 178). While Craig marvelled at Loutherbourg's illusionist spectacles, he also rejected them as akin to sheer entertainment, since his vision of the theatre strongly negated mimetic representation and the actor's presence on the stage:

> Yet the aim of the Theatre as a whole is to restore its art, and it should commence by banishing from the Theatre this idea of impersonation, this idea of reproducing Nature; for, while impersonation is in the Theatre, the Theatre can never be free. (Craig 1980: 75)

In his 1908 essay *The Actor and the Uber-Marionette*, Craig would indeed wish for the actor to 'leave' the stage, since due to man's 'imperfection', body and mind would always be chained to emotion. 'Art only arrives by design', said Craig in the essay (published in his journal *The Mask*, 1908, Vol 1, No 2: 3) and by necessarily representing nature and reality, the actor must involuntarily destroy art. German writer Heinrich von Kleist had, as early as 1810 in his essay *On the Marionette Theatre*, attributed more grace and dignity to the artificial puppet, the marionette, than to the human dancer. While Kleist's essay more than supported Craig's concept of the non-human performer, his notion of the 'Uber-Marionette' and the banishment or destruction of the actor should not, however, be taken literally.[3] What Craig sought was not 'no actor' but rather an actor with a different kind of physicality that would amount to a total spiritual immersion into the scenic event:

> The Uber-marionette will not compete with Life – but will rather go beyond it. Its ideal will not be flesh and blood but rather the body in Trance – it will aim to clothe itself with a death-like Beauty while exhaling a living spirit. (Craig 1908: 12)

In Craig's vision of a theatre characterized by architectural, dramaturgical and rhythmical harmony, the 'body in Trance' is no longer master of his movements but is directed as if on strings, by (one might say) the pervading spiritual mood or energy of the theatrical event. To achieve such harmony, simultaneously ancient and forward-looking, Craig went beyond theoretical musings and manifesto-type polemics to build rigorous, tactile methods for testing and constructing stage elements, lighting design and choreography. Between 1907, when he first experimented with the mobile elements later patented as

'Screens', and 1921, when his so-called 'Model A' was to become the Screens' complete simulation model, Craig used models and the modelling process as iterative and experimental tools to arrive at precise artistic articulations.

The notion of the artist as an experimenter and sole author of both material elements and atmospheres came to Craig through his early encounters with the theatre experiments of German émigré landscape painter Hubert von Herkomer (1849–1914). Royal Academy member and Slade Professor of Art Herkomer's financial success as a narrative painter of idyllic peasant scenes and portraits, ranging from robust German realism to a subtle English idealism, enabled him to realize his lifelong dream of a theatre of his own, which he opened beside his private art school in Bushey in 1883. A passion for Wagner's music and dissatisfaction with the tired conventions of contemporary commercial stagecraft prompted Herkomer to seek scenic innovations in a non-commercial experimental setting. His interest in music and composing led him to embrace the theatre as a painter to whom the stage was 'an extension of the easel' (Herkomer 1908: 316).

Herkomer's auditorium seated 150 people with a raked stage, and a stage opening four metres wide and three metres high. In effect, it was little more than a miniature theatre, yet it provided him with a theatrical playing field, a model stage and teaching tool in one. Herkomer called his experiments 'pictorial music plays' (Herkomer 1892: 316), a term that referenced Wagner's music-dramas but emphasized, in contrast to Wagner, the priority of the image. Musical considerations were of secondary concern, with narrative as an 'excuse for the whole thing' (Herkomer 1908: 316). His first production, *The Sorceress* from 1887, he called a 'plastic picture, of varying groups of figures, with an annotation (so to speak) both of song and instrumental music' (Herkomer 1908: 151), later noting that the lighting techniques for the night sky and moon transiting the stage had been his and his students' 'triumphs' (Herkomer 1908: 151). To the painter Herkomer, light was

> the most potent factor in scenic art. By its magic, the most trumpery materials are transformed into priceless fabrics; tinsels into gold and silver; and a few feet of canvas into vast distances. (Herkomer 1908: 199)

After performances, Herkomer would lead members of the audience onstage to explain his mysterious lighting effects, but admitted that few cared to know the technique behind his famed lunar illusions.[4] In his second production *An Idyl*, from 1899, another 'pictorial music-play' set in a thirteenth-century English pastoral landscape,[5] Herkomer extended his stage to fourteen metres deep, ten wide and twenty high, to incorporate the full potential of the moonlighting. This time, the orb was to rise in the distance, 'a great, red harvest moon – and gradually increase its light as it rises higher and higher in the darkening sky' (Herkomer 1908: 159). The young Craig, accompanied by the actress Ellen Terry (his mother) and Henry Irving, actor-manager of London's Lyceum Theatre, witnessed at close quarters after a performance the apparatus developed by Herkomer and his students for producing the moon-illusion. Craig's son Edward is purported to have said that his father, with the rest of the audience, were sure they had witnessed the real moon – revealed merely by removing the theatre's back wall.[6] Edward also notes that the twenty-year-old E.G. Craig, after attending Herkomer's lecture 'On Scenic Art' at London's Avenue Theatre in January 1892, had written in his autobiography *Index to the Story of My Days* that this lecture had 'first opened my eyes to the shortcomings of the established theatre' (Craig 1957: 9). Further, he had preserved the published lecture in his scrapbook (Craig 1957: 9–10). Herkomer's lecture (received enthusiastically by the press and public alike) promoted scenic innovation from the perspective of a painter who seeks the best possible views for his two-dimensional work. In the lecture, he critiqued present-day theatre architecture and the fixed proscenium, the importance of stage lighting and an understanding of the scenic artist as an experimental artist and worker. To Herkomer, the complete 'plastic stage-picture' (Herkomer 1892a: 259) could be realized only in a renewed architecture informed by Wagner's Bayreuth Festspielhaus,[7] to be complemented by highly controlled stage lighting that sought natural representation of the actor and the creation of a variety of atmospheres. The scenic artist, says Herkomer, 'must be a born experimenter' (Herkomer 1892a: 262), that is, one who follows an initial idea through iteration and experimentation, failure and success. His copious experiments (beyond the mechanical moon so admired by Craig) included modelled uneven wooden stage floors and the abolition of footlights in favour of an ensemble of lights that allowed realism or spectacle, as appropriate.

Herkomer's influence on Craig can be seen not only in the direct application of several of his scenic ideas but crucially in his overall pictorial approach and experimental and iterative working methods. In all his writings, Herkomer, the self-styled theatrical outsider and undisciplined perceiver, set out to rethink scenic representation from the painter's perspective, always based on the paradigm of the visual. This approach resonated with Craig, whose dual background as graphic designer and actor let him combine visual art techniques and the scale model as key instruments for developing and representing scenic ideas. In his first opera as director and designer, Purcell's *Dido and Aeneas* in 1900, Craig, inspired by Herkomer, employed coloured lights with gauze hung in front rather than a fixed, painted backcloth, creating a seemingly infinite, atmospheric stage effect. In subsequent designs he continued to explore – very much the experimental visual artist on the stage – how to produce painterly effects with light, in order to have actor and scene merge in a single metaphysical realm. From 1906 onwards, Craig developed both methods and instruments for achieving mastery over the stage's visual elements, with 1907 to 1913 being a particularly intense and productive period:

All came along this year – 1907: Screens, and SCENE, the 'Ubermarionette', Black Figures, *The Mask*. (Craig 1957: 297)

Model and experiment: Mobilizing the stage

Edward Gordon Craig: *Hamlet*, **Moscow Art Theatre 1912**

Edward Gordon Craig: *Scene*, **1923**

In early 1907,[8] Craig began to experiment with elements that would enable a stage to move in a single rhythm according to setting, mood and music. From early ideas on curtains and drapery, he developed a stable system of mobile rectangular wooden frames that he called screens. These were covered with cotton in monochrome colours to enable differentiated and coloured lighting. Craig began to make notes and sketches of the concept of an overall mobile stage he called *Scene*.[9] In these (finally written up in Rapallo in 1922 and published in 1923), he radicalized the idea of mobility in all scenic elements by devising an 'instrument' that inscribed utmost flexibility in them all. Craig's first, and central, step in the design of *Scene* consisted in making hundreds of models that sought to arrive at the basic architectural condition of a 'home' within which his design process could take place. Craig explained the genesis of *Scene* as a continuous stripping away of artificial, cultural and symbolic layers – achieved by a sequence of models of man's habitation structures between 5000 BCE and 1900 CE. By comparing structures and through continuous iteration, he was to arrive at the base elements of the dwelling. Craig, perhaps unsurprisingly, found these to be the floor and ceiling, elements that denote architecture's primordial task of providing shelter:

Having rejected in the two hundred and fifty models any piece which cannot be found in every other piece, I find I am then left with the essential parts which form the habitation of man. The walls remain:
The floor.
The ceiling ... nothing else. ...
So now you see how it is that my screens, my SCENE is composed as it is of plain flat walls. I wished to reduce scene to its essentials and I found it reduced itself. I have but done as ordered.
I then added mobility to it. (Craig 1923: 22)

Craig's innovative reverse iteration process, that is, systematically and comparatively removing design elements to arrive at architecture's origin, let him conceptualize the basics of the *Scene* (stage floor and ceiling) and subsequently mobilize them. *Scene* (which Craig also called an 'instrument' or a 'device') initially comprised four, six, eight, ten or twelve monochrome screens of the same height that could fold and unfold in two directions. Lighting complemented the mobility of the screens and helped create an intricate choreography of architecture and movement. Craig understood the screens as neutral surfaces that delivered a myriad of meanings through the lamps' different angles, intensities and colours. The overall impression would be of a mobile scenography and lighting in concert with mobile architectural elements:

> Scene and light then move.
> I may have any number of pieces in my scene and I may have any number of lamps.
> For the moment we will speak of a scene with five pieces – five screens and of ten lamps.
> Having rehearsed a small set of these on my model stage in my room, I come to my theatre and my larger screens and lamps. I place my screens in their first position. I now pass each screen through its drill – that is to say, my eight or ten manipulators of the screens will practise each screen to see that it is flexible and each man in trim. That done, I myself go to my switchboard and test each tap, each lamp – the force of the light, the smoothness of each pulley, wheel, grove, and so on…
> When I am well assured that my screens and my lamps are quite ready, I commence the rehearsal. (Craig 1923: 25)

From the eleven pages of notes and sketches dated 1906–1907 (that Craig had put between the final pages of Serlio's 1575 Book II of *Tutte l'opere* …) to the publication of *Scene* in 1923 lay a path of continuous experiment with scale models and (increasingly) with black wooden character figurines made by Craig himself, as well as etchings, sketches and drawings. Craig expertly employed representational media for diverse purposes, such as the eighteen etchings published in *Scene* for the portrayal of atmospheres, and scale models with figurines to precisely visualize the choreography of the screens in conjunction with the moving performers. Serlio, in Book II of his seven-volume *oeuvre*, was concerned with perspectival issues, that is, the scenographic representation of architecture and theatre. To demonstrate to his readers the construction of central perspective, Serlio divided the stage floor into perspectival squares, a technique that inspired Craig to conceive the stage as a hydraulic instrument with mobile cubic elements on both floor and ceiling that could be raised and lowered to individually differing heights.[10] The proposition of mobile floor and ceiling elements demanded the vertical extension of the stage and their seamless operation to enable the complex composition and rhythmic coordination of music, stage and performer. The etchings published in *Scene* show multiple and visionary architectural volumes of varied heights and depths. These either appear in spatial configurations of density, compression and vertical orientation or depict deserted, abstracted landscapes with horizontally oriented scattered cubic elements.

The three-dimensionality of Craig's scenic environments, however, must be seen as speculative and propositional rather than as blueprints for production. They are meant to represent a single scene, in the sense that out of one base configuration, all other spatial situations could unfold by means of the hydraulically operated cubes, the turning and repositioning of the screens and the coordinated lighting plot. In Craig's continuous exploration of the stage's kinetic potential,[11] his hands-on work with the model was always central. The models he built until 1921 fulfilled different roles: enabling the director-designer to accomplish intimate conceptual work, offering a persuasive medium for actors, theatre collaborators and the press, and for speculative proposals that were never to be realized (see Figures 3.1 and 3.2). In September 1908 Craig

FIGURE 3.1 *Gilded model screen 39 cm high by Edward Gordon Craig, Model A Extra-Pieces and Other Models, MSS. Book 14 1913.*

FIGURE 3.2 *Gilded model screen 39 cm high by Edward Gordon Craig, Model A Extra-Pieces and Other Models, MSS. Book 14 1913.*

began to build, in the disused theatre of Arena Goldoni in Florence, several small-scale model theatres with simplified versions of the *Scene* – comprising the screens but not the mobile cubic volumes. From 1909 onwards he developed a generic portable version of the model stage for demonstration purposes. In a collaboration with Irish writer W. B. Yeats, whose play *The Hour-Glass* Craig was to design for Dublin's Abbey Theatre in 1911, a scale model of the screens, built specifically for the dramatist, served as a creative stimulus and spatial framework during Yeats' writing process. Yeats wrote that the model enabled him to

> 'produce' my play while I write it, moving hither and thither little figures of cardboard through gay or solemn light or shade, allowing the scene to give the words and the words the scene. (Yeats 1911 as cited in Fleischer 2007: 162)

For a planned production of *The Merchant of Venice* in Florence starring Ellen Terry, he constructed a model stage for the testing of screens and lighting that now included individual woodcut character figurines.[12] Despite Craig showing Terry exhaustive configurations of the eighteen screens with lighting, including a persuasive 1:1 version, they were not used, presumably due to the complexity of handling.

The only fully realized production with the screens as singular scenic elements apart from *The Hour-Glass* in Dublin in 1910–1911 was to be his 1912 Moscow staging of *Hamlet*. Craig had his screens patented[13] at a time where his scenic inventions and costumes for *Hamlet* at Konstantin Stanislawski's Moscow Art Theatre (MAT) were in danger of being ignored by that theatre's Board. Meanwhile, he exhibited a full-sized model at his London studio and demonstrated to the press the workings of the screens and lighting:

The model screens exhibited were all in monochrome, which was practically the 'self-colour' of the material of which the models were made: but indoor and outdoor scenes alike were made each in a few seconds in two or three movements, and the purport of each was unmistakable. Quite extraordinary effects of space and spirit were obtained: and in this the lighting played a very important part. For one advantage of these screens is that the light can be directed from almost any point, and a change of light makes a change of mood, or even of place. ... A proscenium that can be easily enlarged or reduced forms a subsidiary part of the scheme; and sloping stages could, if necessary, be made flat for the reception of the screens. It is claimed that the new scenery is cheap, easily and quickly provided, simply and quickly worked, and adaptable to practically all needs. It is certainly of wonderful effect in the suggestion of place and mood; and experiment with the models only whets the appetite to see a stage equipped with the new scenery on the full scale. (Stage Scenery, *The Times*, London, Saturday 23 September 1911: 8; Issue 39698)

The full-sized model served here as a particularly persuasive tool, just as an architect would offer a building model to a client to convince him of its design and function. Contrary to the traditional architectural or stage model, Craig's screen model operated as a performative architecture providing numerous settings and moods in one. The London full-sized version was, therefore, an autonomous model and prototype, which did not point towards a future production but rather demonstrated the functioning of the scenic screen system. Craig's full-sized functioning model was inherently performative in the dynamic working of the screens, and at the same time comprised a performance when set in motion by the model-maker.

Craig's second large-scale model for an envisaged production of *Hamlet* at MAT was built in 1910 to the specifics of the theatre's stage and lighting rig, but both its purpose and effect on cast and crew make it one of history's more elaborate models. Divergence between Craig as designer and Stanislawski as director quickly arose. The latter's psychological realism would not align with Craig's fundamental scepticism as to whether Shakespeare could ever be staged without destroying it. This, along with his apparent inability to make firm decisions in rehearsal, extended the work to almost two years, with Craig banished from the last rehearsals.

Craig had been introduced to Stanislawski in 1908 by the American expressive dancer Isadora Duncan, after which the plan to stage *Hamlet* arose (see Figure 3.3). After initial talks in Moscow, Craig returned to the Arena

FIGURE 3.3 *Etching for* Hamlet *in Edward Gordon Craig's handwritten notebook entitled* Hamlet ECG 1910 *for Craig and Stanislawski's production of* Hamlet *at the Moscow Art Theatre 1911–1912.*

Goldoni in Florence to start making the models and setting out the entire choreography with the screens. He wrote to Stanislawski, asking his carpenters to experiment with ways to turn the screens, demanding that they fold and unfold quickly and discreetly in full view. Back at MAT (from March 1910), Craig set up in a rehearsal room a large model of the theatre and proscenium, to the scale of 1:12 (also called the 'one-inch scale'), complete with a scaled-down copy of the MAT's eight-row lighting system. Craig had brought his screen models with him for placement on the large model (see Stanislawski in Benedetti 2008: 289). He proceeded to produce copious sketches in situ for the theatre's directing students to translate into small maquettes and then show to Craig for his approval. During this iterative method, involving the production of what seemed to ensemble and crew to be endless numbers of models, those approved by Craig were quickly scaled up and positioned on the model stage for testing under lights. Craig wanted the stage architecture to form an extension to the theatre's architecture, and the lighting to be highly expressive. Duplicating the MAT's lighting allowed him to define and rehearse, in sequence, every lighting position in tandem with screen transitions and actor movements. At this stage, the main actors were invited to a demonstration of the production's entire choreography. Craig brandished a long stick that held wood or cardboard figurines which he moved according to his directorial concept, and he apparently simultaneously indicated the 'tone' (i.e. voice) to be used. Mardzhanov, one of his MAT assistants, outlined Craig's complicated system for communicating during rehearsals:

[Craig] would read the English text of Hamlet, discuss his interpretation of it, analyse the psychology of the characters, and then by means of wooden figurines he had roughly cut out, would act out a given scene [moving them with a long stick with a hole at the end] … We, that is Stanislawsky, Sulerzhitsky and myself, were supposed to grasp all this, master it and then prepare the actors along these lines for performance. … Craig was working on Hamlet for the second year now, but one peculiarity of this clever artist was his inability to set a stopping point, to break off and move on to a realized concept – and this brought us no nearer to production. (Mardzhanov 1910 as cited in Senelick 1982: 101)

Indeed, Craig continued to use his model for the overall spatial narrative of the screens as a substitute for engaging with the creative team and the ensemble. He appeared to withdraw into the model room rather than oversee the transitions to full scale on the stage. Laurence Senelick, in the 14 April diary entry resulting from his direct observations of the *Hamlet* rehearsals, states, all the screens and set pieces that had been made in the previous year were to be set up on the main stage and 'more recent experimental screens were to be set up on a platform in the small theatre to act as the model' (Senelick 1982: 111), which means that final decisions on screen positions were still being left open. In February 1911, following the long break in rehearsals due to Stanislawski's typhoid illness and recovery period, Stanislawski wrote to his assistant Suler with some of the urgent talking points for a possible meeting with Craig in Dresden, the first of which was to ask Craig to find 'arrangements for the screens on the stage itself, looking for a general mood and not scrupulously reproducing his models' (Stanislawski as cited in Senelick 1982: 125).

Increasingly, MAT's creative team, crew and ensemble began to see Craig's models and his continuous experimentation with figurines, screen and lighting positions and transitions as counterproductive and paralysing, a sign of his inability to lead technical rehearsals towards the final product. Indeed, Craig had already noted in April 1910 in his production copy of *Hamlet:* 'The quiet work in the room with the models ... I enjoy the most' (Craig 1910, as cited in Grund 2002: 99). To the poet and visual artist Craig, the model offered not merely utterly persuasive potential for a 'future' production (possibly even commercial success, as with the London full-scale model) but, in fact, a refuge for immersion in his creation without any real consideration for its realization into a living piece of theatre. In Moscow, in a cruel twist, the screens that had worked so seamlessly on the model stage turned out to be too cumbersome and unstable to be manoeuvred on the real stage, and on opening night the curtain had to come at each scene-change, extending the performance to a leaden five hours, and reminiscent of Vitruvius' tale of the unlucky architect Callius whose war machine could not operate at full scale, yet had been utterly convincing in miniature. Conceptually ahead of technological development such as hydraulics that are able to lift and lower volumes imperceptibly and perfectly timed without interrupting the action on stage, Craig's visionary ideas were to remain compromised when realized manually in the theatres of his time.

Following *Hamlet* and perhaps partially as a result of the technical difficulties and artistic conflicts experienced in Moscow, Craig withdrew from theatre practice as a designer, yet continued to explore theatrical space through the construction of models in diverse scales. These included the 1913 four-metre-high labyrinthic, Piranesi-like model for a staging of *St Matthew Passion* and a 1914 model for the staging of Plato's *Dialogues*. While these were shown in exhibitions of his work through the 1920s, neither was ever realized. Nor was Model A – intended to show all the inventions of *Scene* in one model, including adjustable proscenium, mobile platforms and screens – ever concluded.

The significance of Craig's theatre work is inextricably linked to his understanding of the model as a knowledge-producing tool that can be as autonomous and experimental as it can be purely functional. In the 1923

Scene, Craig had granted the actor freedom to arrange and re-arrange the mobile shapes differently on stage every night, much in the way that he played with the cubes and screens on his model stages.[14] Such an offer stands in contrast to his rigid (and finally unsuccessful) rehearsal methods for *Hamlet* in Moscow, where he had kept the actors away from any decision-making or spatial improvisation. These facts point again to the disparity between Craig's visionary theory and his comparatively rigid and uncompromising design practice. And while Craig had gained formal and technical inspiration from Loutherbourg's mechanical theatre *sans* the actor, and from Herkomer's experiments for the creation of atmosphere, the notion that the model should be at the centre of the designer's experiments, that it should be able to simulate mobility, was his very own discovery. It led to what is, in today's terms, best defined as the first genuinely performative stage architecture.

4

Staging the Future:
The Model as Performance
of Inhabitation

The previous chapter closed with the observation that Craig's rigorous and hands-on experimentation with stage set models was chiefly responsible for his development of a performative stage architecture defined by mobile elements. Abstraction was one of the key principles of Craig's modernist architectural and scenographic imagination and aesthetics, and his 1:1 models comprised mobile stages that allowed him to perform scenography rather than to build it. Modernist architecture of the time, with Mies van der Rohe as one of the movement's prime protagonists, came to understand the value of the 1:1 playing field in the form of model houses and model house exhibitions that included the 'new' functional rather than decorated interiors, in a distinct move away from the bourgeois intérieur of the nineteenth century, famously compared to a 'box in the world theatre' that equally consumes and overwhelms its inhabitants in Benjamin's essay 'Paris, Capital of the Nineteenth Century' (Benjamin 2002b: 14–26). Benjamin writes:

> The interior is not just the universe of the private individual; it is also his etui.... He has a marked preference for velour and plush, which preserve the imprint of all contact. In the style characteristic of the Second Empire, the apartment becomes a sort of cockpit. The traces of its inhabitant are molded into the interior. (Benjamin 2002b: 20)

In direct contrast to Benjamin's so acutely described closed-off and purely reflective interior of the late nineteenth century, the modernist exhibited model building or interior propelled the interior from an intimate domestic scene to the public stage.

Its predecessors are found in the competition entries for civic buildings from the mid-nineteenth century onwards, where exhibited architectural models at full scale had already been associated with the viewer's direct and immersive experience of architecture in a new mode of representation and promise that shifted the exhibited architectural object from one of sheer observation towards one where space was 'practised',[1] activated by the visitor's behaviour. The newly emerging genre of the architectural model or 'model home' rapidly became a vehicle for new architectural typologies, material experimentation and the communication of socio-political agendas in addressing issues such as housing affordability, community, social housing, methods of prefabrication, technology and sustainability and must be seen in parallel to the model's use in the 'show home'[2] as a commercially motivated form of experience-based marketing.

The inclusion of the model home in international fairs and expos, as well as increasingly in a critical context in biennales, exhibitions and museums of art and architecture worldwide, attests to its effectiveness as supporting a cultural and commercial spatial strategy in the dissemination of ideas and concepts around domestic futures and the future of the city at large.

The performative nature of the model has been discussed in previous chapters, including Scamozzi's linkage of architectural and scenographic models in the *Teatro all'Antica* in Sabbioneta resulting in the spatialization of absolutist governance, and with regard to Craig's 1:1 experiments leading towards a performative stage architecture. In the following, the development of scenographic and performative space-making strategies of exhibited full-scale architectural and urban models in Germany and the United States from 1927 to 2013 is discussed in dialogue with curatorial, social and spatial concepts in order to understand their central importance in the dissemination of new housing types.

The format of the full-scale architectural model in exhibition, as an enterable and material artefact to aid the advancement of social agendas, can be traced back to the end of England's industrial revolution and 'the first major international exhibition in 1851 at the Crystal Palace in London' (McQuaid, Bee and Droste 1996: 9). *The Great Exhibition of the Works of Industry of All Nations* set the format 'for future industrial exhibitions by the display sections within the Crystal Palace: Manufactures, Machinery, Raw Materials, and Fine Arts' (1996).[3]

Erected adjacent to the Crystal Palace was a full-scale model exhibit, titled *Prince Albert's Model Lodging House*, built by the Society for Improving the Conditions of the Labouring Classes (SICLC) and designed by the architect Henry Roberts. This small brick apartment block for four families was awarded one of the 170 Great Exhibition Council Medals and was included in the exhibition's magazine *The Crystal Palace and Its Contents of 1851:*

An Illustrated Cyclopaedia of the Great Exhibition, published weekly from October 1851 to March 1852. The project marked the first exploration of a new architectural strategy of using 1:1 models within an exhibition context in parallel to the Great Exhibitions' claim of being the 'first international exhibition of manufactured products' (vam.ac.uk, 2017), and thus assuring exposure to greater cross-sections of society. While *Prince Albert's Model Lodging House* was the first model house to be attached to an international exhibition, Henry Roberts had already designed stand-alone model houses for the SICLC, notably the 1844 Bagnigge Wells Estate model houses in Pentonville, London. Significantly, the Society agreed in May 1844 on changes to its charter, including a name-change from the Labourers' Friend Society (founded in 1827) to the SICLC. Beyond its mission to address the plight of agricultural labourers, the Society now additionally included the concerns of the urban poor, while seeking to work at the 'intersection of the built environment and print culture' (Tarn 1974: 14). This expansion marked a shift from its previous focus on the printing of books, pamphlets and posters to the dissemination of their social interests through the model home. The 1844 meeting produced three 'modes' of assistance: pursuing the development of an urban allotment system, the clustering of houses and a system of controlled loans. The 'means' for achieving these modes included the 'arranging and executing plans as models for the improvement of the dwellings of the poor, both in the metropolis and in the manufacturing and agricultural districts' (Tarn 1974: 15).

The rise of industrial production and globalization with its associated rapid urbanization and growth of working-class populations near centres of production in Europe and America, following its early adoption in Great Britain, raised many of the social challenges that the SICLC had identified in London. The format of the model house, in response to some of these concerns, was taken up by concerned associations and societies globally in an attempt to propose domestic solutions for the urban poor.

As discussed in the following in this chapter, organizations such as the Deutscher Werkbund (1907–1934) in Germany and the Congrès internationaux d'architecture moderne (CIAM) in France (1928–1959) were key to developing a strong international architectural exhibition culture across Europe in the twentieth century. In America, the Department of Architecture and Design at The Museum of Modern Art in New York (MoMA),[4] whose first director was influential American architect Philip Johnson, was crucial for similar developments. MoMA has been key in promoting 'Good Design', an American concept closely linked to the 'international style' that developed out of the 1930s and reached prominence in the post-war years through the support of designers such as Charles and Ray Eames and Marcel Breuer and championed by curator Edgar Kaufmann Jr.

With the 1950s seeing the export of American design to Europe in the form of touring exhibitions, 'the US State Departments disseminated MoMA's gospel of global modernism abroad' (Castillo 2010: 111). Under sponsorship from the Marshall Plan, the exhibition *American Home Furnishings*, chiefly sourced from the 1951 MoMA exhibition *Good Design*, toured Europe from 1952 to 1953 with significant contributions also being shown in the 1952 exhibition *We're Building a Better Life* (Berlin). The original *Good Design* exhibition was revisited in 2009 at MoMA under the title *What Was Good Design?... MoMA's Message 1944–56*, organized by Juliet Kitchen and curated by Aidan O'Connor in an affirmation of the importance and influence of these mid-century housing exhibitions.

In 2008, MoMA created a 1:1-scale exhibition of architecture entitled *Home Delivery: Fabricating the Modern Dwelling*. It included five full-scale models from five international architects in the tradition of MoMA's earlier full-scale projects in the MoMA gardens, namely the Marcel Breuer house from 1949, Gregory Ain's house from 1950 and the Shofuso (Pine Breeze Villa and Garden) from 1953. Curated by Barry Bergdoll, the exhibition 'paid homage to the tradition of exhibition houses so integral to the history of innovation in modern architecture' (Bergdoll in Broadhurst and Oshima 2008: 09). Projects were commissioned as 'occupiable model buildings' (2008) that explored prefabrication, sustainability, mass customization and advanced manufacturing techniques. Reflecting on the model's persuasive nature, MoMA architectural curator Barry Bergdoll argues:

> The reason to do 1:1 scale temporary architecture ... is because it creates a more powerful experience for a greater number of people to enter into a debate about whatever is important. I think of the 1:1 project as a discursive tool more than an object per se.[5] (Bergdoll in Arpa and Andel 2013: 72)

The immersive, immediate and performative quality of an occupiable model building engages its audience in a spatial experience through its ability to create a discourse about space. Bergdoll's notion that this form of model-making 'is a discursive tool more than an object per se' is borne out in each of this chapter's examples, where the primary architectural intent in creating the model or model home is demonstrably the creation of new typologies to generate discourse around issues critical to architects' understanding of their role in society. Sociologist Virág Molnár observes:

> The twentieth century was marked by a stern conviction in the power of architecture to fundamentally change social reality ... it was assumed that radical new housing design would lift workers out of their culture of poverty and uplift society. (Molnár 2013: 7)

The model in exhibition has enabled architects 'a degree of freedom precluded in private or government commissions' (Zimmerman 2014: 185) where discursive spaces are created, which allow form and idea to emerge simultaneously in built form in order to advance a social, cultural and political discourse beyond issues of design or materiality. The performative quality of the model that is fully realized with the movements and actions of its temporary inhabitants has made this format particularly attractive to designers, curators and audiences alike.

Model and domesticity: Staging the new typologies

Mies van der Rohe and Lilly Reich: *The Dwelling*, **Stuttgart 1927**

Mies van der Rohe and Lilly Reich: *The Dwelling of Our Time*, **Berlin 1931**

The Deutsche Werkbund, or German Association of Craftsmen, was formally founded in 1907 out of dissatisfaction with the historicist approach to architecture and design prevalent in the mid- to late nineteenth century. German architect and author Hermann Muthesius published a series of lectures reproaching the design establishment and in support of a group of forward-looking designers provoking a concerted effort to have him removed from his government post. In refusing to comply, state officials gave tacit support for Muthesius to initiate an opposing association of architects, artists, designers and manufacturers that were to become a seminal twentieth-century organization for design and architecture. *The Third German Applied Art Exhibition* in Dresden in 1906 had been organized by architect and urban designer Franz Schumacher, who engineered the selection process to favour designers, artists and companies that supported design and manufacturing concepts that were to become the Werkbund's vision of modern design. Muthesius, strongly influenced by the English Arts and Crafts movement, brought together a network of individuals who had been involved in key secessionist and breakaway groups of the late nineteenth and early twentieth centuries. They included Joseph Maria Olbrich, strongly connected to Jugendstil; Josef Hoffmann, an influential member of the Vienna Secession; Max Liebermann from the Berlin Secession; and Franz Von Stuck from the Munich Secession. Completing the group were some of the most renowned designers of the early twentieth century, namely Peter Behrens, Theodor Fischer, Wilhelm Kreis, Max Laeuger, Adelbert Niemeyer, Bruno Paul, J. J. Scharvogel, Paul Schultze-Naumburg and Fritz Schumacher, working together with twelve Munich-based manufacturing companies.

The purpose of the alliance was to improve the quality of goods manufactured in Germany by encouraging cooperation between producers, tradesmen and art professionals. It sought to represent artists and architects by leading commissions their way, and to serve businessmen who saw a competitive edge in the use of artists' designs. (Schwartz 1996: 09)

With state support, the Werkbund went on to significantly reform German applied arts in the fields of production, design and economic practice, and, by the outbreak of the First World War, had 1,870 members across six countries. The Werkbund continued to privilege exhibitions and displays of design and architecture as a primary method of dissemination, and as Claire Zimmerman points out in her study on Mies van der Rohe: 'In the history of exhibition architecture from 1907 to 1935 the Werkbund played an influential role as the sponsor of multiple exhibitions of which *The Dwelling* was the most prominent' (Zimmerman 2014: 184).

Architect Ludwig Mies van der Rohe joined the Werkbund in 1924, becoming its vice-president in 1926. He became director of the Bauhaus from 1930 and finally left Germany for the United States in 1938. His long-term collaboration with modernist designer Lilly Reich resulted in some of Mies' best-known early works, including the *Barcelona Chair* and the *Brno Chair*. Reich had from an early age directed her own studios in Vienna and Berlin. In the Werkbund, where she was tasked with curating and designing exhibitions, her contribution 'was crucial to the elevation of modern exhibition design as an art and as a discipline, which was determined not only by products that exemplified a superior standard of design but most dramatically by the exhibition itself using only the essential elements of presentation' (McQuaid, Bee and Droste 1996: 9).

In 1927 in Stuttgart, 'under the artistic supervision of Werkbund board member, Ludwig Mies van der Rohe' (McQuaid, Bee and Droste 1996: 22) Reich and Mies conceptualized and designed parts of the Werkbund exhibition *Die Wohnung* (The Dwelling) as inhabitable interiors. In the Central Exhibition Hall, fragments of future buildings were constructed, complete with furnishings, as part of a 'four-part exposition whose centrepiece was the *Weissenhofsiedlung* (Weissenhof Housing Settlement), built on a hill above the city of Stuttgart' (1996). It included permanent houses from some of the key modernist architects of the time, including Le Corbusier and Pierre Jeanneret, Walter Gropius, Bruno Taut and Hans Scharoun amongst others. This 'showcase for the most representative modern architecture ... led to the inclusion of an international selection of architects and to the appointment of Lilly Reich' (1996) to design the layout of the exhibitions. Ultimately, she was responsible for eight of the nine exhibitions.

Described in a 1927 review as 'tasteful provisory buildings',[6] the scaled fragments were to perform a new way of living, made easy and efficient through the use of mass-produced lighting, heating systems and kitchens. These represented the staging of the future of daily life rather than a mere display of desirable objects. The exhibition was favourably received and understood as a tangible answer to the question on the exhibition poster: *Wie Wohnen?* (How to Live?) With its fragmentary inhabited interiors, it shifted the future of housing and living persuasively closer to reality.

Mies and Reich continued to expand their exhibition practice, including the 1931 *Die Wohnung unserer Zeit* (The Dwelling of Our Time) in Berlin (see Figure 4.1) as part of the *Deutsche Bauausstellung* (German Building Exhibition) which as an organization sought to establish a permanent building exhibition in Berlin. However, 'this new exhibition would be taking place indoors, in a hall where 1:1 models were built based on the design of the participants' (Gameren and van Andel 2013: 93). In total, 23 living units were constructed, clearly reflecting the economic crisis strangling Europe: a 'dwelling for the minimum existence', a 'spatial program for the family of an intellectual worker', a 'house for a sportsperson' and a 'house for a childless family'.[7] Around the main exhibition of 1:1 models was an exhibition of building materials following a design by Lilly Reich, who also designed two of the model houses in the main exhibit.

While the exhibition was heavily criticized for seemingly advocating an 'impoverished' way of living in such economic times due to its minimalist

FIGURE 4.1 *Exhibition house by Mies van der Rohe at* Die Wohnung unserer Zeit *(The Dwelling of Our Time), German Building Exhibition, Berlin 1931.*

interiors, statements such as that by Wilhelm Lotz in 1931 below show that Mies' intention to create an exhibition as a site of experience and discovery succeeded. *Die Wohnung unserer Zeit* pointed to a different, more hopeful, modernist future, freed from the burden of representing nineteenth-century plush:

> It is important and significant, that such beautiful things as these residential houses with open spaces and lively connection between interior and outside space have been created by a hand driven by an artistic and innovative sense. Here, one likes to breathe; here one feels that there are still powers that have the courage to think freely and unhindered into the future. (Lotz 1931)[8]

In a surprisingly innovative and theatrical approach, actors were employed to sit in chairs, smoke pipes and walk about, turning the exhibition artefact into a stage. Rather than representing abstraction through scaled models, plans and drawings, Mies and Reich created a fragmentary double of the future: a unified entity of building, interior and furniture.

As architect Bruno Taut wrote in the Russian newspaper *Izvestia:* 'what was seen in Stuttgart in 1927 as audacity, here is seen as having arrived' (Taut in Gameren and van Andel 2013: 93). Modernism and the representation of modernist ideas through exhibition and 1:1 full-scale models in Europe had reached a high point, only to have its international trajectory curtailed in the political upheavals of 1933.

Model and mobility: Staging America's urban future

Norman Bel Geddes: *Futurama*, New York World's Fair 1939

The immersive and the performative as attributes of 1:1 full-scale models can also be seen in extremely large models, even if these are at smaller scale and cannot be entered in the same way as the examples cited earlier. In the case of the 3,200-square-metre modelscape *Futurama*, created by American designer Norman Bel Geddes for the *General Motors Highways and Horizons Pavilion* at the 1939–1940 New York World Fair (see Figure 4.2), it is not the experience of an enterable interior that makes it immersive but its sheer size. This vast scheme featured half a million buildings, a million trees and 50,000 cars that 'immersed his audience in a carefully-orchestrated theatrical experience' (Speck 2012: 293). Audience members sat in compartments

FIGURE 4.2 *The* Futurama *exhibit by Norman Bel Geddes at the* General Motors Highways and Horizon Pavilion, *New York World's Fair 1939–1940.*

comprising two blue mohair upholstered chairs, equipped with individual sound systems and attached to a moving conveyor system constructed by the Westinghouse Elevator Company, that made its way around the models in a carefully orchestrated 420-metre, 16-minute ride simulating a flight over this city of the future. By the end of the two seasons at the New York Fair, 25 million people had seen the exhibit.[9]

Bel Geddes (apart from a three-week stint at the Art Institute of Chicago) was a self-taught designer who 'moved easily from the design of theatre and movie production to scales and stoves to automobiles and trains to huge public buildings and entire landscapes' (Hauss-Fitton 1996: 55). His extensive knowledge of the scenographic techniques of scale, effect and atmosphere combined with decades of architectural and industrial design projects culminated in this vast vision of an American city set twenty-one years in the future. Here, many of his previous singular designs could be realized in model form. Through careful framing of the visitor's gaze together with individual location-based sound relating to one's position in the model sequence, Geddes structured a complex, immersive urban narrative aided by the visitor's predetermined movement through his miniature world. The use of animated and moving elements, including 10,000 moving 'teardrop-shaped motor cars and buses and streamlined trains designed by Geddes in the early 1930s' (1996: 58) and ambient lighting that created 'the atmosphere from dawn to midday, through sunset, into dusk, and midnight' (1996), added a level of realism in coalescence with the model's detail, and physical size allowed the visitor to suspend disbelief and enter its world.

Ultimately, the quality of the carefully constructed immersive experience enriched the exhibit's success: 'all of its components contributed to the creation of a unified effect' (Hauss-Fitton 1996: 55). The resultant space was as much a theatre as an exhibition, with audiences passive participation activating and creating the world. Beyond representing a vision of a future city, *Futurama* was a highly self-referential world of interrelated objects that on one level operated as entertainment but on another as a focused ideological marketing tool. The *Futurama* conveyed a distinct ideology that was shaped not only by the client General Motors, but by Geddes himself, as he makes clear in his book *Horizons:* 'Industry is the driving force of this age' (Geddes 1977: 06).

As America was emerging from the Great Depression, the New York World Fair generally and *Futurama* specifically, took the 'opportunity to convince the public of the trustworthiness of corporations and the brighter future offered by industrial capitalism' (Speck 2012: 291). They offered the public 'an extraordinary, optimistic image of a utopian future' (2012: 302). Geddes and his team had been working on designs of interstate motorway and urban road systems for years preceding the World Fair and combined with hundreds of realized and unrealized projects (partially documented in Geddes' 1932 publication *Horizons*),[10] the material for *Futurama*, developed over decades, delivered a fortuitous ideological convergence. The rational and repetitive nature of the urban planning of *Futurama*, the monolithic skyscrapers on a grid-based plan and abundance of parkland have led some observers to comment that it 'bore strong resemblances to Le Corbusier' (2012: 296) in terms of its urban form, with particular reference to the Swiss architect's 1924 scheme, *Ville Radieuse* (The Radiant City).[11]

Projects such as *Futurama* show that models are highly persuasive vehicles for socio-political concepts and ideas that transcend its immediate form and present specific agendas defined by its creators. *Futurama*, commissioned by an automobile manufacturer, put the car unequivocally at the centre of the urban experience. Vittorio Gregotti observes in *Rethinking Architecture* that Geddes 'realizes the Bauhausian dream of a civilization made from the use of the culture of objects' (Gregotti 1996: 05). In the format of the large-scale model, Geddes found in this exhibition an 'extraordinary opportunity for an expressive coincidence with the American Dream' (1996).

As visitors left the exhibition, they were given a pin that stated, 'I have seen the future'. Perhaps they had since many of the concepts concerning mobility in the 1960s had appeared before them in Geddes' staged future of the American city.

Model and Marshall Plan: Staging the Cold War

US Department of State: *We're Building a Better Life*, Berlin 1952

US Department of State: *American National Exhibition*, Moscow 1959

The historical ascension of the full-scale model as discursive device and socio-political tool reached a peak in the 1950s, as 'model homes offered an accessible formula, instantly recognizable across national borders and extremely suited to the synthesis of industry and culture' (Floré and Devos 2014: 33). In Europe, the model became a traditional stage with a live performance with the inclusion of actors inside the model playing family members and an audience viewing the theatrical display through the windows, reminiscent of the setting and viewing conditions of Maeterlinck's 1894 symbolist drama *L'Interieur*, originally intended for marionettes where the audience watches the action from the outside, through the windows of the protagonists' house.

The model remained enterable (though not for the public) and had become a set-piece in an ideological spectacle, a post-war design strategy that served as 'a bulwark against the Soviet bloc' (Oldenziel and Zachmann 2009: 07). Here was a very public face for the economic concepts of the Marshall Plan,[12] with its ambitions for a 'European economy based on a New Deal-Fordist-Marshall Plan that encouraged individual patterns of (mass) consumption' (2009). Seeking to address European 'perceptions of a degraded American 'non-culture' (Castillo 2008: 65) the US Department of State (through the Marshall Plan) in the early 1950s engaged MoMA curator Edgar Kaufman Jr[13] to oversee a number of its sponsored exhibitions in Europe, including the 1952 *Wir Bauen ein Besseres Leben* exhibition in West Berlin (see Figure 4.3).

The exhibition featured a full-scale model of a detached suburban house without a roof (which would have hindered the audience's view from above). A narrator in a white coat stood on a custom-designed tower praising the domestic wonders below and explaining the workings of the kitchen to the audience. All objects were designed and manufactured in countries belonging to the Marshall Plan[14] with many from Kaufman's annual *Good Design* exhibition at MoMA in New York, which had been touring Europe under the title *American Home Furnishings*. A variety of appliances, furnishings and other objects originating in Europe filled the living room, bathroom and bedrooms. However, the 'calculated mix of products from the Marshall Plan member nations ended at the kitchen door' (Castillo 2008) with almost the entire kitchen contents being imported from the United States. In the model home of the early 1950s, the new fully stocked and 'well-equipped kitchen was a key modernist indicator for society's civilization in the twentieth century' (Oldenziel and Zachmann 2009: 07).

FIGURE 4.3 *Full-scale model house from the exhibition,* Wir bauen ein besseres Leben *(We're Building a Better Life) in West Berlin as part of German Industrial Trade Fair 1952.*

The exhibition opened as part of the German Industrial Trade Fair in West Berlin's George Marshall-Haus,[15] and in three weeks was viewed by half a million people before it travelled to Stuttgart, Hanover, Paris and Milan. While the model home was the centrepiece, the remaining space displayed over 6,000 manufactured objects, including all objects in the model home – each labelled with country of origin, price and hours worked to purchase it. The exhibition's strategy and its acceptance by Europe's public saw the model interior or the model home as a powerful didactic instrument with which to draw attention to the idea of successful post-war reconstruction, a new national identity or a promising future. (Floré and Devos 2014: 33)

The home, in particular, the kitchen, had been pushed to the centre of the political stage, no better illustrated than in the 1959 televised 'kitchen debate' between US Vice President Richard Nixon and USSR State Secretary Nikita Khrushchev. This staged exchange took place in one of the four American kitchens exhibited in the American National Exhibition in Moscow's Sokolniki Park, alongside displays of fashion, cars and fine art (mainly Abstract Expressionist). Featured here also was a full-scale model house titled 'X–61', cut in half so that visitors could walk through. The exhibition, a direct result of the Soviet–American cultural agreement signed a year earlier in 1958, attracted around 2.7 million visitors.

The kitchens featured professional actors playing the idealized role of full-time housewife, 'keeping a serene home to which the male breadwinner could retreat' (Reid 2008: 154) surrounded by the latest American domestic technologies. Leaning on the barrier to this display, the two politicians delivered what has been referred to as 'the most iconic encounter of the cold war' (2008) with a clash of views on whether communism or capitalism provided the best living standard for the greatest number in their respective societies. Leaving aside the space race and arms race, this 'living standards race' centred on 'the kitchen as a techno-political node that linked the state, the market, and the family' (Oldenziel and Zachmann 2009: 3).

The model house had become occupied by actors and politicians in a bid to both stage and influence the future, driven by opposing political systems that desired to own it. The model had become a highly visible propaganda tool that promoted specific utopic ideas for political purposes.

Model and discourse: Staging the 1:1

Barry Bergdoll: *Home Delivery: Fabricating the Modern Dwelling,*
New York 2008

The exhibition *Home Delivery: Fabricating the Modern Dwelling*, curated by Barry Bergdoll at the Museum of Modern Art, New York (MoMA) between July and October 2008, comprised its first 1:1 full-scale exhibition of architecture in fifty years. The exhibition was divided into two components: the first comprised five 1:1 full-scale models assembled on a 1,700-square-metre vacant lot in mid-town Manhattan that illustrated 'the many paradoxes of the prefabricated house' (Bergdoll in Broadhurst and Oshima 2008: 7). The second, shown in parallel at MoMA, comprised an exhibition of fragments, drawings, photographs and scale models that charted the history of prefabrication and its path from mass standardization to mass customization. The exhibition's point of departure was the Sears Catalogue homes from 1908 to 1940, and included designs ranging from modernist architects Le Corbusier, Walter Gropius, Adolf Meyer, Marcel Breuer, Charles and Ray Eames to utopic 1960s schemes from Archigram, Moshe Safdie and Matti Suuronen to the pioneers of 'computer-generated architectural forms' (Bergdoll in Broadhurst and Oshima 2008: 174) including Greg Lynn. Additionally, four fragments were commissioned, three exploring digital modelling output via a laser cutter or CNC router, and the fourth by Japanese Architect Kengo Kuma proposing flat-packed water-filled blocks with 'the potential to compose dwellings of infinite configurations' (2008: 187). The five 1:1 full-scale models or 'occupiable model buildings' (2008: 9) included the *Digitally Fabricated Housing for New Orleans* by MIT Professor Lawrence Sass,[16] the *Cellophane House* by American architects Kieran Timberlake Associates, the *Micro-Compact Home* by British architects Horden Cherry Lee Architects and German architects Haack + Höpfner, *SYSTEM3* by Austrian architects Oskar Leo Kaufmann and Albert Rüf, and *Burst*008* by New York-based architects Jeremy Edmiston and Douglas Gauthier.

Sass' *Digitally Fabricated House for New Orleans* (see Figure 4.4) addressed the exhibition's core themes by proposing a low-cost solution in

FIGURE 4.4 *A 1:1 full-scale model house by Lawrence Sass/MIT,* Digitally Fabricated House for New Orleans *in* Home Delivery: Fabricating the Modern Dwelling *at the Museum of Modern Art, New York 2008.*

the wake of the devastation wrought by Hurricane Katrina in 2005. The house, based on the traditional New Orleans Shotgun house with filigree ornamental style, is uniquely rooted in African-American culture. The proposal, beyond providing pragmatic and quick shelter solutions, reinforces in its reinvention of traditional ornament the identity of a community at a time when many such symbols had been destroyed. As Sass points out, 'the styling as a shotgun house was selected to call attention to social, visual and historical issues' (Sass 2014), while juxtaposing the intended devastated New Orleans site with the exhibition's midtown Manhattan location.

Sass' structural proposition explored the use of planar construction and comprised of 7,000 interlocking plywood components cut with a CNC router.[17] The entire structure was held together by friction and gravity alone and could be constructed with a single rubber mallet. To check the components and structural logic of the full-scale model, a 1:6 scale model was produced from masonite using the same digital files as the full-sized version with only minor modifications. In terms of testing the compatibility, functionality and structural integrity of all components, the smaller model was integral in the process of verifying and producing the full-scale variant. It was displayed inside the 1:1 occupiable model, serving both as an on-site referent during construction and as a representation of its full-sized cousin. During the exhibition it acted as an enclosure, offering the visitor a simultaneous external and internal view, creating a double of the building as a unified entity. Sass' dual models, displayed at two different scales without the loss of detail typically associated with a smaller model, are exceptional in that they are not an abstracted representation of reality[18] but a material manifestation of a digital phenomenon where the original and the copy are indistinguishable from one another. One could presumably 'print' multiple copies at different scales; the only limiting factor in the creation of perfect facsimiles would be the technical capacities of the machine used to output the data.

American architects KieranTimberlake Associates contributed an occupiable model building known as the *Cellophane House*, a four-storey solar-powered structure comprising off-the-shelf components including aluminium framing, polypropylene sheet walls and polyethylene terephthalate film, held together with horizontal and vertical steel connectors. Central to the discursive nature of this model was an argument on sustainability and waste minimization. With a focus on designing a system rather than an object, the architects' argument centred on retaining the integrity of elements[19] that could be demounted and reused when the building has no further use.

British architects Horden Cherry Lee Architects and German architects Haack + Höpfner's seven-square-metre *Micro-Compact Home* argued for the 'absolute extraction of domestic vestiges of a pre-digital age' (Bergdoll in Broadhurst and Oshima 2008: 190). This came in the form of an advanced-engineered cubic form constructed off-site and deposited by helicopter or truck, its small footprint allowing delivery to sites with little disturbance to the ecosystem. Needless to say, all components were recyclable. Responding to growing post-materialism, it was designed for no books and minimal clothing, embracing, with a digital generation in mind, the immaterial nature of digital content as a space-saving solution.

Austrian architects Oskar Leo Kaufmann's and Albert Rüf's *SYSTEM3* was a refinement of a building system segmented into four producers, namely skin producer, solid element producer, serving units producer and window producer. These elements were brought together in an elegant, timber-based, rectangular volume.

The fifth commissioned project, New York-based architects Jeremy Edmiston and Douglas Gauthier's *Burst*008* focused more on 'creating a system of production than in creating form. They use the computer and collateral technologies as tools to draw and fabricate architecture that is not merely a digitization of hand-drawn and traditional production' (Bergdoll in Broadhurst and Oshima 2008: 204)'.

As Bergdoll writes in the preface of the *Home Delivery* catalogue, the project 'paid homage'[20] to the tradition of the twentieth-century modernist housing exhibition, reviving the established modernist format and presenting us with 1:1 full-scale models, commissioned fragments and contextual material in the form of videos, photographs, drawings and fine-scale models. However, it was the digital, social and environmental concerns embodied in the five projects that brought the models conceptually closest to its twentieth-century antecedents. Presented with new forms of manufacturing, new challenges concerning sustainability, affordability and social responsibility, the projects tackled the issues of our time through new typologies represented by 1:1 full-scale models, to stage a future we have not yet fully grasped.

Model and *doppelgänger*: Staging identity and interpretation

Robbrecht en Daem: *Mies in Krefeld*, Krefeld 2013

Beyond the architectural model's functional ability to propose new typologies lies the more fundamental question as to how it can operate as an epistemic tool. Closely linked to such truth-finding, for example, through iteration and optimization, is the question of how the model itself presents a realm of accessible knowledge and whether it belongs to the realm of ontology or epistemology. Ontology, on the one hand, considers what things are and what the nature of things that are is. Here the question may be: what is the nature of the full-scale model? An epistemological approach, on the other hand, seeks methods for discovering its nature. In the process of truth-finding through the model, the 2013 Krefeld Golf Club project allows linking both, not by proposing new typologies, but by reflecting on existing typologies from a performative (space) paradigm and blurring the borders between architecture, art and performance.

The 2013 full-scale model of a golf clubhouse by Mies van der Rohe is a convergence of Mies' unrealized 1930 plans and Ghent architecture firm Robbrecht en Daem's contemporary interpretation built near Mies' proposed site. Robbrecht en Daem's redefinition of an architectural programme, from the practical clubhouse to temporary exhibition and event space, infused the enterable model with a performative agenda requiring the visitor's participation and reflected on the role of the architectural model's ability to stage the past. The Krefeld Golf Club project is used here as an instance of an autonomous model freed from the responsibility of proposing a new typology and results in a highly nuanced and referenced reflection on the nature of the occupiable model.

In 2010, art historian and curator Christine Lange, great-granddaughter of the Krefeld silk industrialist Herrmann Lange, founded Mies in Krefeld (MiK), a society that aimed to create an occupiable model building that would mediate between modernism and contemporary architectural intervention. A spatial *doppelgänger* beyond 'original and copy', it was to be designed by more than one architect, built at a different time and located on a different site. Lange's concept was to realize the unbuilt golf clubhouse as close as possible to its original site, in a rare convergence of Mies' original plans, a contemporary interpretation and her curatorial brief for an occupiable model building defined by similarity and difference.

By relating original and cited articulations of scale, materiality and detail in search of the 'essence' of Mies' formal and architectural language, the architects emphasized the model's epistemic functions while also spatializing its ontology as a work-in-progress tool. In their wish to reveal the 'essence', and by the decision to make it 'enterable', they asked visitors to experience their search. Their work was thus firmly based, conceptually and programmatically, on an 'unfinished' project by Mies: 'it was a work in progress' (Robbrecht in Lange 2014: 104).

It is here argued that rather than being a 1:1 representative model, the golf club structure presented a highly referential autonomous scale model informed by design and curatorial strategies employed to fill the 'gap' between Mies' incomplete original plans and the final built structure. The model thus embodied and questioned existing knowledge in the form of an unbuilt precedent combined with contemporary formal and material interventions. It enabled the development of an argument comprised of fragments of Mies' existing plans together with a number of realized projects, including the re-created Barcelona Pavilion from 1986 and some of the architect's theoretical writings on the relationship between built-form and nature. The resulting architectural object was on display as a 1:1 full-scale model. However, its diverse modes of influence, citation and interpretation took it beyond the 1:1 representative model towards an autonomous structure. This notion was strengthened by the key change in the Krefeld project's architectural programme: from a practicable clubhouse to a temporary exhibition space, embedding a performative agenda that required the visitor's live participation in a continuous reorganization of the building's interior (see Figure 4.5).

Curator Christiane Lange's conceptual precedent is to be found in the re-creation of the 1929 Barcelona Pavilion from 1983 to 1986. A temporary exhibition, it was demolished barely a year after its opening. A group of Spanish architects reconstructed it on the basis of black-and-white photographs and original plans. The subsequent *Interventions* programme commissioned by the Mies van der Rohe Foundation saw artists and architects such as Ai Weiwei, Kazuyo Sejima, Ryue Nishizawa, Enric Miralles, Antoni Muntadas and Jordi Bernadó restructure elements of the Pavilion, including the pools,

FIGURE 4.5 *Full-scale model* Mies 1:1 Golf Club Project *realized by Architects Robbrecht en Daem based on the incomplete drawings of Mies van der Rohe, Krefeld 2013.*

basement and doors, in temporary installations and performances. The Pavilion's identity now included its history of construction, *disassembly* and reconstruction followed by periods of temporary artistic deconstruction and conscious misuse of the building. Examples include Ai Weiwei's 2010 filling of the water pools with milk and coffee, and Andrés Jaque's 2013 showing of the Pavilion's underworld of objects stored in its secret basements, which included vacuum cleaners, broken glass and so on, displayed as museum artefacts in the representative spaces upstairs. Perception is ever dependent on a contextual system of relations, as Nelson Goodman points out in *Languages of Art*:

> There is no innocent eye... Not only how but what [the eye] sees is regulated by need and prejudice. [The eye] selects, rejects, organizes, associates, classifies, analyses, constructs. (Goodman 1976: 7–8)

Central to Goodman's positioning of an analytical aesthetics and theory of art as one of symbols, the history of a work's production is integral to its identity. Since architecture uses a certain notation in the codified form of architectural plans and thus is an allographic or 'repeatable' art form, any building built after a specific plan shares the same identity. Goodman deduces, however, that due to the 'autographic' origins of architecture where the difference between original and forgery is significant, architecture cannot be categorized as either fully autographic or fully allographic, thus presenting as a 'mixed and transitional case' (Goodman 1976: 221).

The 'reconstruction' of a Mies van der Rohe building, therefore, serves as a case study for both the autonomous architectural full-scale model and its epistemic functions: between past and present, and between autographic and allographic categorizations.

Mies van der Rohe, then director of the Bauhaus,[21] and Krefeld architect August Bierbricher were the only two architects invited in August 1930 by directors of the newly founded Krefeld Golf Club to compete to design an expansive clubhouse with full facilities, a restaurant with bar and dining area, a multi-purpose hall and a terrace. Mies was no stranger to wealthy Krefeld, having built two villas (Haus Lange and Haus Esters) for industrialists Hermann Lange and Dr Josef Esters between 1927 and 1930.[22] Lange, later a lobbyist for the German textile industry in the Third Reich, commissioned ten projects from Mies between 1927 and 1938 with half of them realized, namely the 1927 *Café Samt und Seide* at the Berlin trade fair *Die Mode der Dame*,[23] the Krefeld villas and Mies' only industrial project, the Verseid AG in 1931. Kleinman and van Duzer observe that Lange used his influence to introduce Mies to von Schnitzler, Reichskommissar, for Germany's contribution to the 1929 Barcelona World Exposition (Kleinman and van Duzer 2005: 20). By contrast, under a world economic crisis, the golf club competition was never decided and the clubhouse never built.

The site was to be on Egelsberg hill, near Krefeld, with proposed dimensions of 87 × 92 metres. Mies' notes, project sketches, perspectives, sections and detailed layout plan were uncovered by chance by Christine Lange in the Ludwig Mies van der Rohe Archive at New York's MoMA. Mies' plans showed an open sequence of spaces in an asymmetrical cross form, both exhibiting the landscape while nestled in it – typical of his approach to site:

> Nature, too, shall live its own life. We must beware not to disrupt it with the color of our houses and interior fittings. Yet we should attempt to bring nature, houses, and human beings together into a higher unity. (Mies van der Rohe in Neumeyer 1991: 235)

Complementing Mies' position on the relationship between built form and nature, the Krefeld project displayed only neutral tones of plywood, whitewash, grey gravel and chrome-plated pilotis. The architect's plans reveal that a 50 × 7 metre projecting roof, stabilized by seven pilotis, was to form the entrance. Stretching wide into the landscape was both the dramatic gesture of the awning and the locker room on its left side. The visitor was led along a 20-metre glass front, through a hall and incidental spaces to the central 240-square-metre hall, entirely glazed but closed to the east. Mies observed:

> The wide cone of land needs a flat, expansive building that will blend in with the landscape. The view demands that the building should be open to the south, the west and the north. (Mies in MoMA Archives, cited in Lange and Robbrecht en Daem Architects 2014: 72)

A site adjacent to the original (today a nature reserve) accommodated architects Paul and Johannes Robbrecht's temporary approximation of Mies' design. They decided on a steel frame with fully visible chrome-plated pilotis, with the ceiling alone clad in wood. Non-load-bearing walls were of wooden planks, while ceilings and walls were painted white. Inside and outside floor areas were covered with concrete tiles or gravel. Areas left unspecified by Mies were identified as such, but not 'filled in' or speculated upon. Cross-formed chrome pilotis simultaneously promised a single 'complete' detail that juxtaposed with the structure's overall provisory character. Neither devoted reconstruction nor autonomous object, Robbrecht en Daem's structure oscillated between architectural interpretation and citation, a strangely provocative object that seemed to both engage in dialogue with the landscape and be entirely alien to it. From May to October 2013, the Krefeld Egelsberg became a site for re-examining the sustainability of Mies' basic principle of open, flowing space in dialogue with its surrounds. The project ended with architecture students from Aachen and Krefeld dismantling the structure and using its materials to build temporary structures within a design studio, entitled 'Recycle Mies'.

The Krefeld Golf Club investigated 'the model as tangible representation'[24] beyond the singularity and temporality of the project. With the stated aim of building an 'enterable architecture model' (Lange 2014: 43), Robbrecht en Daem's task may have seemed straightforward, yet questions of context, scale, material and detail soon arose. While Mies' drawings, perspectives and plans were labelled and annotated as to the programme and internal layout, the architects note that it was not clear what Mies wanted to 'achieve' with the building (Robbrecht in Lange 2014: 104). Their primary challenge thus lay in finding an approach that would move beyond a 'first construction' and offer a built discourse on Mies' architectural language. In their catalogue essay 'Figures in a Landscape', they describe their approach in musical and literary rather than architectural terms, that is, the 'score' and 'essay' (Robbrecht in Lange 2014: 102–112). They compare their reading of Mies' plans to a conductor whose reading of the score and internal audial construction of orchestral sounds sets in motion a dynamic process of interpretation, focus and intention. In their essay, the authors' vision is set out to privilege their subjective argument over a comprehensive academic treatment. The term 'essay' is used to establish the architects' conceptual approach as subjective and reflective since the built result was to be 'a model, an exercise, or a three-dimensional structure' (Robbrecht in Lange 2014: 106). Such unrestricted free flow enables essential questions to be asked of the model as an inventive and reflective tool in design and architectural history.

Robbrecht en Daem's realized scheme relied not only on the accessible documents but on architectural citations from other realized buildings by Mies, specifically the Barcelona Pavilion (1929) and Brno's Villa Tugendhat (1929–1930). The strategies of simulation and citation produced an autonomous model referencing an abstracted interpretation of space and a rendition of specific architectonic elements. In approaching the commission to 'build' an unbuilt Mies, Robbrecht en Daem employed strategies from their practices, which have included architecture, furniture and object design, allied to a conceptual and artistic approach formed in collaboration with the curator. This project from the very start had the visitor's experience in mind. In fact, as Johannes Robbrecht puts it, visiting the Golf Club was to be 'like visiting a ruin'.

That ruin, as a site of past construction and destruction, invited the visitor to revel in what might have been and what might be linking the romantic topos of the architectural ruin to the notion of the architectural model as hovering in a liminal state between past and future, reality and wish. In contrast, building a contemporary ruin collapsed the temporalities between original and copy, between intention and realization, and such a building, or rather a model *of* the past and *for* the present, is autonomous and inhabits its site.

The architects' strategy lay not in the construction of the whole and its subsequent demolition, but rather by the careful omission of some elements and finishes and the detailed citation of others already realized by Mies. In the completed project, framed windows without glass are included, as if in a state of incompleteness – a suspended building site. An additional reading meanwhile confirms that the presentation of the window frame acknowledged a Mies hallmark, namely transparency, but denied another, that of reflection. By omitting the glass surface, the visitor encountered transparency without reflection. Such intended rupture between transparency and reflection captured the autonomous nature of the Krefeld *Mies*. Some walls have been omitted while others leave their framing exposed. Freestanding walls were finished with varnish while other planes, including the external walls, were painted with a white pigment not seen in any of Mies' realized buildings. Sections of the roof were also omitted; it was defined merely by 'I' beams spanning a void, allowing light and the elements to enter. The architects used chromed cruciform pilotis throughout, arguing that 'the chromed cruciform columns are the only "real" materials' (Hick 2013).

Cruciform columns from Mies' Barcelona Pavilion were thus cited in their positioning, detail and materiality. The two projects are bound by their temporary nature (in fact, the Golf Club's opening coincided with the eighty-fourth anniversary of the other), and both buildings have been created, recreated and interpreted from the plan to represent a simulation of what may have been, affirming Robbrecht en Daem's assertion:

We decided to make an abstraction that claims its own autonomy, while revealing the essence of Mies' architecture. (Robbrecht in O'Toole 2013)

In *Mies 1:1 Golf Club Project*, with the inclusion of material and formal citations from built structures by Mies, the architects designed and constructed an autonomous model. The resulting model of both 'autographic' and 'allographic' character[25] was closer to a fragment or sketch that alluded to Mies' ideas about nature, materials and space while playfully denying the significance of detail. Thus, rather than designing and building an autonomous structure, and intrigued by the possibility of referencing other iconic buildings in the history of the International Style (and in the process, freely exploring other architects' languages), Robbrecht architects brought other dimensions to the Golf Club: the architectural *doppelgänger*, and the performative and performance space. This represents what the authors have in past writings identified as a *doppelgänger* space,[26] namely the application of formal and material architectural citation combined with an original floor plan was manifest in the Krefeld project. On entering, visitors walk this double space: mentally, according to the footprint of Mies' plans, and physically in regard to Robbrecht en Daem's realization. Further, the architects' citations in the form of pilotis, frames and gargoyles operated as architectural doubles and performative markers, shifting the visitor's act of walking from the 'here and now' towards participation in an architectural *mise en scène* between past and present. And in successfully evoking the continuous emergence of a performative event through the intended interaction of visitor, architectural object and landscape, *Mies 1:1* was conceptualized as a temporary yet practicable performance space.

In sum, the Krefeld autonomous architectural model, while staging its presence, staged other absent architectures that influenced its form and materiality, while operating seamlessly and autonomously between a rigidly genre-bound architectural history and contemporary convergences between architecture, intervention and performance. As a temporary architecture that referenced other reconstructed buildings by Mies such as Brno's Villa Tugendhat and the Barcelona Pavilion, *Mies 1:1* was both autographic and allographic, thus possessing a unique production history that ultimately defined its identity as object.

In the trajectory of this chapter, from the modernist model home to the contemporary performative re-enactment of a propositional Mies building, the residential model has been shown to promote the future of living. At no other scale does the model present the future as temporarily inhabitable and render the visitors as performers rehearsing a life yet to come. The model house became occupied by actors and politicians in a bid to both stage and influence the future, driven by opposing political systems that desired to own it. The full-scale model had thus become a highly visible propaganda tool that promoted specific utopic ideas for political purposes.

5

Performing the Past:
The Full-Scale Model
and Mock Up

Typically, the 1:1 architectural model, prototype or mock-up promises to truthfully represent a future construction. No model, however, can claim to be complete and accurate at once; rather, each model comprises diverse, selected levels of simulation and approximation in form, function and material, depending on the designer's intention. Where the 1:1 model is placed in a real urban context or is part of a simulated urbanity as on the stage or in the post–Second World War propaganda home model exhibitions discussed in the previous chapter, its scope of reference increases such that its inscribed narratives extend from memories and 'lost' places to envisioned futures in relation to the present. The model's inherent performativity, that is, its ability to fashion a (new) reality, makes it particularly productive in the service of political, social and cultural commentary, persuasion and critique.

In the theatre, a scenographic trend can be observed in favour of model dwellings situated on the stage, and with it a re-articulation of the nineteenth-century convention of the fourth wall (understood as an imagined boundary between stage and auditorium). This is to be viewed in the context of postmodernism and its rejection of modernism's grand narratives, and even where scenography embraces the representation of detail and ornament, it does so without seeking a unified and harmonious visual narrative, but rather comprises a critical and representative device:

Through the use of discordance, ugliness, and juxtaposition – what postmodernists would call rupture, discontinuity, disjuncture etc – the spectator of postmodern design is constantly made aware of the experience of viewing and, at the same time, in the most successful examples, made aware of the whole history, context, and reverberations of an image in the contemporary world. (Aronson 2008: 14)

Meticulously designed and furnished sets by collectives such as The Builder's Association with the production House/Divided from 2011, by director Katie Mitchell with the multimedia stagings of Miss Julie in 2010 at Schaubuehne Berlin and The Forbidden Zone at Salzburg Festival in 2014, or by scenographer Bert Neumann (see detailed discussion on The Idiot and Hotel Neustadt below) and by scenographer and director Anna Viebrock with Medea in Corinto (Bavarian State Opera 2010) or Riesenbutzbach (Avignon Festival 2009), became fully functional yet collaged and abstracted found architectures, complete with stairs, doors and windows. These elements physically re-establish the fourth wall that allows or forbids viewing access. As found architectures, they bring with them residues of their past, that is, they extend the reference system of the stage to memories that originate from their architectural form or detail while including past lived realities. The 1:1 model as a site of involved narratives is most evident where its architectural form recalls others of the same genre, and here interpretation depends on how the past is articulated in the present and on the model's immediate and wider contextual placement in history and the present. The onstage model or mock-up is capable of making precise cultural, social or political statements by its material status and by its conjunction with the 'here and now' of live performance. Where the 1:1 or mock-up is defined not only by a façade but by the articulation of an enterable interior volume, the model becomes the stage itself and the viewer the participant in a narrative comprised of its movement possibilities and its architectural, aesthetic and material language.

The model and mock-up, as physical objects and simulators of the real, can convincingly invent past, present and future – in fact, to combine these into one physical and temporary construction. The 1:1 in architecture, while also made for structural and material testing, and display and staging of future habitation (as discussed in Chapter 4), is by its sheer scale and visibility always a public statement in built form. It needs no mental translation from a smaller, more abstracted scale into reality, but relates immediately and directly to viewer and environment.

The 1:1 temporary model is also the exact scale where architecture meets theatre, and the borders between the genres merge in its construction and display. Such merging often comes at the hands of scenic artists, concerned only with façades or details to be photographed, collaged into 'reality' or seen from an auditorium. Nowhere is empty theatricality more evident than in the German National Socialist (NS) regime's photographs of façade mock-ups of future representative buildings, surprisingly often taken from such angles that the wooden scaffold and fake nature of the front wall were clearly visible.

The scaffolding that holds the mock-up rather than the mock-up itself reveals its overall simulative purpose such that where the scaffold is intended (on a stage or in a gallery) to be a feature rather than the hidden backside, it acts as a visual marker and symbol for falsity and betrayal.

Model and nation: The large and full-scale model as propaganda tool

Albert Speer: *Great Hall, Germania,* **Berlin 1939/44**

Albert Speer: *New Reichs Chancellery,* **Berlin 1940**

In the first decades of the twentieth century, the ability of large and architectural models to claim a built reality before their actual construction allowed artists and architects to project a new social and political order. By example, the model Tatlin had made in 1919–1920 to be exhibited as the 'Monument to the Third International' was not confined to the artist's studio or exhibition hall but became a symbol for the ascendance of the working class when carried on their shoulders in the 1925 May Day Procession in Petrograd. Albert Smith concludes in his study on the architectural model as 'machine': '[I]t is clear that the constructivist scale model was a machine needed to destroy the old capitalist system while constructing a new Marxist society' (Smith 2004: 107), and '[s]pecifically Tatlin's tower and Lissitzky's Prouns were seen by the constructivists as scale models needed to develop the new architecture' (2004).

The strategy of constructing a new social order through the world-creating power or large-scale model and mock-up (not through single objects but rather their rapid and orchestrated construction and display) was perfected in Germany and put to systematic and nationwide use in the propaganda politics of the Third Reich. Between 1933 and 1945, the German National Socialists designed a distinct scenography of state. To ensure the population's enduring trust in the value of the NS project, architecture was elevated as a mainspring of a centralized propaganda system in the form of imagined, modelled and realized monumental buildings and grandiose master plans.

The architectural vernacular of the Third Reich diverged into a medievalist typology of a romanticized pre-industrial Germany typified by regional towns, and a monumental representative architecture for the capital Berlin and the city of Nuremberg (since 1933 the site of Reich Party Assemblies and mass rallies). The typologies of NS architecture ranged from neoclassicism to traditionalism and heritage and refused modernity as advocated by the Bauhaus architecture and movement.

Propaganda, governmental and party buildings, in particular, were designed in a neoclassicist style with Roman and Greek elements[1] in an effort to associate the glorious past of the Roman Empire and the achievements of Athenian democracy with the projected future of National Socialism. Models and mock-ups were strategically used as carriers of an imagined national collective past and future that could easily capture the public eye.

Mock-ups and models thus adorned the National Socialists' panoply of propaganda media that would convince the populace of the unique value of the symbolic architecture of the Third Reich. The NS authorities had recognized early that the rebuilding or rebranding of Germany through architecture (as much as it was hastened under their chief architect Albert Speer) was going to take time, and its primary function of symbolizing national socialist unity, community spirit and political power would emerge only little by little. Architectural models and mock-ups, however, could be produced quickly and at any scale, offering an immediate vision and tactile comprehension of the future world-governing Germany.

An innovative and all-encompassing use of modern propaganda media was closely linked to the rapid rise of National Socialism in Germany. From 1933 on, NS propaganda had promoted the nation's internal mobilization and external branding through uniforms, rituals, rules and insignia, while the press, radio and film were synchronized to operate as ideological tools in the service of the regime. The relentless display of NS symbolism through flags, torches, mass-choreographed uniformed processions and the mass chanting of slogans and songs became the instrument of continued political presence, seduction and threat. Public spaces were transformed into overwhelming temporary urban scenographies, especially in the capital Berlin and in Nuremberg,[2] all planned and staged with precise intent. The urban mise-en-scènes created by theatre and film scenographer Benno von Arent from 1936 onwards, following his elevation to *Reichsbühnenbildner* (Reich Scenographer), were typically dark and steeped in the NS' nebulous medieval and folklore symbolism. Germany's public spaces became arenas for ephemeral stagings of the NS narrative of domination and submission, collective and leadership. The immaterial elements of theatre such as atmosphere, sound and light were relentlessly exploited for the staging of Reich Party Assemblies, rallies and processions.

Beyond the ephemeral mass performances celebrating NS spirit and community, a precise national architecture of assembly and leadership was to become the visual symbol of the National Socialists' political will, power and presence.

The architect and urban planner Rudolf Wolters, a close collaborator and colleague of Speer, described in 1941 the link between NS scenography and the future architecture of German cities under the regime:

Flags, masts, tribunes, and the light cones of the spotlights were the first architectonic media ... From these grew the new design of German cities. (Wolters 1941: 11, trans. from German by the authors)

The 28-year-old Speer was appointed chief designer for the future Germany, initially as outdoor lighting designer for the May Day NS gathering on Berlin's Tempelhof Field in 1933. Here, his experiments with dramatic outdoor effects, which would culminate four years later in his iconic 'Light Dome' at the Reichs Party Rally at Nuremberg in 1937, were achieved with the use of 130 newly developed two-metre-wide military spotlights that sent powerful rays upward to a height of several kilometres (see Figure 5.1). From 1936, Speer was responsible for the new design of Berlin, and received on 30 January 1937, as a testament to his largely unlimited architectural and urbanist authority, the newly created title *Generalbauinspektor fuer die Reichshauptstadt* (Inspector-General of Buildings in the Reich Capital (GBI)). That same day, Hitler announced his grand plans for rebuilding and restructuring Berlin, with Speer as principal architect for 'Germania', a master-planned metropolis defined by two major axes, North–South and East–West. All major national and governmental institutions were to be placed along the North–South axis, a kind of Berlin Champs-Élysées

FIGURE 5.1 *Light dome over the Zeppelinfield, NSDAP Reichs Party Assembly, Nuremberg 10 September 1937.*

that extended from the Südbahnhof on the southern end to the Great Hall at its northern end over a distance of five kilometres. Designed by Speer to hold 180,000 people, the Great Hall's cupola was to begin at 98 metres from the ground with a high point at 220 metres, an ambitious design (and possibly technically unachievable at the time) in accordance with his mandate to create ever-larger places of assembly as symbols of NS power, vigour and ideology.

The 1930s saw the unprecedented fabrication of large models that epitomized the NS politics of representation and celebration. These were constructed, used and promoted in numerous ways and scales: as 1:1 façade models and detail models, collaged into propaganda films, photographed and published in mass media and professional magazines such as *Deutsche Baukunst*, and displayed at mass events such as rallies, processions and exhibitions. A gilded large-scale model of the *Germania* Triumphal Arch, designed after a 1925 sketch by Hitler, was given to him on his fiftieth birthday as an acknowledgement of both his architectural talent and his role as 'architect' of the regime's inexorable triumph.

In his extensive 2016 study *Albert Speer (1905–1981)*, Sebastian Tesch emphasizes the active role of the contemporary press in promoting the usefulness of the architectural scale model and in praising Speer's professionalism and diligence, of which his large models were deemed proof (2016: 198). With Speer's city of *Germania* destined to be the NS world capital, numerous large models were produced under his guidance, to be then used in exhibitions and photographs in mass media and professional publications. Models in large scales ranging from 1:20 to 1:5 and 1:1, as well as façades and corners of future buildings, were constructed in the typical film architecture technique of painted cardboard mounted on wooden scaffolds.[3] NS architectural models had a dual function, namely as a persuasive tool for Hitler and, for a lay public, as an ideological tool predicting a victorious NS future transcending the perceived humiliating defeat of the First World War.

For the public, detailed architectural scale models were publicized via not only print media but film – another industry the regime recognized at the outset as an efficient medium for mass dissemination of its messages. Model photographs and model animation films, in particular, were ideally suited for blurring distinctions between built reality and utopian future – between what was dreamed and what had already been built – by their capacity to conjure what appeared to be an objective representation of reality. One of the most iconic extant images of the *Germania* model from 1939, shows the Great Hall, framed by dramatic cloudscapes, photographed through the semi-circular monumental Triumphal Arch (see Figure 5.2). This idealized model photograph resembles a film still, and thus shifts the architectural ensemble from its utopian state to a perceived full scaled reality.

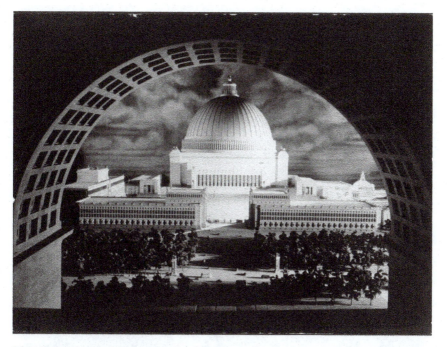

FIGURE 5.2 *Model photograph of* Grosse Halle *(Great Hall)* Germania *by Albert Speer, 1939/1944.*

Models were used in propaganda films, notably in the 1939 Ufa newsreel *The Word of Stone*[4] that showed four grand building schemes including *Germania*, a model of Munich's new Opera House and the new Odeon at Hofgarten Munich. Model stills were animated and montaged between real streetscape scenes so that the spectator could not differentiate between the buildings' present and future states. In scales of up to 1:10, architectural models were regularly exhibited along with representations of their interiors. A notable example was the 1938–1939 *Second German Architecture and Art Exhibition* in Munich's House of German Art. This exhibition, including over 120 large models and 150 big photographs of the models, their antetypes in antiquity and some completed buildings, was staged to summarize the architectural successes of five years of Nazi rule (1933–1938). Overwhelmingly, the message for the visitor was that of a stable government in control of its internal and external representations, and of an aesthetic coherence and harmony modelled on early Athenian democratic and sacred places of assembly. The artefacts, in conjunction with the overall exhibition scenography, thus achieved a double coding of political reality and ideologically based deception. This was evident in the media representation of the New Reich Chancellery, adjacent to the planned *Oberkommando der Wehrmacht* (High Command of the German Army).

The New Reich Chancellery from 1940 was Speer's only building realized in the framework of the megalomaniac project of *Germania*, and there was little time to complete even this. This fact explains the construction of numerous 1:1 models of its façade and their subsequent dissemination in published photographs. These models had been built by craftsmen of the cinema studios in Berlin-Lichterfelde and served the immediate purpose of testing materiality, dimensions and proportions (see Figure 5.3). Typically, a human

FIGURE 5.3 *1:1 façade model of New Reich Chancellery by Albert Speer, set up in Teuplitzer Strasse Berlin-Neukölln.*

being (possibly Speer himself) in either civilian clothes or uniform would pose at the foot of the model to indicate how the architecture dwarfed the individual, thus emphasizing the state's grandeur. While the skill of the scenic builders meant that the models or mock-ups looked entirely realistic, the supporting scaffolding visible through window openings and side views undercut this ambition, unmasking the architectural proposition as something akin to a partial theatre or film set.[5] Other 1:1 models such as the tribune sections of the planned Nuremberg German Stadion in the Hirschbach Valley (built from September 1937 onwards) served the dual purpose of demonstrating NS efficiency in transforming the nation's architectural landscape and testing and optimizing Speer's designs. To this purpose, he had five rows of bleachers built at different angles to determine optimum viewing axes. From the concrete blocks and wooden seating constructs of the original model, only the concrete bases remain, and today enjoy heritage status in memory of a totalitarian regime's ambitions and failures. The Stadion, the world's largest of its kind, like so many Speer designs was never to be built.

Large-scale models were also carried through city centres in public processions, for the first time at the 1933 Munich *Tag der Deutschen Kunst* (Day of German Art) displaying a model of the Haus der Deutschen Kunst designed by Paul Ludwig Troost[6] and again in Munich during the 1937–1939 revivals of the *Tag der Deutschen Kunst* (see Elser and Schmal 2012: 104–105). These acts show the potency of a newly developed national architecture and art that appealed, with its distinct anti-modernist aesthetics, to both NS elites and the attendant masses. An extant photograph of the 1933 Munich procession shows the public display of Troost's model choreographed into the overall scenography of the event. The large-scale all-white model was placed on a platform decorated with fantasy banners and textile borders and carried at shoulder height by 32 men in medieval costume. Through such historicized staging, the model gained prominence and symbolic value as a promise and a gift.

Significantly, the mediatization and mass dissemination for propaganda purposes of NS-regime models had already been meticulously planned at the time of their construction. Firmly linked to an overall media politics designed to seduce and manipulate the masses, the architecture models of the Third Reich were singularly teleological; that is, they relentlessly depicted a victorious NS movement, symbolized by its monumental architectural achievements in a deliberate blurring of reality and illusion, present, past and future. The large models and mock-ups of representational buildings and complexes thus operated in a complex coding that invoked Imperial Rome's glorious past in their monumental architectural dimensions and proportions adorned with contemporary NS symbols, in an effort to artificially construct both a nation's collective memory and its future.

Model and memory:
Venetian theatres of the world

Vincenzo Scamozzi: *Teatro del Mondo*, Venice 1597

Giovanni Antonio Rusconi: *Teatro del Mondo*, Venice 1593

Aldo Rossi: *Teatro del Mondo*, Venice 1979–1980

Theatre, to the Italian architect Aldo Rossi,[7] comprises an architecture of memory; it exists as a site of memory and stands as a metaphor for the vitality and ephemerality of life and its transformative aspects. But unlike Camillo's memory theatre for an individual orator-in-training discussed previously, Rossi understands memory in the theatre and memory in the city as formed by individual memories and resulting in a collective, sited memory. This collective memory, to Rossi, defines the *locus* of the city and affords the city its specific quality and character.

In 1979, the Pritzker Prize winner designed a temporary theatre, titled *Teatro del Mondo*, for the 1980 Venice Theatre and Architecture Biennales, as part of the exhibition *Venezia e lo Spazio Scenico, Architettura, Teatro*.[8] This theatre, moored in the San Marco Basin for the duration of the Biennale, positioned itself in the tradition of Venetian floating *Teatri del Mondo* since the sixteenth century. It moved beyond their representative nature in its architectural conception as a model of all past, present and future *Teatri*, encompassing the collective memories of their appearances, performances and spectators. Rossi understood theatre and architecture to be spaces for unforeseen events as well as for habitation, and theatre in particular as a catalyst for comprehending an entire city as a space 'burdened with memory' (Rossi 1981: 30). Following Maurice Halbwachs' concept of a *mémoire collective* (collective memory),[9] Rossi understands the city, its artefacts and places to be formed by the collective memory of its inhabitants and its architecture, past and present. In his reflections on architecture, a fascination with the ephemerality and uncertainty of theatre and the translation of these into built form (that is, the city at large) plays an essential part:

> The theater, in which the architecture serves as a possible background, a setting, a building that can be calculated and transformed into the measurements and concrete materials of an often elusive feeling, has been one of my passions, even if I do not always like to admit it. (Rossi 1981: 33)

The *Teatro* embodied Rossi's concept of theatre and architecture, and it is not surprising that it became his best-known building: a structure that straddled

Venice's past and future as well as enabling and comprising a performative event. Rossi describes theatre as a whole as

a vehicle for an event we desire, whether or not it actually occurs; and in our desiring it, the event becomes something "progressive" in the Hegelian sense. (Rossi 1981: 3)[10]

The potential for theatre and architecture to be both sites for an event and comprise the event itself, and thus to present Hegel's 'progressive nature of history', lies at the centre of Rossi's Venice design. It explains why rather than proposing a contemporary version of a traditionally open and inviting floating theatre for entertainment, he presented the *Teatro* as a sombre and internally oriented structure. Pared down to a formal horizontal composition of cube, pyramid and sphere, with an internally articulated void for a performance space, the *Teatro* drew out Rossi's core ideas on collective architectural and theatrical memory as instrumental in forming the city. For Rossi, architecture and theatre are instruments that enable an event to occur and to be viewed, and the defining parallel between the disciplines is that through their practices and conventions they allow such events to unfold continually. Thereby, the sum of these events creates the *locus* or site of the 'analogous city'.[11]

The temporary, floating theatre thus embodied past and present through a construction of collective memory. Rossi achieved its model character through formal abstraction, citation of architectural elements common to the historical Venetian floating *Teatri*, and an inversion of exterior and interior (see Figure 5.4).[12]

These strategies enabled the *Teatro del Mondo* to operate as both object and autonomous model, designed not to iterate into a future object but to remain what it is. If the *Teatro* is understood to be a highly referential but autonomous model in the conceptual tradition of the baroque cosmology of the *theatrum mundi* (theatre of the world),[13] that saw the world as a stage populated by actors who perform a play devised by the divine author-god, then its additional function as a visual and conceptual referent in the San Marco Basin becomes evident. The *Teatro* on its raft-like base was built in the shipyards of Fushino, before being moved along the lagoon to a site in the San Marco Basin that triangulates iconic Venetian landmarks: the maritime customs house Punto della Dogana, San Marco, and Palladio's imposing Redentore church on the Giudecca island opposite. It remained moored here for the duration of the 1980 Biennale's theatre section, and at its conclusion travelled down the Adriatic coast to Dubrovnik where it moored briefly before being disassembled.

The *Teatro* redefined and repositioned Venice's major sites of civic, commercial and spiritual architectures as relational rather than hierarchical (which would see San Marco in the centre). At the same time, it was the

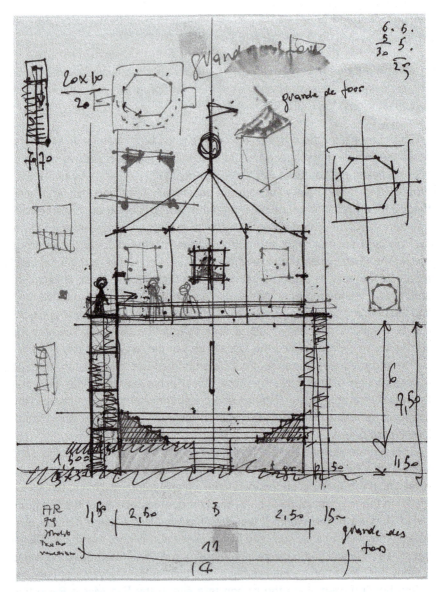

FIGURE 5.4 *Sketch of* Teatro del Mondo *by Aldo Rossi 1979–1980.*

spatial manifestation of Rossi's notion of theatre's and architecture's capacity to collect, contain and communicate a collective memory that in totality forms the (analogous) city at large.

Its title, its design and its very site connected the *Teatro* to Venice's long tradition of producing ephemeral architectures and water scenographies for civic and religious festivities and royal entries into the city.[14]

Contemporary iconographic and written documents show that the *Teatri* typically moored at Venice's civic centre, Piazza San Marco, thus offering good visibility from the piazza and barges nearby. Preceding the sixteenth-century circular, oval or octagonal *Teatri* were rafts populated with actors and musicians, performing mainly allegorical topoi such as the one described in a letter from Beatrice d'Este to her husband Ludovico Sforza, dated 27 May 1493:

All of our ladies shook hands with the Prince, and we set out again on our journey, meeting an infinite number of decorated galleys, boats, and barks. Among others, there was a raft with figures of Neptune and Minerva, armed with trident and spear, seated on either side of a hill crowned with the arms of the Pope and our own illustrious lord, together with your own and those of the Signory of Venice. First Neptune began to dance and gambol and throw balls into the air to the sound of drums and tambourines, and then Minerva did the same. Afterwards they both joined hands and danced together. (d'Este in Cartright 1903: 458–459)

The Venetian *Teatri del Mondo* themselves were thought of as cosmologies, models of the world so that the theatre metaphor became prominent in all disciplines concerned with the communication of knowledge and imagination to describe man's position in the universe.[15]

The theatres were spectacles and playhouse-worlds in themselves. They had evolved from the single actor of the so-called *momaria* (masked displays), often performed on barges, into elaborate allegorical spectacles on highly decorated floating stages designed to be seen from the civic centre of the *Serenissima*.[16] While the public congregated on the shore and at windows and balconies of buildings nearby, invited guests were placed within the floating structure and on accompanying barges and gondolas. The *Teatri*'s typical viewing conditions were those of a public looking onto and inside the wide open structure, with the musicians, actors and guests on the raft both watching the dramatic action from the raft and looking out to the shore. These mirrored design strategies, reinforcing the notion of inclusion and exclusion, and exaggerated in Rossi's *Teatro* by rows of strategically placed little windows, made the Venetian *Teatri* a public spectacle while firmly remaining an entertainment of the ruling Venetian patrician-aristocrats. Rossi's design playfully cites and appropriates several design aspects of the historical *teatri* such as the cupola crowned by another, smaller decorative element and the durational aspect of the floating theatres and with this strategy subsumes the theatre's histories as theatres of the world into his contemporary theatrical and architectural articulation.

In 1564, a *Teatro del Mondo* designed by Venetian architect and hydraulic engineer Giovanni Antonio Rusconi (1515 or 1520–1579), decorated by the sculptors Ludovico and Troiano Modenesi, with performances by the

Compagnia degli Accesi (see Paduan 1966: 142) moored in Venice (see Figure 5.5). Three extant contemporary images – a 1564 drawing signed Tintoretto, a 1590 engraving by Giovanni Grevembroch and an engraving by Andrea Vecellio from his book on costume, *Habiti* – show the theatre from the (frustratingly similar) perspective of the lagoon looking towards San Marco. On the ground floor of the circular raft-like platform, sixteen *telamoni* (larger than life-size figures of Atlas that function architecturally as structural support) with their arms held high above their heads support a round cornice and balustrade. All three images show that the second tier acted as a practicable platform for numerous musicians and guests. In its middle rises a smaller cupola with a roof lantern on top that allows light to enter the cupola beneath. The lantern itself is crowned with an unidentified statue (see Paduan 1966: 142). The cupola reappears in Rossi's theatre with the statue replaced by a metal flag, and in a direct reference to the Venetian celebrations lasting for several days, his model theatre – as the abstracted essence of all *teatri* – navigated the Venetian lagoon for the duration of the Biennale.

At the end of the sixteenth century, several entrances for the *dogoresse* (the Doge's brides) provided spectacles on land and water that typically lasted several days. Extant iconographic documents, in particular a monumental painting by Andrea Vicentino[17] and Giacomo Franco's three engravings from

FIGURE 5.5 *Anonymous drawing of a naval procession passing the Doge's Palace in Venice; gondolas in the foreground and figures lining a bridge at right. The present example is similar to the* Teatro del Mondo *made for the Compagnia degli Accesi in 1564 by Ludovico and Troiano Modenesi after a design by Giovanni Antonio Rusconi.*

1610, depict the 1597 coronation of Morosina Morosini, wife of Doge Marino Grimani, and the *Teatro del Mondo* designed by Vincenzo Scamozzi for this event (see Figure 5.6). Scamozzi's floating *Teatro del Mondo* accompanied the

FIGURE 5.6 La serenissima Dogaressa dal suo palazzo...Bucintoro *from* Habiti d'huomeni et donne Venetiane, *showing the* Teatro del *Mondo by Vincenzo Scamozzi in 1597 (engraving by Giacomo Franco, c. 1610).*

Dogoressa's *bucintoro* (state barge) and several other *macchine* (machines) along the Grand Canal to San Marco, where the party descended to the Basilica for the traditional prayer Te Deum, then on to the Ducal Palace for Morosina's actual *insediamento* (inauguration). The theatre's base is variously described as oval or octagonal (which would make it seem a neat precedent for Rossi's octagonal roof) in the literature. Pulled by four barges shaped as fish with a large figure of Neptune at the rear, the *Teatro's* overall composition comprised a balustraded inhabitable level connected by twelve vertical columns to a domed roof crowned by a roof lantern and statue, reminiscent of Palladio's symmetrical plan for the Villa Rotonda in Vicenza,[18] Scamozzi's *Teatro* had four equal sides with a portico each (rather than one privileged façade), and with a cupola in its centre that functioned like the Villa Rotonda's *oculus* (eye of God) as both a light-giving architectural element and a cosmological reference. Scamozzi's *Teatro* carried two dozen musicians and several of the Dogoressa's gentlewomen and was surrounded by several barges carrying guests. On land, the spectacle of the Dogoressa's arrival was viewed, as Vicentino's painting shows, by many spectators from windows and balconies of the two-storey Doge's palace as well as surrounding two- to three-storey buildings and a nearby bridge. The curator's note from the 2004 Vicenza exhibition *Architettura è Scienza. Vincenzo Scamozzi (1548–1616)* explicitly links Scamozzi's design with Rossi's *Teatro* in that his *Teatro* denoted the return of the Venetian tradition of the ephemeral *apparati* (apparatuses) and *Teatri del Mondo* in our own time.[19]

Rossi's relationship to the historical *Teatri* was antithetical to the open, circular form of the earlier floats. Instead, he set a fully enclosed horizontal structure with a central empty space denoting a stage and a single window looking to the outside. In this cultural and geographic context, his *Teatro* presented itself as the performance of a model as it comes into vision and disappears again with the motion of the waters of the San Marco Basin. Further, by its proximity and viewing axes to the neighbouring architectural landmarks, the *Teatro* added another, consciously hermetic, temporary spectacle to Venice's urban scenography. Reflecting on *Venezia e lo Spazio Scenico*, Marco Dezzi-Bardeschi draws attention to the theatricality of Venice:

> its theatrical mechanisms, its use as a convenient and colossal stage extension, as the object of a constant play of trompe-l'oeil ... The tradition of building the Great Machine confirms the perfect historically-established interconnection between architecture and theatre. (1980: 13)

Rossi's *Teatro* and its 'prototypes' (Dezzi-Bardeschi 1980), the Venetian floating *Teatri del Mondo* from the sixteenth, seventeenth and eighteenth centuries, also called (grande) *macchine* or *apparati*, were architectural and scenographic expressions in one, both using and temporarily extending

Venice's urban scenography. His structure surprised due to its formal severity and strict geometry, and at the same time delighted in its whimsical nature in confidently and playfully citing Venice's architectural and theatrical histories. Located amid some of Venice's most iconic buildings from the Italian Renaissance and Baroque,[20] it contrasted its small figure of a rigid geometrical volume topped by a very small sphere and fixed metal banner, with the surrounding extravagant, confusing and hectic display of architectural and sculptural skill and mastery. Manfredo Tafuri describes Rossi's attitude and gesture as 'Palladian' in its internalized formal language and autonomy towards the architecturally heterogeneous context of its site in a 1980 issue of *Domus* that he titled, programmatically, *The Ephemeral Is the Eternal*:

> What is Palladian ... is his refusal to be dragged into the vortex of involvement towards which Venetian spatiality tends to exercise its attraction. The only adventure Rossi allows himself is that engendered by the dangerous encounter between the rigorous consistency of his object and the triumphal fullness of the 'chorus', which accompanies the 'solos' of the Piazzetta, the Salute, and the churches that give thickness to the 'edge' of the Giudecca. (Tafuri 1980: 7)

Against the Baroque abundance of the surrounding representative buildings, Rossi posited the severe geometry and reduced colour palette of the *Teatro*, in a gesture read by Tafuri as an intervention as radical as Palladio's architectural symmetrical clarity. The 25-metre-high horizontal object was constructed from tubular iron scaffolding fixed to a raft-like structure and covered with wood. This related back to Venice's wooden foundations as well as to maritime constructions in general; and in particular, as Rossi explains, 'to the black wood of gondolas' (Rossi in Gallanti 2010). The structure was topped with a six-metre-high octagonal pyramidal roof covered with galvanized sheet iron. In colour and materiality, it referenced its immediate surroundings:

> The Venetian green contrasts with the cold color of iron on the roof of my theater. This metal is reflected in the gray of the lagoon, while above it stands the ball and the slowly creaking metal banner. (Rossi 1981: 67)

The building's main body – the theatre itself – was a cube 9.5 metres long and 11 metres high, whose top opened to a terrace allowing wide views of the lagoon, and beyond, an imposing and diverse architectural context. Inside the single-axis symmetrical structure capable of holding an audience of around 200, the central stage comprised a space flanked by a staircase block with three-tiered galleries on either side and three lines of windows. These windows corresponded to sea level, to the level of surrounding buildings and the sky. Rarely used as a performance space during the Biennale, this strange object comprised a performance in itself, as a spectacle that allowed itself to be viewed as it appeared and disappeared from view, and that transformed the surrounding buildings, seascape and sky into a scenography that could be experienced over time. Meanwhile, a window in the centre of the stage, divided into four equal parts, was, as Paolo Portoghesi claims in his chapter on Rossi in *Architettura e Memoria*:

> a symbol for an architecture that wishes to 'discover the eye in all things' [a quote by Giorgio di Chirico] and help to see unsparingly, but with trust, the notion of the human condition. (Portoghesi in Gottardo 2006: 387)

Rossi's *Teatro*, itself a cosmogony, that is, a model that explains the origin and core functions of theatre and architecture, their relation to each other and the site, was pared back to the essential typology of the floating theatre. The structure operated as an 'instant object' (Tafuri 1980: 7) that drew the viewer's eye, crowned by a cupola or sphere at the top, as a symbol of the theatre as macrocosm and the world as a stage upon which man's fleeting life is played out. The autonomous yet highly referential model theatre operated as a temporary architectural 'dwelling' and as a place that embodied theatre's visual key parameters, namely to 'observe and to be observed' (Rossi 1981: 67). It has come to symbolize Rossi's notion of the existence of collective memory in theatre and architecture in its relatedness to the urban, social and cultural history of Venice.

Model and reality: Bert Neumann's mock ups as an imitation of life

Bert Neumann: *The Idiot*, Volksbühne Berlin 2002 and 2007

Bert Neumann: *Neustadt*, Volksbühne Berlin 2002 and 2007

At Berlin's Volksbühne theatre, the mock-up has become something of a trademark, whether as a multifunctional stage or (since the 1990s) as trashy façade city. Bert Neumann, Head of Scenic Design at the iconic Volksbühne Berlin[21] from 1997 till his untimely death in 2015, worked with stage models on the stage that used remnants of past and found architectures to deliver critique through architectural citation.

Designed to be demonstrative rather than realistic, these operated as performative and autonomous mock-ups that invoked memories of past places. All were instantly recognizable by their architectural typology: apartment blocks, airports, brothels or road stops to name a few. They comprised what anthropologist Marc Augé has influentially defined as the 'non-places of Super-modernity' (Augé 1995) in that they are simulations of reality that induces imitative rather than individual behaviour.

In Neumann's mock-ups, all structural and decorative elements were selected to uncover the political dimensions of architecture. Life within the mock-ups was shown to be a reductive citation of life within an architectural citation, and it was only at the 1:1 scale that the postmodern subject on the stage could be convincingly shown as trapped in architecture. The built fourth wall completed the notion of architectures of control and surveillance, and thus acted as an architecture of isolation and confrontation that unhoused rather than housed both subject and dramatic action.

Besides his articulation of theatrical space as a conflicted site made up of found architectures and elements of popular culture, Neumann was chiefly responsible for the Volksbühne's iconic visual branding, both on stage and in public view. He created the Volksbühne's logo, a rusty sculpture in front of the building at Rosa-Luxemburg-Platz that depicted a walking wheel on legs, which reportedly referred to a medieval warning sign etched into trees signalling danger in the covert thief's language of *Rotwelsch*. The East German-born Neumann also designed T-shirts, matchboxes and posters with the Volksbühne logo that, in a playful and ironic use of capitalist marketing strategies, soon became a symbol of artistic resistance against commercialism in all its forms.

In his many collaborations with Berlin stage directors Frank Castorf and René Pollesch, Neumann repeatedly returned to 1:1 mock-ups of desolate petrol stations, shabby hotels, anonymous apartment buildings or shady bars. The son of German Democratic Republic (GDR) architects who fought vainly for recognition of the 1920s and 1930s modernist aesthetics of the Bauhaus movement (defamed in the GDR as elitist), Neumann preferred to be named an architect[22] or a 'visual artist who works in the theatre' (Neumann in Mueller-Tischler 2010: 9) rather than a scenographer. Typically conceived without directorial input by Castorf or Pollesch, the set was first encountered in fully built form by the directors and actors in rehearsal. Rather than designing a set for a director, Neumann created autonomous environments that by their very layout and construction deliberately hindered the performer's movement and circulation, as well as obscuring the audience's full view of the stage. Pollesch, in his homage to Neumann at the awards ceremony for the prestigious Hein-Reckroth Set Design Prize in 2015, praises above all the autonomy of Neumann's stage spaces as political, in that they seek by artistic means to subvert and change capitalist production structures prevalent in state-financed theatre in Germany:

Each room that you have built speaks of this autonomy, dear Bert. And let's build our autonomy. And this is not just about a boundless impetus to design but rather the establishment of an own practice and the subversion of a governing and hierarchical practice. This is the reason why one makes a theater: by making it completely anew. Not for reasons of originality but rather to change the parameters in a way that allows one to work. Then one can say that one has done it, in the real sense: one has made the Volksbühne. Not because one simply potters about in there, but because everybody in there has changed the parameters. (Pollesch 2015)[23]

Neumann developed his trademark gritty aesthetics using a jarring collage of architectural fragments and details from soulless, prefabricated and crumbling GDR buildings and interiors, as well as architectural typologies seen in 1950s and 1960s American B-movies. The mode of construction in Neumann's scenographies, often deliberately cheap and makeshift, was always visible and formed part of their aesthetics. Neumann's set designs have shaped the image of Volksbühne as a site of political discourse according to artistic and aesthetic modes of production and presentation and are here defined as mock-ups. Should one invoke the meaning of the verb 'to mock' (from which 'mock-up' is derived), synonyms such as 'ridicule', 'deride' and 'taunt' emerge. A potential chasm between what is 'true' and 'false' opens up, as well as the notion of a motive behind the 'mocking'. To define Neumann's set designs as 'mock-ups' rather than as 'models' means to apprehend them as interpretive, taunting, provocative 'imitations of life'. Neumann himself spoke of his works as fakes and outlined how they can be discursive tools to make visible the façades of contemporary living:

My spaces are what they are. They are not trying to create illusions. Locations that are undisguised and where the illusion is so obvious that it is quite clearly recognised as fake... There is illusion in my spaces only if you are allowed to also see the backside.... The disparate is one thing that's simply important to me as a stylistic device. The undisguised, the roughened, indeed, and also the used up. But also the question: to what degree does pretence mould our everyday lives? How are we fooled by our cities' façades? Here is the power of the fake. (Neumann in Asmuth 2012)

The mock-up served Neumann as an instrument to explore the postmodern dilemma of whether one 'imitates life or whether one lives an imitation' (Neumann in Hurtzig 2001: Foreword n.p.). The notion of life as a blatant imitation with unwritten rules governing social interaction and behaviour, along with its spatial implications on the stage, led Neumann to name his set design master-class at Bochum Art Academy 'Imitation of Life'. With his design students, Neumann worked in a former industrial building where they were able to build 1:1 constructions of houses they had researched and photographed in the Ruhrgebiet. The students filmed the resultant cardboard city, then developed narratives informed by the spatial characteristics and placements of their temporary mock-up. Their films ironically rendered the fake as real, in an inversion of experienced reality and mediated filmic image (see Neumann in Hurtzig 2001: Foreword n.p.).

Neumann first encountered the concept of human existence as an 'imitation of life' in a 1959 film (with the same title) by German-American theatre and film director Douglas Sirk. Sirk's films, highly popular at the time but condemned by critics as unsavoury and melodramatic, uncovered moral corruption in 1950s America. As the subject of recent screenings, such as the 2011 MoMA series that looked at the reinvention and subversion of Hollywood cinema,[24] they are increasingly invoked by film theorists according to their scathing social critique, specifically, the portrayal of people who are 'trapped in their houses and their moral values'.[25] Sirk described his melodrama *Magnificent Obsession* in an interview with Jon Halliday as

a combination of kitsch, and craziness, and trashiness. But craziness is very important, and it saves trashy stuff like *Magnificent Obsession*. This is the dialectic: there is a very short distance between high art and trash, and trash that contains the element of craziness is by this very quality nearer to art. (Sirk 1971: 96)

Parallels between Sirk and Neumann are evident in their intention to demonstrate rather than to seduce. Sirk distanced himself from the narrative in the almost Brechtian sense of portraying the social construction of human lives rather than examining individual lives, while Neumann chose to articulate the 'imitative' character of life through stereotyped yet incomplete and temporarily habitable mock-ups rather than fully articulated individual environments.

In 2002 and 2007 at Volksbühne, an ensemble of several fake architectures formed the multifunctional stage and auditorium for Castorf's six-hour adaptation of Fyodor Dostoevsky's 1868 novel *The Idiot*. Neumann placed the audience on the Volksbühne's revolving stage, on scaffolded seating that denoted a shady hotel-cum-brothel crowned with the pink neon sign 'Romantic World'. He transformed the auditorium into a *Neustadt* (new city) with several 1:1 inhabitable mock-ups of buildings, complete with a fake skyline above and three blocks of apartments in which most of the action occurred (see Figure 5.7). A supermarket, a brothel, a hairdresser and bar completed the new city erected around the revolving stage. The audience entered through this city and took designated seating positions on the scaffold as if walking through a film set, where a series of façades on practicable scaffolding evoked the sense of a Potemkin village.[26] The distinct style of this mock-up

FIGURE 5.7 *Set design by Bert Neumann for* The Idiot *after Fyodor Mikhailovich Dostoyevsky, Volksbühne Berlin 2002 and 2007.*

connoted the modernist legacy of Mies van der Rohe's and Le Corbusier's architectural living machines[27] as much as the depressing remnants of the socialist *Arbeiterstaedte* (worker's cities) in the former GDR.

Despite its many walls, this new city admitted no privacy. Video cameras installed in apartment rooms transmitted the evening's intimate scenes onto large screens above the buildings, thus offering up the private as popular entertainment. Relationships full of conflict, love and high emotion turned into their simulations, played out in architectural mock-ups built in such a way as to offer no shelter. Central to Neumann's mock-ups infiltrated with media was that the media was able to be paused and stopped, thereby distancing the dramatic action from immediacy and refuting the spectator's desire for immersion and identification. Further, the distancing device of video expanded the performance's temporal axis towards the past – a second simultaneous presence – as well as to the future. Such extension allowed the creation of multiple spaces in one, testifying to the unique capability of theatre that Foucault in his 1967 lecture 'Of Other Spaces: Utopias and Heterotopias' expressed as the production of 'heterochronies' or 'slices in time':

The heterotopia is capable of juxtaposing in a single real place several spaces, several sites that are in themselves incompatible. Thus it is that the theater brings onto the rectangle of the stage, one after the other, a whole series of places that are foreign to one another. (Foucault 1984: 9)

To Boris Groys, the video image implies a space of the past that does not rest with the sites of the dramatic action but includes the body of the actor that in the projection is now considered dead. It is the past life of the actor that is pulled back into the present by its projection on the stage:

always somehow referring to their transmission into an afterworld or afterlife ... We assume that what is shown on the screen is being shown post mortem. The actor on the screen is being thought of as already dead and what remains of him is his transformation into a virtual figure. (Groys 2007, trans by the authors)

Constructed as integral architectural elements within or on top of the mock-ups, Neumann's large video screens cited the visual overload in contemporary urban life through commercial media projection and electronic façades. By projecting private scenes, the loss of privacy and the ubiquitous nature of media for both communication and surveillance were shown to be part of the city's architecture.

Following Wartofsky's assertion of the model as purposeful and directed towards the future, Neumann's multimedia mock-ups presented as models *of* reality in their adaptation and collaging of real-life architectural elements. They operated as models *for* a future where a different society demands a different architecture.

Neumann proposed an aesthetics of the real that exhibited its imitative nature through the mock-up or 'fake'. The fake, however, not only presented a concept but was built to copy, to resemble or cite the original. Neumann's emphasis in his work on the 'building' rather than the 'design', links him to Bertolt Brecht's 'stage-builder' (Brecht 1967: 635) Caspar Neher and his work of the 1920s and 1930s. This relation is evident not only where both seek a social critique using unfinished, incomplete and crudely built stage architectures that display their mode of construction. Neumann enhanced Neher's legacy in that his stage architectures required the spectator to not simply look at an open set through its 'fourth wall' but rather be confronted by the fourth wall as a built structure that physically included or excluded performers, and that permitted or forbid the spectator's view. Neher's 'curtain', set at two-thirds of the stage height and level with the proscenium, either allowed or obstructed the view at distinct points during the action or enabled it to 'pause'. Neumann extended this principle by using video technology, microphones and large-scale projections embedded in the mock-ups, to permit or deny visual and auditory access to actions occurring behind closed walls in offstage areas or back rooms invisible from the auditorium.

Neumann's strategies for spatial production on the stage resound with Jane Rendell's notion of a critical spatial practice as 'work that intervenes into a site in order to critique it' (Rendell 2009: 2). Following this definition, Neumann's mock-ups were an intervention into architecture: its deconstruction, disassembly and critical reassembly on the stage. Neumann critiqued the imitation of life through the mock-up, unmasking the dwelling as an oppressive social construction. The mock-up served to exhibit the subject on the stage rather than to support and envelop it, and the capacity of this was used to awaken spatial memories and recognition in the viewer. As 'fakes', they rudely imitated the real and put it on the stage, thus enabling the performance of an imitation of the real. The 'power of the fake' emerged from citation and abstraction, from feeding on the original and thereby uncovering its fragility, achieved through temporary constructions made from nothing but façade, scaffold and the flicker of the video.

Throughout the history of theatre and architecture, fakes, models or mock-ups have been used as intentional constructions, not only as future referents but even more so as significant and symbolic carriers of memories and past narratives. They are linked in that the model invokes a reality by its sheer physical presence and by a high degree of architectural similarity and approximation to 'real' built structures. Scale, however, is independent of intention, and underneath the imaginative appropriation of historical precedents and urban concepts in Rossi's floating theatre, the hyper-real presentation of capitalism's non-spaces on Neumann's stages, and the terrifying yet utterly persuasive presence of NS representative buildings lie the diverse ideological landscapes of the twentieth century and their representation in architecture. Thus autonomous models unfold their scenographic and performative qualities at exactly the junction between memory, reality and promise – steeped deeply in the politics of space between the past, present and future.

6

Staging the White Cube: The Autonomous Model as a Performance of Space

In reading the history of exhibition through the model, the parameters of scale, materiality and context that have been identified throughout this project as instrumental for the model's capacity to produce, communicate and store knowledge appear again. The many shifts in the relationship between viewer, object and space since the beginnings of the collection and showing of artefacts, which can be summed up as oscillating between the convention of the distant observation of exhibits and the privileging of interaction and tactility, are reflected in the overall rise of the model in exhibition. This rise to prominence is most notable in the exhibition history of the model in designated theatre and architecture exhibitions throughout the twentieth century, but must be traced back to the significance given to the architectural model in the subjectively authored and eclectic art chambers of the sixteenth to eighteenth centuries. The architectural models exhibited had mostly travelled north across the Alps from Italy to the aristocratic and patrician art chambers located primarily in Southern Germany and Austria[1] and were testament to the collector's subjective sense of aesthetics. At the same time, as discussed in regard to Furttenbach's collections, the models, as miniature copies of existing buildings, formed a scaled reconstruction of the collector's journey. In miniature, and mostly made from wood prior to the Italian fashion of manufacturing miniature models in cork for easy transport in the eighteenth century,[2] viewing and close examination of the models extended, besides providing the obvious pleasure of viewing, the architectural knowledge of the time in addition to knowledge derived from the much more widely distributed architectural drawings and etchings. Beyond proving the design skills of the architect of the original building, the model reflected closely the model-makers' skill in its mode of construction and assembly, the selection of detail and abstraction, chosen scale and materiality.

Designed with the visitors' movements through the exhibition in mind, the art chamber comprised an interactive theatre and performance of knowledge[3] where models (and other objects) could be touched and contextualized through other present media such as books and drawings. In contrast, the classifications and systematic displays of architecture models (typically encased) in the nineteenth-century museum forbade any interference or even close contact with the exhibits. At the same time, however, architectural details were exhibited for competition purposes in public space, and the link between scale and persuasion became evident. In the first designated theatre exhibitions of the early twentieth century, the scenographic model, at the scale it had been produced originally, assumed its place next to drawings of set and costumes, and, when exhibited in retrospect, could be viewed in combination with production photographs and actual costumes.[4] The first rupture to this convention came with the exhibition of Frederick (Friedrich) Kiesler's 1:1 model of the Railway Theatre in the Vienna Konzerthaus as part of the 1924 Ausstellung Internationaler Theatertechnik. Constructed for exhibition yet comprising a functioning stage at the same time, Kiesler's autonomous model at full scale prefigured future scenography and architecture exhibitions where the exhibited object was neither remnant nor reconstruction but existed as an enterable architecture or scenography. The potential of the scenographic and architectural model to possess performative agency began to unfold in a delayed response to the emergence of museums and galleries as discursive platforms since the 1960s and the subsequent development of interactive and participative exhibition formats, and only occurred with the rise of the large international survey shows such as the Venice Architecture Biennale and the Prague Quadrennial for Performance Design and Space (PQ) from 1980 onwards.

The beginning of an overall discourse on the politics of space in exhibition, and thus the theoretical reframing of the exhibition space from a passive Euclidian container to an active environment capable of purposeful actions, occurred with the 1976 publication of three provocative essays by critic and installation artist Brian O'Doherty.[5] In *Inside the White Cube*, O'Doherty claims that the gallery is a historical and ideological construct where the object must be seen as contextual rather than as an isolated 'treasure' shut away from social and political realities. Recognition of the exhibition's potential to operate as a discursive platform located within society rather than as an exclusive entity can be traced to the subsequent change in the understanding of the model in exhibition practice since the 1980s, that is, its evolution from a sheer representative object of display to an autonomous model that possesses performative agency. In the context of the exhibition as the result of an authored and conceptual process, the curator emerges as a single figure or curatorial team responsible for an overall theme and the selection of practitioners whose work relates to it.

Provocatively, art critic and philosopher Boris Groys positions the single artwork as mute, reliant on the curator to make it speak within the context of exhibition:

It is no coincidence that the word 'curator' is etymologically related to 'cure': to curate is to cure. Curating cures the powerlessness of the image, its inability to show itself by itself. Exhibition practice is thus the cure that heals the originally ailing image, that gives it presence, visibility; it brings it to the public view and turns it into the object of the public's judgment. (Groys 2009)

Just as the art object, once put into curatorial context can transcend its 'weak' status, the exhibited model progresses from a merely representative object to an active agent in the overall curated space. This development not only has steered the model's spatial organization in the exhibition towards thematic clusters and the inclusion of iterative, imperfect models but has, significantly, changed its scale. Architectural and scenographic models made specifically for exhibition have shifted increasingly towards large and full scale; they are often enterable, thus offering an immediate, tactile environment for the viewer. At such scales, the model created for exhibition becomes an experiential interior space and volume, rendering it both performative and autonomous. Beyond the mere representative display, it is constructed increasingly for exhibition alone, asserting its autonomous status as a cosmopoietic or world-making physical object or environment.

To fully comprehend the shifts in the exhibition history of the model, its relatedness to the visual arts genre 'installation' in scale, materiality and form affords mention. The genre's origin may be traced from Kurt Schwitters' ever-unfinished paper assemblage of the so-called *Merzbau* (1923–1937), where the artist as maker becomes integral to the work. The genre underwent a resurgence in 1960s and 1970s performative actions, as well as in the environmental compositions and stagings of land art. In general, installations comprise spatial mise-en-scènes that are often site-specific. They are built or compiled, often involving sound, light and movement. Not bound to specific materials or media, they may or may not be interactive, or may at least invite or enable interaction. As an artwork that often literally takes place over time, the installation is closely related to performance, often demanding a performative act from the viewer such as operating an installative element or simply entering the structure. The object thus lies in direct relation to its surrounding and is understood contextually rather than as an isolated and passive construction. Installations and staged spaces in the gallery and museum that invite interaction and participation do not necessarily follow political or socially oriented artistic strategies, yet since the 1990s a trend can be observed that favours the installation as a physical basis or starting point for envisaged actions by the visitor in the actual creation of the artwork. Nicholas Bourriaud, in *Relational Aesthetics*, a collection of seven essays published in English in 1992, first articulated the notion of a relational art engaged in bringing social and cultural practices rather than finished objects into the gallery:

> The possibility of a *relational* art (an art that takes as its theoretical horizon the sphere of human interactions and its social context, rather than the assertion of an autonomous and *private* symbolic space) is testimony to the radical upheaval in aesthetic, cultural and political objectives brought about by modern art. (Bourriaud 2002: 60)

By questioning the role of art and the status of the art object in a contemporary society of accelerated global economies and cultures, artists experimented with new positions and strategies in terms of the temporary production of social encounters. They subverted the viewing and behavioural conventions by positioning their works outside the gallery in everyday urban contexts. Bourriaud cites projects such as Angela Bulloch's 1993 café in the Centre pour la Création Contemporaine in Tours that activated a recording by *Kraftwerk* as soon as visitors sat down, or Rirkrit Tiravanija's 1994 chill-out space for participating artists in the exhibition 'Surfaces de Réparation' in Dijon.

There is no clear line to be drawn between the genre of 'installation' in the visual arts and 'model' in architecture or scenography exhibitions, and there exists no typological difference between an installation and an autonomous model built specifically for exhibition. Groys (2009) points out that it is indeed the installation (and, this study argues, the model) that claims autonomy and is 'space itself'. Both installation and model transform the notion of the exhibition as a collection of single artworks and redefine the relationship between object and viewer to a performative one:

> [T]he installation is material *par excellence*, since it is spatial –and being in the space is the most general definition of being material. The installation transforms the empty, neutral, public space into an individual artwork – and it invites the visitor to experience this space as the holistic, totalizing space of an artwork. Anything included in such a space becomes a part of the artwork simply because it is placed inside this space. The distinction between art object and simple object becomes insignificant here. (Groys 2009)

Installation practices have significantly expanded traditional architecture and scenography exhibitions from representative overviews into performative spaces of action, in a development that originated in discourses by practitioners and curators in relation to their disciplines' current social roles and functions.

This has resulted in many shows where all aspects of practice were brought into the exhibition hall rather than simply represented, and where research and theory entered in the form of libraries, reading areas and presented contextual material.

The redefinition of exhibitions in both disciplines as traced here through the changing role and increased attention given to the model has demonstrably influenced the exhibition practices of the Prague Quadrennial of Performance Design and Space (PQ) and the International Architecture Exhibition of the Venice Biennale. In Venice, curatorial positions have increasingly questioned the role of architecture in society, selecting projects that address issues of communication, inequality, sustainability and globalization in both the main thematic exhibition (in the Arsenale and Central Pavilion) and the nationally curated pavilions (in the Giardini and across the city). Issues of scale, materiality and audience interaction have always been pertinent in Venice since its topography demands that the exhibition is distributed to many venues that require visitors to discover their route between them on foot. This allows visitors to construct a personal exhibition narrative interwoven with the city's heterogeneous urban scenography. As discussed, Rossi's 1980 Venetian *Teatro del Mondo* constituted a spectacular and deeply relational full-scale model, and ever since, the exhibition of specifically designed architectures in Venice has resonated strongly with practitioners, curators and audiences. Realized as large-scale models, these structures, while referential and contextual, are autonomous in that they simultaneously comprise the initial and final artefact.

In the case of the Prague Quadrennial (PQ), a shake-up of the exhibition and curatorial strategies and thus a re-evaluation of the model in exhibition, occurred only recently with its 2007, 2011 and 2015 editions, due primarily to the PQ's regimented institutional exhibition history that was upturned for the first time by artistic director Sodja Lotker and General Commissioner Arnold Aronson in 2007 in a pronounced shift from the exhibition of stage model boxes with accompanying drawings to newly imagined scenographic spaces and performances in the exhibition hall and throughout the city of Prague, as discussed in detail below, and in 2011 with a name change from *Prague Quadrennial International Exhibition of Stage Design and Theatre Architecture* to its current name *Prague Quadrennial for Performance Design and Space* in a programmatic move that acknowledged how the expanded field of scenography demands new and discursive exhibition formats, a development that scenography scholars McKinney and Palmer succinctly describe as an expansion

from an exclusive function as a craft-based practice serving the performance of a theatrical text to incorporate autonomous art practices that operate in contexts beyond buildings and engage directly with social as well as the cultural dimensions of contemporary experience. (McKinney and Palmer 2017: 3)

For both scenography and architecture curators, the most pertinent question that arises when rethinking modes of exhibiting models is that of 'how to transcend the representation of the practice in forms of remnants and fragments', and, while the Venice Biennale engaged with this question earlier, that is since its inception in 1980,[6] each scenography or architecture curator finds themselves asking this same question anew with each exhibition, closely interrelated to the conceptual search of how the genre of exhibition can be best utilized to redefine the discipline in today's world.

Model and exhibition: Performing architecture

Paolo Portoghesi: *La Presenza del Passato*, Venice Biennale 1980

St John Caruso and Thomas Demand: *The Nail House*,
Venice Biennale 2010

Valentin Bontjes van Beek: *Maison Dom-ino*, Venice Biennale 2014

Shumi Bose, Jack Self and Finn Williams: *Home Economics*,
Venice Biennale 2016

The First International Architecture Exhibition in 1980 marked the independence of the former architecture section from the Venice Biennale. The Exhibition, as a biannual event housed in dedicated national pavilions in the Giardini gardens and interiors of the Corderie and Arsenale,[7] emerged from the 1967, 1975 and 1978 architecture exhibitions of the Art Biennale. Since 1980 it has been led by a duo of a president and a different director for each edition, who is at the same time the curator for the Arsenale and central exhibition in the Giardini, a choice that emphasizes curatorial agency. The Biennale's international influence has grown steadily, as it aimed to show and discuss current practices related to aesthetic, social, cultural and political issues in the field and beyond.

In a spectacular gesture by director Paolo Portoghesi, and titled *La Presenza del Passato* (The Presence of the Past), the 1980 exhibition featured twenty full-size façade models by twenty architects, arranged as in two sides of a street along the interior of the vast Corderie Dell'Arsenale. The rows of linking façades, built by scenic artists from Rome's Cinecittà film studios, represented the eclectic style and transhistorical formal language of postmodern architecture, intended to be experienced up-close and over time by means of a street walk. Each façade was built to dimensions of 7 × 9.5 meters, forming a street of about 70 metres in length.[8] Titled *Strada Novissima*, the exhibit recalled the first fixed Renaissance sets depicting façades of the ideal Renaissance city built in perspective on a raked stage.[9]

In contrast to previous architecture exhibits in the framework of the Art Biennale, where plans, drawings and small-scale models dominated the halls, Portoghesi in 1980 affirmed the relevance of the architectural curator in showing that by refuting traditional notions of scale and materiality and adhering to postmodern architectural ideas of citation and theatricality, an architectural movement as complex as Postmodernism[10] could be reimagined and represented in a purpose-built interior. According to architecture historian Léa-Catherine Szacka, it also signalled a 'return to the traditional city' and a reaffirmation of its social aspects:

There was a clear link between the idea of the street and the return to the traditional city, as it was proclaimed by some postmodernists. In the case of the 1980 Venice Architecture Biennale, the concept of the exhibition and its scenography, in tune with upcoming theoretical discourses, was far from being a generic and neutral form of display. It was a strong declaration of intentions, in favour of the return to traditional city planning and to the use of basic urban elements fostering sociability. And that is why, in 1981, when the exhibition was presented in the Paris Salpêtrière's chapel, the space of the street was transformed into another component of traditional cities: the piazza. (Szacka 2012: 19)

In the confined space of the Salpêtrière and the vast corridor of the Corderie dell'Arsenale, the exhibition space was reconfigured into a complete scenography with its stage populated by visitors.

Each International Architecture Exhibition since *La Presenza del Passato* has had a distinct conceptual and thematic focus articulated by the Director. The field's diverse representations increasingly mirror pressing questions about the role and responsibility of architecture in national and global contexts.

Beginning with *Strada Novissima*, the curation of autonomous models, that is, such models built specifically in response to an exhibition's theme as opposed to retrospective representative models, has become a fixture of the International Architecture Exhibition. With the rise of the 1:1 model in architectural and scenographic exhibitions in the last decades, architectural discourse has embraced notions of performance and performative space as fundamental to its discipline. It was in the 2010, 2014 and 2016 editions in particular that the autonomous model appeared in a way that staged space and enabled its performance as the models were constructed at full scale. They extended Portoghesi's bold formal and aesthetic focus into the spatial and participative aspects of architecture, placing the model in direct interface with the visitor.

In 2010, architect and curator Kazuyo Sejima set out to curate a diverse 'set of encounters' (Sejima 2010) between people, as much as between people and space. Far from articulating an explicitly theoretical language, the aim of the 12th International Architecture Exhibition of the Venice Biennale, titled *People meet in Architecture*, was nothing less than to explore how architecture could

help people relate to architecture, to help architecture relate to people, and to help people relate to themselves. (Sejima 2010)

Sejima's Exhibition posited that architecture's role and responsibility was to enable communication and interaction in physical spaces. For the curator, the physicality of architecture is closely linked with the subjective experience of space. This concept gave rise to several full-sized enterable models, one of which was the *Nagelhaus* (*Nail House*), a first-time collaboration between London-based Caruso St John Architects and German visual artist Thomas Demand. Demand is known for full-size cardboard models of boardrooms constructed after his photographs; he subsequently photographs his models then exhibits the photographs in highly staged settings.[11]

Situated in the Exhibition's main space, *Nail House* was a hybrid object in that it referenced a historical Chinese precedent and an unrealized architectural design by Caruso St John's Zurich office in the form of an enterable scenography.

Nail House thereby became the 'artificial memory of an event twice replaced' (Caruso St John 2013). This 'event' was the architects' viewing of a media image of a so-called 'nail house' in the Chinese city of Chongqing. It stood alone in the centre of a huge building pit, cut off from water and electricity. In China, such buildings have come to symbolize resistance in the form of a singular building or 'nail' in the midst of overwhelming new development. The image of the Chongqing house standing proudly provided both precedent and inspiration for Caruso St John's 2007 design for a competition in the city of Zurich. One step removed from the precedent, their deliberately modest Zurich design comprised a twenty-four-hour cafe and amenities. Outraged by the proposed cost and following a populist media campaign, the residents of Zurich voted the project down, and (as so often happens in architecture competitions) even though Caruso St John had won the competition their winning entry was never built.

It was perhaps the experience of their own failure to insert their small building into Zurich as much as the stubbornness and pure theatricality of the original 'nail house' poised on its precipitous mound amid a busy Chinese construction site, which inspired Caruso St John, now in collaboration with Demand, to realize their full-sized model or mock-up (now twice removed from the original image) at the Biennale (see Figure 6.1). Their Venice *Nagelhaus*

FIGURE 6.1 Nail House *by Caruso St John Architects and Thomas Demand, Venice Biennale 2010.*

retained a key feature of the proposed original: at the Zurich site, Escher-Wyss-Platz, their design would have just fitted under the overpass, indicating its creators' dwarfing under institutionalized concepts of progress and mobility. Similarly, at Venice, the structure seemed to duck under the Palazzo dell' Esposizione's ceiling. Built as a full façade model with wooden bracing just like a theatre set, the *Nail House* could be entered, so that people meeting within the structure (according to Sejima's motto) would be as if actors in the same play. In this case, though, they were largely unaware of the narrative context in which they had been placed.

The strangely seductive 'power of the fake', seen in Bert Neumann's highly referential scenographic mock-ups (see Chapter 5), also came into play in the *Nail House*, as it stood, promising shelter but unable to do so, drawing attention to the links between the realization of architecture and political interest.

Rem Koolhaas' 2014 International Architecture Exhibition at the Venice Biennale, *Fundamentals*, reversed the focus from a subjective experience of architecture to an attempt to 'reconstruct how architecture finds itself in its current situation' (Koolhaas 2014) by situating its contemporary practice within the history of modernism and modernization in the twentieth century. For the first time in the Biennale's history, national curators were given a topic, 'Absorbing Modernity: 1914–2014', and asked to interrogate issues of modernity through the lens of their countries' architectural and political histories and cultural practices. The goal, as Koolhaas said, was to acknowledge the heterogeneous uptake and manifestation of modernist principles and technological innovations in a refusal of a harmonizing master narrative (2014) In the encyclopedic display 'Elements of Architecture', in the Central Pavilion, Koolhaas revealed a comprehensive spatial catalogue of architecture's elements – doors, windows, stairs, walls, corridors and airport security systems – as architectures of inclusion and exclusion. Mock-ups were created and entire rooms dedicated to diverse stair configurations of past and present. The exhibition then extended to the Central Pavilion's front lawn where a particular icon of modernism was displayed as a full-size model constructed in alternative materials.

Titled *Maison Dom-ino*, the open two-storey structure with two connecting internal stairs made from engineered wood was conceived by architect Valentin Bontjes van Beek and built by his students from the Architectural Association (AA) in London. *Maison Dom-ino* constituted the first physical construction of a set of extant 1914 drawings with the same title by iconic modernist architect Le Corbusier (see Figure 6.2). *Maison Dom-ino* relates

FIGURE 6.2 Maison Dom-ino *by Valentin Bontjes van Beek, Venice Biennale 2014.*

to the Dominoes board game, where twenty-eight wooden blocks numbered with dots are combined in numerous ways by four players. Le Corbusier had developed a modular prefabricated building system that could be arranged and added to, both vertically and horizontally, facilitating mass-produced buildings. Devised in response to the depletion of Europe's housing stock after the First World War, Le Corbusier's *plan libre* (open plan) structure allowed for the free placement of external, internal or loadbearing walls, windows or any other form of fit-out.

The 2014 *Maison Dom-ino* operated as a spatial re-enactment, which brought to the fore a key parameter of the model in its difference to the architectural drawing, namely the model's experiential quality and its capacity to become a practised space: the model as performance. For the visitor, the experience signified a 'double walking' in an 'architectural doppelgänger space'. Provoked by Le Corbusier's system of spatial relations, the visitor thus temporarily inhabited this abstract structure, while their expected unique spatial experience evoked an uncanny and fragile architectural *déjà vu*.

The change in material from Le Corbusier's envisaged reinforced concrete to timber renounced any notion of permanence for that of a temporary demountable installation. Indeed, the model arrived in Venice's Giardini in Ikea-style flat packs, to be shipped to new displays in London and Tokyo once the Biennale ended. Its lightness and immateriality added to its success, not by realizing or replacing the 1914 plans, but by invoking that earlier unbuilt project. As an architectural 'double', the re-enacted *Maison Dom-ino* inferred its unseen architectural other.

Active inhabitation of the model was encouraged, with platforms to cross and space to linger, sit and read. The visitor's temporary inhabitation activated the model and shifted its immediate purpose to one not of distant contemplation but to the immediacy of the performative 'here and now'. In scenographic terms, structure (environment and stage) and visitors (performers) engaged in the co-producing of space. The space incessantly authored here was performative, shifting, permeable and dynamic: unstable as long as its purpose, its programme, remained unclear.

Such making of space was mirrored in Caruso St John's and Demand's Venice *Nagelhaus*. Its scenographic relation was even more transparent due to its method of construction. Unlike *Maison Dom-ino*, the *Nail House* was constructed in the fashion of classical theatre scenery (coulisse) with front and sides fully articulated and its interior revealing an uncertain purpose. As an enterable scenography, it welcomed its visitors as actors, invited to perform the roles of Zurich commuters who would have entered and exited the kiosk and restaurant twenty-four hours a day.

In the response of national curators to Alejandro Aravena's theme *Reporting from the Front* for the 15th International Architecture Exhibition in 2016, interaction with and through the exhibited model continued to be a key curatorial strategy for communicating architectural concerns. Aravena's mission statement emphasized the impact that diverse perspectives, such as those from the 'frontline' of contemporary life, have on the advancement of the discipline and thus on ways of living together:

> The forces that shape the built environment are not necessarily amicable ... the greed and impatience of capital or the single-mindedness and conservatism of the bureaucracy tend to produce banal, mediocre and dull built environments. These are the frontlines from which we would like different practitioners to report, sharing success stories and exemplary cases where architecture did and will make a difference. (Aravena 2016)

Called the 'Biennale of the Model' by many visitors who were surprised by the sheer number of small-, large- and full-sized models, Avarena's theme evoked responses from curators and architects regarding the effects of globalization, housing crises and climate change on small and intimate scales of living. The representation of interiors and interiority on the local level became a leitmotif of *Reporting from the Front*. For example, British curators Shumi Bose, Jack Self and Finn Williams' *Home Economics* in the British pavilion consisted of five heterogeneous architectural propositions for a new domesticity in Britain, according to the vision of invited artists, designers and architects. Installed as enterable 1:1 models in the five rooms of the 1895 pavilion, the spatial responses were ordered around new notions of the home according to five temporal dimensions – hours, days, months, years and decades – with the central room proposing an ideal communal meeting space:

> *Home Economics* is not about designing better versions of established housing models that are already broken. It is about designing new ideas for the home understood through the duration of occupancy. That is why we have chosen room designers and advisers who are working outside of traditional models, pushing boundaries and challenging the status quo. We believe that British architecture is not responding to the challenges of modern living – life is changing; we must design for it. (Bose, Self and Williams as cited by the British Council 2016)

On entering the pavilion through an oversized black door that references Queen Elizabeth I's dictum that each British family should have their own home to prevent the spread of infectious diseases, the visitor was invited to explore each of the full-scale models. These dealt with shared living (*Hours*, by Jack Self with Shumi Bose and Finn Williams), mobility and personal space (*Days*, by åyr), the politics of domesticity in the global city (*Months*, by

Dogma and Black Square), resistance to property speculation at a domestic level (*Years*, by Julia King) and adaptable, experiential spaces (*Decades*, by Hesselbrand).

The model environments of *Home Economics* shifted the visitors' reception from a purely theoretical engagement to the immediacy of inhabiting and testing the idea in situ. As with *Maison Dom-ino* and the *Nail House*, a performative, dynamic and ever-changing performative space emerged. As much as these models operated as visualizations and embodiments of ideas, they also gave form to untested speculations and propositions, claiming their reality at the moment of activation in the here and now of their performance.

Model and exhibition: Performing scenography

Muriel Gerstner: *Muriel Gerstner Presents: Number Nine Barnsbury Road, Soho,*
Prague Quadrennial of Performance Design and Space (PQ) 2007

Intersection: Intimacy and Spectacle, PQ 2011

Romeo Castellucci: *Persona, Intersection,* PQ 2011

Monika Pormale: *Exhibit No. 17, Installation for Two People, Intersection,*
PQ 2011

Anna Viebrock and Tim Exit: *THE THINGS/DIE DINGE, Intersection,* PQ 2011

The Prague Quadrennial of Performance Design and Space (PQ) originated in Czechoslovakian artist František Tröster's winning entry to the 1959 São Paulo Art Biennial. Tröster's exhibit, which highlighted Czech and Slovak stage design and theatre architecture after the First World War, resulted in an offer for Prague to stage an international exhibition of theatre design and theatre architecture for the first time in 1967. In the years following, the Prague Quadrennial was seen as a mediator beyond the Iron Curtain, and a means for artists from East and West to meet and communicate. With the dissolution of the Soviet Union in 1991, PQ was in search of a new raison d'être, and in 2007 under director Sodja Lotker and General Commissioner Arnold Aronson, it began to open up to new contemporary and interdisciplinary forms of theatre and performance design. With this came the question of how to represent a new scenography that incorporated new technologies and occurred both within and outside designated theatre and performance spaces. Compared with the International Architecture Exhibition of the Venice Biennale, the PQ, due to its complex political and institutional history (it has always been administered by the city of Prague and the Czech Ministry of Culture), was until 2007 thought to represent the best in international theatre and performance design. While providing an overview of current practice, it was not centrally curated but depended on national curators' selections of participating artists. The persistent result was the display of scenographic remnants, and as Arnold Aronson remarks, it was the paradox of the PQ that 'it exhibits artefacts of process, but the event itself is missing' (Aronson 2008).

The PQ's 2007 edition under Aronson and Lotker saw the first ruptures in traditional set-ups of costume, props, small-scale models and accompanying video displays, notably in the Student Section where many contributions showed a new understanding of the exhibited object's scenographic role by shunning the display of representative models altogether. Instead, they devised conceptual models of interaction and participation, with an open dramaturgy driven by a raw aesthetics. Cases in point included *Forest*, the Finnish contribution that resembled a 'chill-out lounge' and the Hong Kong exhibit that invited visitors to build small paper boats, to be left on the floor to form an installation. The latter highlighted the collaborative nature of scenographic practice by making the once-passive visitor a co-actor and creator. Students from the United Kingdom devised a rotating workshop programme that was framed around a response to the notion of 'Collaborators', the title of the SBTD (Society of British Theatre Designers) national UK exhibit. It invited students from different theatre and performance design courses to collaborate live in the form of performative designs and without producing any stationary exhibits. One group even debunked the very notion of national representation by setting up an 'international pavilion' where everybody could show their work or simply meet. As in the Finnish tent and Hong Kong floor installation, the rawness of execution and presentation guaranteed success, and perfection as an aesthetics became irrelevant. Instead, scenography's performative aspect, its ability to conjure space and place, took priority over the presentations or attempted reconstructions of a past or future performance event.

Many exhibits in the 2007 National Section meanwhile adhered to the conventions of scenographic exhibitions, with one notable exception. Switzerland was represented neither by several scenographers' works nor an individual retrospective or theme, but by one deeply resonant project from scenographer Muriel Gerstner. Contrary to most other national exhibits, it lacked any identifying link with its country of origin, being enigmatically titled *Muriel Gerstner Presents: Number Nine Barnsbury Road, Soho.*[12] Gerstner deposited a 6 × 6 × 3 metre enterable black model box into the 'white cube' of Prague's Industrial Palace exhibition space, generating an immediate productive dissonance amid the collections of small-scale objects (see Figure 6.3). Just outside the model's entrance, visitors found a small black simply titled booklet, and on the last page read 'Muriel Gerstner and the

FIGURE 6.3 Muriel Gerstner Presents: Number Nine Barnsbury Road, Soho *by Muriel Gerstner, Prague Quadrennial 2007.*

Swiss Federal Office of Culture.' The construction comprised several sparsely furnished rooms, while the booklet suggested a narrative of strange past events to do with male twins dressed in little girls' clothes, along with their writing activities. Smashed white ceramics were lined up along one wall, yet no explanation of the destruction or collection process was forthcoming. The last room comprised a bookshelf and comfortable chair. Facing the chair was a model within the overall model that rotated within a glass box.

Gerstner's enterable model fell into the classical definition of models by Stachowiak (1973), in that it was an abstracted representation, however, not of reality (as would be the case in a scientific model) but of a fictional story. Reduced in complexity and materials with a focus on visualizing specific elements and attributes, Gerstner's model interrogated the phenomenon of the scenographer's working processes.

The visitor first witnessed Gerstner's model set-up before retracing the artist's steps as he or she navigated through the model's elements. The conclusion came in the confrontation with the rotating scale model under glass. It was understood that the stage set model is constantly in flux and that the scenographer's work is an open-ended investigation in the translation of text into three-dimensional space, diversely explored with each new model:

This project ... seeks to convey a visual image of language as a permanent building site and archaeological dig: a kind of commentary on our theatre work... I see our task largely as a question of translating: from language into image and music, and back again, in a never-ending process. (Gerstner 2007a: 27)

As the physical representation of an idea, Gerstner's model was autonomous, comprising a final artefact and creating its complete world in a single object and as a set of relations that aimed to simulate the designer's conceptual process. It was both creative and teleological in that it sought to understand and communicate the scenographer's design process, and it was performative in that it could only be read by the visitor's physical engagement. The small model set within the library is described by Gerstner as 'the scale model of the castle of a Romanian Duke who, we suspect, is involved in these rather strange events' (Gerstner 2007b: n.p.). It comprised the result of the scenographer's concept and design, but since it was trapped in a constant rotating movement, it could never be fully apprehended. The model could only ever represent one possible interpretation of a given dramatic original – in this case presumably the opera *Bluebeard's Castle* by Hungarian composer Béla Bartók.

Gerstner's black box was a discursive space that situated pressing questions within an enterable full-scale model: how to arrive at a textual representation in the form of a three-dimensional set model, how to find a language to describe it, and (perhaps the central question) how to represent scenography. Gerstner's 'wicked house' (Hegel in Gerstner 2007a: 25) artistically transformed the scenographer's search for images into voyeurism (to be in someone else's house), discovery (the jewel in the box), and theoretical inspiration, analysis and reflection (the chair). While the house was closed on three sides, the library was open, presenting the fourth wall. This model configuration thus revealed the viewer as having been a participant of the scenographer's internal research and visualization. While its material subject, the set model, resisted both touch and dissection, the theory and process of finding images was continually challenged in an exchange with the outer world.

Gerstner's contribution to the PQ, while popular with audiences, was thought of by the community as obscure, theoretical and guilty of bringing the genre of installation into an exhibition of theatre and performance design and by 2008, Lotker had become acutely aware that the PQ was in danger of falling out of step with current theatre and performance design practice. Lotker subsequently assembled a group of theorists and practitioners to map out the future of the PQ. In this debate, Gerstner's work, the installations and participatory works of the Student Section and the national contributions that replaced scenographic objects with scenography itself (such as Hungary's border transit station) guided the discussion.

To advance the critical discourse on the future of scenography in exhibition, Lotker and Aronson changed the PQ's name to Prague Quadrennial of Performance Design and Space for the 2011 edition. This gesture sought to make clear the transdisciplinary nature of the production of space and to acknowledge that theatre and performance belong together but are distinct. Aronson contextualized the significance of this in *The Disappearing Stage*, an introduction to the PQ's 2012 publication. His reflections on the 2011 Quadrennial reveal that traditional scenographic elements and artefacts appeared in no more than half the exhibits, giving way to installations and immersive environments, sound machines, fashion shows, workshops and talks:

I would like to think, however, that the variety of performative and installation displays was, in fact, a reflection of the contemporary state of stage design and perhaps of theatre in general. I have titled this book *The Disappearing Stage*, which most obviously refers to the increasingly vexed position of theatre within culture and society at large. And it also references the encroachment of digital and electronic media which for many people is the primary, if not sole, source of performance and generator of our imagistic vocabulary. (Aronson 2012: 9)

In 2011, in a departure from previous editions of the PQ, Lotker added and curated a new section titled *Intersection: Intimacy and Spectacle*, located in Prague's city centre in the Piazzetta between the National Theatre and New Stage Theatre, the former Laterna Magika by famed Czech scenographer Josef Svoboda. With its title drawn from Michel de Certeau's definition of space as 'composed of intersections of mobile elements' (De Certeau 1984: 117), *Intersection* comprised a labyrinth of thirty white cubes and black boxes in a seemingly arbitrary spatial organization by architect and scenographer Oren Sagiv that required the visitor to physically enter it and to open oneself up to an experiential rather than contemplative exhibition (see Figure 6.4). Intersection's programmatic design reminded of the 2007 Russian exhibit in the National Exhibition Section (that ultimately won the Golden Triga, the PQ's highest award for participating countries) where, in order to see the exhibited models of different Chekhov productions, one had to put on waterproof galoshes and wade through ankle-deep water and become part of a Chekhov exhibition world oneself. In the same way, *Intersection* exhibited performance through the enterable model and model box on an impressive 1:1 scale with 'scenographers, performers, choreographers, film and theatre directors, installation artists, fashion designers, writers and painters' (PQ2011) asked to work within a 3 × 3 × 3 metre space. For eleven days, *Intersection* explored the model's performative potential by inviting the visitor on a subjective, unexpected journey in and between the boxed-in environments.

FIGURE 6.4 Intersection *model landscape by Oren Sagiv, Prague Quadrennial 2011.*

One might, for example, enter through the stage door of the National Theatre and gain the impression that the interior extended into an array of theatrical scenes, each housed in its own model theatre on its own stage. Entering from the street, the visitor became aware of the exhibition's distributed nature, but due to the boxes' height could not get an overview. Thus, with only a printed ground plan with the artists' names on it, one embarked on an exploration – made more mysterious since the boxes carried neither title nor author's name, only a number. The collection of boxes curatorially sought a new hybrid between scenography, performance and the visual arts that had at its centre the activation of models through visitors' direct participation. Sagiv had meanwhile designed a superstructure above the model boxes that he titled the Public Shell. A network of wooden platforms incorporated walkways, a seating area and an open-air cinema, accessible twenty-four hours. The Public Shell offered yet another performance that arose from the scenography provided by the array of boxes. Viewed from above as a topological entity, the visitors became an ever-changing ensemble of actors navigating their way in and out of the spaces and through the 'created' streetscapes. For these 'actors':

This live exhibition talked to you only if you talked back to it. This living and breathing exhibition told you stories, and the more time you spent there the more it spoke to you. It taught you to dance, and asked you to listen. It required positioning and it let you get lost. If you were afraid of intimacy – you better wouldn't have entered. (Lotker 2011)

Lotker's notion of a 'living and breathing' exhibition with theatre and performance design at its centre parallels the ways visual arts increasingly incorporate live performance. This truth underscores the affective potential of a model that enables performance. *Persona*, the model box by theatre director and scenographer Romeo Castellucci, known for his uncompromising concepts and aesthetics, was by all accounts entered with both trepidation and excitement. Inside, a large antique mask was mounted on the wall opposite the entrance, and when the visitor approached, a movement sensor triggered a piercing, frightening sound. The mask thus embodied the contested relationship between audience and performance in a single metaphoric object:

To be brutally frank, the aim of this installation is to induce fear, not of the mask itself, but of the object it is contemplating: we, the audience, the catalogue of the species, both audience and show. The mask is all-seeing. The mask speaks of everything in a summation of all human languages. The human comedy is related with a comic tongue and the human being is looked upon with an inhuman gaze. (Castellucci 2011)

Persona thus spoke of a central parameter of theatre, not in terms of its architecture or materiality, but that by entering and facing the performative object an inadvertent performance occurred – within the model and of the model.

Other boxes such as Latvian scenographer Monika Pormale's *Exhibit No. 17: Installation for Two People* did not refer to performance through a substitutive object or symbol, but demonstrated the making of performative space as an act of social construction, observed from outside. An immediate point of difference was the elevation of its floor by a metre. With three glass fronts and an opaque back wall, *Exhibit No. 17* referenced both the theatre's fourth wall and (by its hard materiality) the strict separation of audience and performer in traditional proscenium stage settings. Very brightly lit by a star-shaped configuration of neon tubes below its ceiling, the box could be entered via a small staircase and door half concealed in a wall. Opening the door, the visitor listened to a pre-recorded stage direction that invited her to enter together with another person. Once inside, they should embrace for several minutes. The provocation lay in the exhibition of intimacy and the implicating of outside spectators as voyeurs to a fragile event. The presentness of such interaction between people who may or may not have known each other constructed the space itself. A brief note further explained the context as an experiment in tension between private and public:

Exhibit No.17 is about the intimacy of the moment of humans being together, people frozen in embrace and talking to each other in 'the language of hearts' in complete silence and solitude. This piece of art is the culmination and the closing of a theme that has been present in Monika Pormale's works for six years. ...In Riga, Monika Pormale made a series of photos featuring the actors of the New Riga Theatre, as well as ordinary people, embracing each other with unusual tenderness in different public spaces – a library, a swimming pool, a supermarket, a church. (Pormale 2011)

Silent and unspectacular, Pormale's social and physical model drew big crowds, with many lingering to observe this subtle interplay between protagonists locked in an embrace inside a closed object. As the partners became actors on a stage, they, in turn, observed the audience witnessing their performance. They expressed this in choreographic and emotional intensities, in the process of their bodies moving into the required position, adjusting and readjusting arms, legs, feet, hips and faces, and in their slow disengagement and departure from the box. The elevated structure of *Exhibit No. 17* acted as a focalized object that staged the presentness of viewer and participant so that the illuminated model was both exhibited object and stage. Not all models required the visitor to perform. Box 12 by German scenographer Anna Viebrock, titled *THE THINGS/DIE DINGE*, was a 1:1 scenographic theatre of memory (Wunderkammer), consisting of remnant objects and architectural elements of a past set design:

This 'residue of space', which is defined by the wood panelling of a theatre production in Cologne, displays a number of things/details/remains, which were significant in various productions. That means these things carry the memory of several theatre performances. ... What happens if one takes these items out of their original, disparate contexts and if one recomposes them into one single room? Which heterotopy is to be created in this way? (Viebrock 2011)

In Viebrock's model box, objects and elements usually left onstage directly after a performance created a new scenography in the presentness of the *Intersection* exhibition. It asked a key question of scenographic practice: how objects acquire meaning through their spatial arrangements in a single space, and how the entire space acquires a meaning that is more than the sum of its objects.

The model landscape of *Intersection* exploited the performative potential of autonomous 1:1 models created specifically for exhibition. Each enterable model box staged its very space, and a myriad of performances emerged from the visitor's actions in and with the model. In total, the thirty boxes formed a heterogeneous landscape, which embodied the desire to imagine, to design, to construct and to apprehend the world through the inherently performative properties of the model, and thus to make the invisible visible. The 2011 Prague Quadrennial, one of its most successful editions both in terms of audience numbers and numbers of participating countries but also, in theory terms, as an exhibition of scenography that aimed at the redefinition of the genre of exhibition itself and, more specifically, at the redefinition of how scenography itself can gain currency and value when exhibited not as mere remnant but when scenography itself becomes a performance. This programmatic ambition could only be achieved through a rigorous redefinition of the role of the model in the scenography exhibition, and its aesthetics and epistemes. By understanding the temporality of the model not as a *before* the performance or *after* but rather as a reality-constructing performative space of action, the model, not only in the *Intersection* component of the PQ but also in several other installation constellations, where the viewer was acting within a model environment, was able to realize its cosmopoietic potential in dialogue with the visitor as participant.

This chapter revisited the model in the context of the extended history of exhibition marked by distinct ideological shifts and trends that have ranged from traditional displays of individual objects to be in favour and, more recently, to overall scenographic approaches in the design of exhibitions and an emphasis on exhibition narratives and immersive, engaging formats. These developments and shifts were discussed in regard to the emergence of the autonomous model in the large, international survey shows, the Prague Quadrennial of Performance Design and Space (PQ) and the International Architecture Exhibitions within the Venice Biennale.

In the detailed discussion of case studies from both institutions, the wish to transform codified communications between the work and the viewer from contemplation to interaction was identified as the prime motivator that led to the emergence of installation, performative and participatory practices and formats. These, in turn, it is argued, have led to the exploration of the autonomous model as comprising and enabling performance, with both viewer and model now active in a co-authored and ephemeral space-making process. The resultant performative space (Fischer-Lichte 2008) was defined in this concluding chapter as forever emergent in the interaction between model, participant and exhibition.

In the wider territory of the model as performance, namely in scenographic practice in theatre and architecture, the autonomous model's agency and performativity render it a provocation to conventionalized exhibition practices. It is the autonomous model, often large scale and often enterable and temporarily inhabitable, that observably proliferates not only in Prague and Venice but across the contemporary exhibition landscape, creating a world beyond the model's material status in a unique cosmopoietic act extending from maker to viewer as witness and participant of that world.

Notes

Introduction

1 See Orton (2004) and Reid (1976) for theatre, and Karssen (2014) and Dunn (2010) for architecture.
2 See Morris (2006) and Moon (2005).

Chapter 1

1 Architecture and set design students study in the studio-teaching format of presentation and critique of drawings, models and plans. They practise the art of design presentation throughout their studies, in a format adhered to since the introduction of the Beaux Arts architecture education in Paris in the late nineteenth century.
2 Model theory is a sub-discipline of mathematical logic, concerned with the relations between formal syntactic expressions of a language and their meaning on a semantic level.
3 'Blurred' is here understood as an approximation of interior spaces and exterior walls and the merging of several past spaces into one. This refutes the accurate representation of a single building and allows for the spectator's memories and narratives to unfold in parallel with the performance, in fact, to become part of it.
4 Camillo's teatro is discussed in detail in the section 'Model and cosmos: Performing the theatres of knowledge'.
5 Some architects and scenographers have adopted design development strategies that are entirely digital.
6 Christopher Wren's 1673–1674 model of St Paul's Cathedral at a scale of 1:25 serves as a prominent example for a costly model produced to convince the client.
7 For a detailed history of the votive model, see Grajetzki (2013).
8 This is documented in descriptions of the building of the West-Attican town of Eleusis in the mid-fourth century BCE.
9 See the sections 'Models and system: Staging the city' and 'Model and cosmos: Performing the theatres of knowledge'.

10 The five books of Serlio's *Tutte l'opere* ... were published non-chronologically between 1537 and 1584. The first English translation under the title *The Five Books of Architecture* was published in 1611.

11 See the section 'Model and cosmos: Performing the theatres of knowledge'.

12 There is no evidence, for example, of stage set models produced by the influential Galli-Bibiena family of painters, architects and scenographers who dominated European scenography from the late seventeenth to mid-eighteenth centuries. In particular, Ferdinando Galli-Bibiena's scenographic innovation of the *scena per angolo* – which extended the Renaissance single perspective to a set with two vanishing points, often constructed from a corner view and showing vast and complex multi-level interior constructions – is documented in drawings and engraving only.

13 Scales of 1:20 and 1:25 for stage set models, established during the nineteenth century, are standard scales today.

14 An example of a multi-perspectival painted backdrop is the set model for Neptune's palace in Dauvergne's *Les Fêtes d'Euterpe* (1758) in de la Gorce (1983: 435). For examples of a staircase, several levels and an Italianite crowning cupola, see the set model for Rameau's *Dardanus* (1760) in de la Gorce (1983: 437).

15 De la Gorce rightly points out that Servandoni had left the Opéra de Paris in 1744, and thus could not have been the author of these set designs.

16 See the section 'Model theatre and model stage: Architecture as laboratory and exhibit'.

17 See the section 'Model theatre and model stage: Architecture as laboratory and exhibit'.

18 In 1849, Wagner published two essays that argue for the reunion of the arts in harmony akin to the antique Greek theatre. They were *Die Kunst und die Religion* (Art and Religion) and *Das Kunstwerk der Zukunft* (The Artwork of the Future). The essay *Oper und Drama* (Opera and Drama) followed in 1852.

19 Herzog von Meiningen 1874–1890. Available at: http://www.wikiwand.com/de/Theatermuseum_Meiningen (accessed 10 September 2016).

20 The representational model continued to be fabricated and collected at diverse scales throughout the nineteenth century and into the twentieth, and a large number of historic and contemporary models can be viewed today in the Architecture Gallery of London's Victoria and Albert Museum, at the Cité de l'Architecture et du Patrimoine in Paris, at the Frankfurt Architecture Museum and, especially for twentieth-century models, in the collection of the Canadian Centre for Architecture (CCA).

21 The Austrian architect Otto Wagner produced a full-scale model of part of the façade of the Historisches Museum der Stadt Wien in Vienna's Karlsplatz, as part of a competition by the City of Vienna in 1910. The German architect Alfred Messel built a full-scale partial façade model, with pediment, of the Berlin Pergamonmuseum in 1912.

22 From around 1930 onwards, Kiesler developed the notion of 'correalism' as the convergence of art, life and the sciences. This is exemplified in the equation 'Design = Stage + Elements × Movement' (Kiesler 1939: 60).

23 See Chapter 3 for details of Craig's co-editorship of the 1921 volumes 6 and 7 of *Wendingen* that were dedicated to marionettes.

Chapter 2

1 See Vitruvius (1999: 1.2, 12).

2 The origins of the concept of the ideal city (or city-state) can be found in Greek philosophical thought. In Book II of his *Republic*, Plato has Socrates say in the dialogue with Adeimantes: '… why don't we start by finding out what sort of thing it is in cities' (Plato 2000: 50, 368e). At the centre of Plato's concept of the ideal city-state lies justice for the individual and the whole. Plato sees the inhabitants of the city-state segregated by class and ruled by 'guardians' who are educated in both warfare and philosophy. Aristotle's city broadly aligns with Plato's ideas of segregation according to class and acceptance of the slavery system. It restates Plato's notion of the body politic, with the city-state as a living organism yet with a single ruler beneficial to the political entity (Aristotle 2008).

3 See, amongst others, Forster (1977), Carlson (1989), Izenour (1996) and Borys (2014).

4 The Baroque art chamber originated in the private cabinet of curiosities of the Renaissance, where the collector's items were arranged in cabinets and vitrines, often closed and only to be opened for special visitors. During the Baroque, the private cabinets grew into exhibition spaces which in turn often became the basis for the modern museum. The cabinet of the London apothecary James Petiver (1663–1718), by example, had been bought by the physician and collector Sir Hans Sloane and was to become the foundation for the British Museum in the late eighteenth century.

5 Kirkbride (2008) points out that the early *studioli*, together with the chambers of curiosities of the seventeenth and eighteenth centuries, might be rightly seen as precursors of the museum. Certainly, their programmes were primarily iconographic and lacked the scenographic inventiveness of the later exhibition settings and environments discussed here.

6 See Zedelmaier (2008: 2).

7 Metonymy is a rhetorical tool by which a concept or object is called by a name closely related to it rather than by its own.

8 The term 'theatrum' came to be used more or less synonymously with the term 'musaeum', and the systematized collections in conjunction with the curator's reflections in catalogues and theoretical treatises, are recognized by museum scholars as marking the beginning of museology. See Findlen (1994).

9 Shortly before his death in 1544, Camillo dictated his central thoughts relating to the theatre to his friend Girolamo Muzio. After Camillo's death, this manuscript and several handwritten notes were integrated into the 1550 publication, *L'Idea del Theatro*.

10 In *De Oratore*, Cicero describes the prerequisites for the *orator perfectus*, the perfect orator. These are, firstly, *natura*, man's natural qualities; secondly, *ars*, mastery of the art of rhetorics including knowledge of its theoretical principles; and thirdly, *exercitio*, the execution of mental and physical training exercises (Cicero, *De Oratore*, 3.57.215).

11 Vitruvius, *Ten Books on Architecture*, Book V, Chapters VI and VII.

12 Yates (1996).

13 Vigilius (1507–1577) was a Dutch lawyer, and ambassador to Karl V. Erasmus of Rotterdam (1466–1536) was a Dutch humanist and scholar.

14 Matussek (2012), Uricchio (2012), Di Benedetto (2012).

15 Most exhibitions in the Venice Biennale are curated by national curators; however, large portions of the former shipyard and military complex, collectively referred to as the Arsenale, are curated by the annually appointed director of the Biennale.

16 The full text of *Architectura Privata* in the original German, including all illustrations, is available online at: http://digital.slub-dresden.de/werkansicht /dlf/1289/1/.

17 See Vitruvius *Ten Books on Architecture*, Book I. Chapter II, 12.

18 The French Studies scholar Marc Olivier follows a similar genesis in regard to Servandoni's *spectacles*; see Olivier (2005).

19 On the development of mediatized presentations and the notion of the virtual throughout Western history, see Grau (2003).

20 See the section 'Model and cosmos: Performing the theatres of knowledge'.

21 Held in French collections, at the library of the Paris Opéra, the Bibliothèque nationale de France, and at the Château de Chambord, these paper models show the perspectival yet uniform symmetry of architecture and nature through the winged configuration.

22 The Theatre des Tuileries was located in the former Tuileries Palace in Paris. The stage machinery, designed by Italian theatre architects Gaspare Vigarani with his sons Carlo and Ludovico, was constructed between 1659 and 1661. It was originally intended for productions staged by Louis XIV. Hardly used by the court, the theatre was given over to the Paris Opéra until 1770. Palace and theatre were destroyed during the Paris Commune in 1871.

23 Servandoni was granted permission to produce his optic spectacles in the Salle des Machines during the Easter weeks in March and April when the other theatres were closed, that is, from 1738 to 1743, and 1754 to 1758. He produced nine spectacles during this time: *La Representation de l'église de Saint Pierre de Rome* in 1738, *Pandore* in 1739, *La Descente d'Enee aux Enfers* in 1740, *Les Travaux d'Ulysse* in 1741, *Leandre et Hero* in 1742, *La Forêt Enchantée* in 1754, *Le Triomphe de L'amour Conjugal* in 1755, *La Constance Couronnée* in 1756 and *La Chute des Anges Rebelles* in 1758.

24 Jerome de la Gorce has confirmed that the twenty set models for the Paris Opera originally attributed to Servandoni must, in fact, be the work of one of his students or successors. See De la Gorce (1983).

25 The programme book of *La Forêt Enchantée* by Servandoni has been digitized and is available online at: http://gallica.bnf.fr/ark:/12148/bpt6k5771989s/f27. image (accessed 4 January 2017).

26 Successful at first, Servandoni's representations were later criticized for their improbable plots and overworking of visual effects. Leaving Paris for London, and in 1751 for Brussels, he finally took up a post at the Court of Wurttemberg where he continued his *spectacles* on a smaller and much less expensive scale.

27 Olivier (2005: 33) mentions the inclusion of a seventy-feet-high vault, but no source is given. Panini's original painting had dimensions of 149.8 × 222.7 cm. The Basilica itself rises to a height of 137.6 metres with a length of 187 metres.

28 Servandoni had been, around 1720, one of Panini's early students.

29 Servandoni was still well known in London for his set designs at Covent Garden between 1747 and 1750, as well as ephemeral structures (particularly the fireworks machine for the celebration of the treaty at Aix-en-Capelle, Green's Park, 1748–1749). The exact productions he was responsible for, however, are disputed in the literature. See S. Rosenfeld, *Theatre Notebook* 1965, 63/64 reprinted in Herbert 2000: 79–82, and Highfill 1991: 260.

30 Loutherbourg nonetheless shows himself to be well prepared, as he states in his letter to Garrick: 'there are seven model scenes to be painted' (Baugh 1987: 127).

Chapter 3

1 Appia (1899).

2 Succinctly, Bablet (1966) calls Craig 'not a rationalist. His principles were not arrived at by the kind of systematic reflection that results in a body of theory' (1966: 117).

3 Excerpts from Kleist's essay were reprinted in E. G. Craig and H. T. Wijdeveld (1921), *Wendingen No. 7 and 8* and supported by photographic reproductions of Javanese, Chinese and Japanese puppets as well as marionette artists such as Richard Teschner.

4 This brings to mind Furttenbach's explanations of the workings of the machines he exhibited in his art chamber. It also affirms the experimental, almost scientific working methods and didactic mission of Herkomer's work.

5 *An Idyl* was premiered in June 1889 at Bushey under the musical direction of the Hungarian conductor Hans Richter, who was renowned for his interpretations of Wagner and Brahms. In 1876, Richter had first conducted the *Ring des Nibelungen* at Bayreuth, and in 1882 he gave the first London performances of *Die Meistersinger* and *Tristan und Isolde*. It speaks for Herkomer's compositional skills and the reputation of his small, experimental theatre to have succeeded in attracting Richter to the production.

6 See Craig (1969: 10).

7 Richard Wagner's Festspielhaus in Bayreuth, built in 1872 by the Leipzig architect Otto Brückwald according to Wagner's ideas, was modelled on the antique theatre, with all seats pointing in the same direction and the illusionist depiction of the antique *vela* or sun sail above the auditorium. The audience had close contact with the singers as the covered orchestra pit, up to twelve metres deep, was largely located under the auditorium. Additionally, Wagner implemented the complete darkening of the auditorium. With his dictum of 'Prima la musica dopo le parole', Wagner was close to Herkomer in the privileging of music over words, although Herkomer's priority was with the visual aspect of the performance.

8 In 1906, Craig had directed and designed Ibsen's *Rosmersholm* in Florence with highly choreographed movements and a distinct anti-realistic acting style. When the production travelled on to Nice, the set was shortened by over half a metre without his approval; thus, the original proportions were destroyed. This event is typically referred to in the Craig literature as the catalyst for his rigorous work leading to the 'Screens'. See Grund (2002) and Innes (1998).

9 Already in an unpublished draft of a manuscript from 1897, according to Bergman (1977: 334) and Bablet (1966: 32–33), Craig had articulated the concept of a theatre without boxes or circles and with a mobile proscenium.

10 Craig had read, during his 1904 stay in Berlin, Martin Semper's *Handbuch der Architektur* and was thus familiar with the Aspheleia System for the raising and lowering of platforms on the stage. See Semper (1904).

11 Craig's work in many respects anticipated Italian Futurist painter and scenographer Enrico Prampolini's 1925 designs for a 'Magnetic Theatre', where expression eclipsed decoration, and the actor was obsolete. Already in 1915 Prampolini had published the manifesto 'Futurist Scenography', where he advocated the stage as a complete 'electro-mechanical architecture' with coloured light as a dynamic and expressive medium.

12 See Newman (1995): 131.

13 Craig applied for the patent of the screens in 1910. For the US application, see: http://www.google.com/patents/US1022020.

14 See Craig (1923: 23).

Chapter 4

1 De Certeau (1984: 117).

2 Also known as a model home, display homes or show apartments are a constant feature in unbuilt subdivisions and apartment buildings, particularly in the Anglosphere. This phenomenon, while interesting, is not the focus of this study.

3 Acknowledged as the first World Fair, it was a periodic event formalized in 1928 into the Bureau International des Expositions, a body that retrospectively bestowed the title on previous fairs and has regulated the fairs (or 'expos') ever since.

4 MoMA was established in 1929 and is recognized as the first museum in the world to have a curatorial department for architecture and design, established in 1932.

5 Interview with Barry Bergdoll: Arpa and van Andel (2013).

6 Schmidt (1927).

7 Tegethoff (1981).

8 Lotz (1931).

9 According to Speck (2012: 293).

10 *Horizons* was published by Little Brown and Company, Boston, in 1932.

11 *Ville Radieuse* (The Radiant City) was a highly influential early modernist city planning concept that formed the basis of Le Corbusier's further urban work. It was published in a book of the same name in 1933.

12 The Marshall Plan was also known as the European Recovery Program. US$12 billion was given in grants and loans by the United States following the devastation of the Second World War.

13 Edgar Kaufman Jr was the director of the Industrial Design Department at the Museum of Modern Art in New York and curator of the annual MoMA exhibition 'Good Design'.

14 Countries belonging to the Marshall Plan included Austria, Belgium and Luxembourg, Denmark, France, West Germany, Greece, Iceland, Ireland, Italy and Trieste, the Netherlands, Norway, Portugal, Sweden, Switzerland, Turkey and the United Kingdom.

15 The George Marshall-Haus had been built as the US pavilion for the 1950 German Industry Exhibition.

16 The *Digitally Fabricated Housing for New Orleans* was designed and supervised by Lawrence Sass in collaboration with MIT researchers Daniel Smithwick and Dennis Michaud, with assistance from MIT students Laura Rushfeldt and Lara Davis.

17 The interlocking plywood components were cut using a multi-axis head on a computer numerical control (CNC) router. This machine can cut timber and other materials into three-dimensional shapes from a computer file.

18 See Stachowiak (1973).

19 By not using permanent systems such as nails or glue to hold the elements in place, the interlocking plywood components emerged undamaged when the structure was demounted.

20 Bergdoll in Broadhurst and Oshima (2008).

21 On the suggestion of Walter Gropius, Mies van der Rohe was appointed director of the Bauhaus Dessau in 1930 as successor to Hannes Mayer who had been dismissed in August by the city of Dessau due to 'communist activities'. In 1932, with a National Socialist majority in Dessau's city council,

the Bauhaus was closed and, despite its name change to 'Freies Lehr – und Forschungsinstitut', dissolved on 10 August 1933.

22 Mies van der Rohe designed seven projects in Krefeld between 1927 and 1939, most notable being the *Haus Lange und Haus Esters* (1927 to 1930). Both designs together with the plans for the golf club were included in the pivotal 1932 exhibition *Modern Architecture: International Exhibition*, curated by Phillip Johnson at MoMA, New York.

23 Commissioned by the German Society for Silk Weavers based in Krefeld, with Hermann Lange a member of the Board, Mies van der Rohe and Lily Reich experimented with a new way of integrating exhibition architecture and exhibits in a complete temporary installation or mise-en-scène. Wide strips of black, orange and red velvet and gold-, silver- and yellow-coloured silk were hung over wave-like, bent metal pipes to create intimate environments within the large exhibition hall.

24 See physicist and philosopher Ludwig Boltzmann on the model: 'The model is a tangible representation, whether the size be equal, or greater, or smaller, of an object which is either in actual existence, or has to be constructed in fact or in thought' (Boltzmann 1974 [1911]: 211).

25 As defined by Goodman (2007).

26 Brejzek and Wallen (2013, 2014a,b)

Chapter 5

1 Architecture historian Helmut Weihsmann (1998: 19–217) identifies several categories of NS architecture, namely classicism for propaganda, governmental and party buildings; heritage for settlements and the so-called 'Ordensburgen' (educational institutions for leading personnel of the NSDAP), a moderate modernist style for private residences and administration buildings; functionalism for military and industry administration buildings; and a new functionalism for technology, industry and factory buildings (1998: 19–217).

2 In 1927, Nuremberg was the location for the first National Socialist 'Reichsparteitag' (party meeting) with 15,000 participants. The building of several colossal structures and connecting axes began as early as 1934 (for instance, the Luitpoldarena, the Congress Hall and the Grand Road that Hitler wished to be understood as a historical orientation towards the Roman Empire and to NS party meetings and processions).

3 In contrast, the complete *Germania* model at a length of fourteen metres had been cast from plaster and is today permanently displayed at the Berlin documentation centre, *Topography of Terror*, site of the former headquarters of the Secret State Police (SS).

4 The eighteen-minute film can be viewed at: https://archive.org/details/1939 -Das-Wort-aus-Stein.

5 For some original photographs from Speer's private archive showing full-scale mock-ups, see the Luxembourg architect Léon Krier's highly controversial attempt at the architectural rehabilitation of Speer (2013: 90–95).

6   Troost (1878–1934) was, until Speer's arrival on the scene, Hitler's favourite architect. Troost's neoclassicist style, while not directly linked to an NS aesthetics, certainly influenced the Nazi architecture to come.

7   Rossi is widely regarded as the founder and leader of La Tendenza, the 1970s Italian neo-rationalist movement that sought to reactivate the typological clarity of eighteenth-century Enlightenment architecture, emphasizing the role of the *locus* (site) of architecture, namely the city itself. Distinct from other Tendenza architects, theatre proved to be a continual inspiration and reference point in Rossi's writing and practice.

8   *Teatro del Mondo* was jointly commissioned by the Architecture curator Maurizio Scaparro and the Theatre curator Paolo Portoghesi (*Venezia e lo Spazio Scenico, Architettura, Teatro:* La Biennale, Venezia, 6 October–4 November 1979, Palazzo Grassi, Venice). Available online: http://www .labiennale.org/it/asac/attivita/2010-.html?back=true (accessed 20 September 2016). See also: https://www.youtube.com/watch?v=REG0eLLJljk&featur e=relmfu (accessed 20 September 2016) for a short, playful animation film commissioned by the Biennale, showing the history of Venice's floating theatres since the *Cinquecento.*

9   According to Halbwachs, the *mémoire collective* is formed by social processes, and the memory thus created is fundamental to the identity-building of any social group. Halbwachs (1992).

10 In his *Introduction to Hegel's Phenomenology of Spirit*, Larry Krasnoff explains Hegel's concept of the progressive nature of history. 'This is the truth in the original idealist assumption that history – understood not as the unfolding of events but as the rational unfolding of events that have already unfolded – is always progressive, an assumption that has been fiercely attacked but can never finally be refuted' (Krasnoff 2008: 157).

11 Rossi discusses the notion of the analogous city formed by collective memories in his 1982 *The Architecture of the City* (128–131).

12 One year before the *Teatro del Mondo*, Rossi had devised another small-scale scenographic installation for an exhibition he called *Il Teatro Scientifico*, the title being an allusion to the sixteenth-century anatomical theatres of Padua and Leiden. In this work, Rossi dissected the key components of theatre itself, explaining it as a multi-medial unity, a notion that is equally true of his Venetian *Teatro*; that is, object, model, scenography and laboratory in one:

> The theatre is thus inseparable from its stage set, its models, the experience of every combination: and the stage is reduced to the artisan's or scientist's work-table. (Rossi 1981: 33)

13 On the notion of the *Teatrum Mundi* in the arts and sciences, refer to Chapter 2.

14 For example, Palladio designed for the 1574 entry of Henri III an ensemble of arches in the waters of the Lido under which Henri's fleet of royally decorated gondolas crossed to the shore. There, Palladio had designed a loggia with twelve Corinthian columns made from fake marble, for the entire ensemble that was to last just three days.

15 In the theatre of Renaissance and Baroque, the notion of a divine world order was taken up by several playwrights, notably Pedro Calderón de la Barca in his 1635 drama *El Gran Teatro del Mundo* (featured in inscriptions of theatre buildings) that has at its centre the staging of a play with God as director. The 1599 inscription above the entrance to Shakespeare's Globe theatre reads as *Totus mundus agit histrionem* (the whole world is a playhouse), and a 1639 epigram by Joost van den Vondels in the painted interior of the Amsterdam Schouwburg Theatre declares that *'De weereld is een speeltooneel,/Elck speelt zijn rol en krijght zijn deel'* (The world is a playground; each plays his role and gets his share) (Smits-Veldt and Spies 2012: 60).

16 *Serenissima* is the abbreviation of the official state title of the republic Venice, *La Serenissima Repubblica di San Marco* (Most Serene Republic of San Marco).

17 Vicentini (1593).

18 Also known as Villa Capra. Construction for the Villa Rotonda began in 1576 and Scamozzi finished the building after Palladio's death in 1580, with some alterations to the original plan.

19 The exhibition *Architettura è Scienza Vincenzo Scamozzi (1548–1616)* was shown in the Palazzo Barbarano in Vicenza, from 7 September 2003 to 11 January 2004.

20 *Teatro del Mondo* was anchored next to the 1678–1682 customs house Punta della Dogana and close to the 1631 church of Santa Maria della Salute, the Piazza San Marco, and opposite the island of San Giorgio di Maggiore, with Palladio's 1610 Basilica and his 1577–1592 Redentore church on the island of La Giudecca.

21 Volksbühne Berlin (*People's Theatre*) was founded in 1914 and is located in Berlin's Mitte (in the former East) at Rosa-Luxemburg-Platz. Financed by member contributions, the so-called *Arbeitergroschen* (worker's penny) from the People's Theatre Movement, the theatre sought independence from state censorship as well as private, commercial theatrical entrepreneurs, all the while providing affordable cultural events for workers. The original building, designed by Oskar Kaufmann, held 2,000 seats. One year after the opening, the director Max Reinhardt (who at the time was already heading Berlin's Deutsches Theater and Kammerspiele) took over from the unsuccessful Emil Lessing, and from 1924 to 1927 the director Erwin Piscator staged several highly provocative political productions such as the *Revue Roter Rummel* (1924). The theatre is closely linked with the history of political theatre in both parts of Germany, and from 1962 until his death in 1966 Piscator was again leading the Volksbühne Berlin that was now located in the capital of the newly founded socialist German Democratic Republic (GDR). From 1992 to 2016, the East German director Frank Castorf elevated Volksbühne to one of the most exciting and provocative theatres in Germany, often in collaboration with Bert Neumann. In 2017 Frank Castorf was replaced by the art historian and curator Chris Dercan amid controversy. For a detailed history of the Volksbühne until the 1970s, see Cecil Davies (2013), *The Volksbühne Movement: A History*, London: Routledge.

22 From a conversation between Bert Neumann and Birgit Wiens, with thanks to Birgit Wiens for sharing this information.

23 In the German original:

Jeder Raum, den du gebaut hast, erzählt diese Autonomie, lieber Bert. Und lässt einen an der eigenen Autonomie bauen. Und es geht dabei nicht um einen unbändigen Gestaltungsdrang, sondern um die Etablierung der eigenen Praxis, um das Umgehen einer herrschenden und hierarchisierenden Praxis. Deshalb und nur deshalb macht man ein Theater, man macht es völlig neu. Nicht aus Orginalitätsgründen, sondern um die Parameter so zu verändern, dass man arbeiten kann. Deshalb kann man sagen, dass man es gemacht hat, also im vollsten Sinne: Man hat die Volksbühne gemacht. Nicht weil man einfach da drin rumwerkelt, sondern weil alle dort die Parameter verändert haben. (Pollesch 2015, trans. from German by the authors)

24 *Drama Queens: The Soap Opera in Experimental and Independent Cinema.* MoMA, New York, 4–19 June 2011.

25 See also Fischer (1991).

26 Neumann's *Neustadt* provided a multi-functional environment for several productions, including René Pollesch's 2002 *24 Stunden sind kein Tag. Escape from New York*, based on the 1980s dystopian science fiction film *Escape from New York* by US director John Carpenter. This came four weeks after the premiere of *The Idiot* in 2002, and in 2003 came *Freedom, Beauty, Truth & Love: The Revolutionary Enterprise*, again by Pollesch.

27 'The house is a machine for living in' (Le Corbusier 1986: 4).

Chapter 6

1 Eminent art chambers of the time include Count Albrecht V in Munich (from 1568); August of Saxony in the Dresden Castle (from 1572); Ferdinand II. Archduke of Austria (1529–1595) in the Ambras Castle, and the art chamber of Palazzo Poggi in Bologna, and Sir John Sloane's botanical and ethnological collections from 1687 onwards that were to form the foundation of the British Museum.

2 Fabricated in great numbers as tourist souvenirs, these were either cork models that showed iconic buildings of Ancient Rome, Greece and Syria in their current ruined state or idealized plaster models.

3 See Chapter 2.

4 See also section 'Making worlds: The emergence of the model'.

5 O'Doherty (1976).

6 The International Architecture Exhibition, as independent from the Venice Biennale, was instigated in 1980 under Paolo Portoghesi and entitled *The Presence of the Past*. Previously, the Venice Biennale had included an architecture section as part of its overall format of fine arts, theatre, dance and music.

7 The year 1980 was the first time the city of Venice had leased the vast space of the Corderie and Arsenale for viewing by the public. The Arsenale comprises several buildings and former warehouses originally used to construct the Venetian naval fleet. Construction began around 1200, with numerous extensions into the late nineteenth century. Today its exhibition floor space totals 50,000 square metres. The Corderie is a building on the Southern side, originally used for manufacturing ropes and cables, and is today an exhibition space spanning 6,400 square metres.

8 *La Presenza del Passato* included façade models by architects Frank O. Gehry, Rem Koolhaas, Arata Isozaki, Robert Venturi, Franco Purini, Ricardo Bofil and Christian de Portzamparc. Behind each life-size façade, solo exhibitions of the architects' work were displayed. Separate exhibitions of the work of Philip Johnson, Ignazio Gardella and Mario Ridolfi (known for their subjective departures from modernist dogma) and an overview of the works of seventy-three young and emerging architects were included, as well as a retrospective on Ernesto Basile.

9 For a detailed discussion on Teatro all'Antica, see section 'Model and system: Staging the city'.

10 Portoghesi succinctly describes postmodernism in architecture as

> a new synchronic vision of History that ultimately becomes an infinite warehouse for images and suggestions from which architects can freely draw shapes, styles and decorative elements. (Portoghesi 1980: 29)

11 For project examples and exhibitions, see www.thomasdemand.info (accessed 11 November 2016).

12 This is the address for Mr Hyde given in Robert Louis Stevenson's 1886 novel *The Strange Case of Dr Jekyll and Mr Hyde*.

References

Alberti, L. B. (1988), *De re Aedificatoria. On the Art of Building in Ten Books*, trans. J. Rykwer, N. Leach and R. Tavernor, Cambridge, MA: The MIT Press.

Alberti, L. B. (2011), *On Painting, A New Translation and Critical Edition*, trans. and ed. Rocco Sinigalli, New York: Cambridge University Press.

Altick, R. D. (1978), *The Shows of London*, Cambridge, MA: Harvard University Press.

Appia, A. (1899), *Die Kunst der Inszenierung*, trans. as *Music and the Art of Theatre*, München: Bruckmann.

Aravena, A. (2016), 'Introduction'. Available at: http://www.labiennale.org/en/architecture/exhibition/aravena (accessed 3 January 2017).

'Architettura è Scienza: Vincenzo Scamozzi (1548–1616)', Available at: http://www.palladiomuseum.org/exhibitions/scamozzi2003/schede/10 (accessed 19 December 2016).

Aristotle (2008), *Poetics*, trans. S. H. Butcher, [Ebook]. Available at: http://www.gutenberg.org/files/1974/1974-h/1974-h.htm (accessed 3 January 2017).

Aronson, A. ed. (2008), *Exhibition on the Stage: Reflections on the 2007 Prague Quadrennial*, Prague: Arts and Theatre Institute.

Aronson, A. (2012), 'The Dematerialization of the Stage', in Aronson, A. (ed), *The Disappearing Stage: Reflections on the 2011 Prague Quadrennial*, 84–95, Prague: Arts and Theatre Institute.

Arpa, J. and van Andel, F. (2013), 'I Think of the 1:1 Project as a Discursive Tool…', in van Gameren, D. (ed), *Woningbouwtentoonstellingen = Housing Exhibitions*, Rotterdam: nai010 uitgevers.

Asmuth, T. (2012), 'Featured: Bert Neumann, Imitation of Life'. Available at: http://contemporaryperformance.com/2012/07/28/books-imitation-of-life-by-bert-neumann/ (accessed 20 September 2016).

Augé, M. (1995), *Non-Places: Introduction to an Anthropology of Supermodernity*, London: Verso.

Bablet, D. (1966), *Edward Gordon Craig*, London: Heinemann.

Baugh, C. (1987), 'Philippe James de Loutherbourg and the Early Pictorial Theatre: Some Aspects of Its Cultural Context', in Redmond, J. (ed), *The Theatrical Space*, 99–128, Cambridge: Cambridge University Press.

Benedetti, J., ed. and trans. (2008), *Konstantin Stanislawski: My Life in Art*, London and New York: Routledge.

Benjamin, W. (1968), 'The Work of Art in the Age of Mechanical Reproduction', in Arendt, Hannah (ed), *Illuminations: Essays and Reflections*, 217–251, New York: Schocken Books.

Benjamin, W. (2002), 'Paris, Capital of the Nineteenth Century (Exposé of 1939)', in *The Arcades Project*, trans. Howard Eiland and Kevin McLaughlin, 14–26, Cambridge, MA: Harvard University Press.

Bergman, G. M. (1977), *Lighting in the Theatre*, Totowa, NJ: Rowman and Littlefield.

Bleeker, M. (2012), 'Introduction: On Technology & Memory', *Performance Research: On Technology & Memory* 17: 1–7.

Boltzmann, L. ([1911] 1974), *Model*, in Brian McGuinness (ed) *Ludwig Boltzmann: Theoretical Physics and Philosophical Problems. Selected Writings*, 211–220, Dordrecht: Reidel.

Bolzoni, L. (1999), 'The Play of Memory between Words and Images', in: Reinink, W. and Stumpel, J. (eds), *Memory & Oblivion: Proceedings of the XXIX International Congress of the History of Art held in Amsterdam 1–7 September 1999*, 11–18, Dordrecht: Springer Science & Business Media.

Borys, A. (2014), *Vincenzo Scamozzi and the Chorography of Early Modern Architecture*, Farnham: Ashgate.

Bose, S., Self, J. and Williams, F. (2016), 'The British Council presents the exhibition Home Economics in the British Pavilion at the 15th International Architecture Exhibition – La Biennale di Venezia from 28 May to 27 November 2016'. Available at: http://design.britishcouncil.org/venice-biennale /VeniceBiennale2016/ (accessed 12 December 2016).

Bouckaert, C. and Salembier, S. (n.d.), Available at: http://www.atelierbildraum .com/i-bildraum-I (accessed 10 December 2016).

Bourriaud, N. (2002), *Relational Aesthetics*, Dijon: Les Presses Du Reel Edition.

Brecht, B. (1967), 'Rede des Stückeschreibers über das Theater des Bühnenbauers Caspar Neher', in *Gesammelte Werke*, Volume 16, Schriften zum Theater II. Frankfurt a.M: Suhrkamp Verlag.

Brejzek, T., ed. (2011), *Expanding Scenography: The Authoring of Space*, Prague: Arts and Theatre Institute.

Brejzek, T. and Wallen, L. P. (2013), 'Subject, Site and Sight: Freud and Tschumi on the Acropolis', in Perren, C. (ed), *Reverse Projections*, 52–57, Berlin: Broken Dimanche Press.

Brejzek, T. and Wallen, L. P. (2014a), 'Derealisation, Perception and Site: Some Notes on the *Doppelgänger* Space', in Perren, C. (ed), *Perception in Architecture*, Newcastle upon Tyne: Cambridge Scholars Publishing.

Brejzek, T. and Wallen, L. P. (2014b), 'The 1:1 Architectural Model as Performance and Double', in *Inarch Conference*, 95–105, Jakarta: Universitas Indonesia (on CD).

Broadhurst, R. and Oshima, K. (2008), *Home Delivery: Fabricating the Modern Dwelling*, New York: The Museum of Modern Art.

Bundgaard, J. A. (1957), *Mnesicles, A Greek Architect at Work*, Copenhagen: Gyllenhaal.

Burke, E. (2008 [1756]), *A Philosophical Enquiry into the Sublime and Beautiful*, London/New York: Routledge.

Camillo, G. (1550), *L'Idea del Theatro*, Venice/Florence: L. Torrentino.

Carlson, M. (1989), *Places of Performance: The Semiotics of Theatre Architecture*, Ithaca, NY: Cornell University Press.

Cartright, J. M. (1903), *Beatrice d'Este, Duchess of Milan, 1475–1497, a study of the Renaissance*, London: J.M. Dent & Sons, Ltd. Available at: https://archive .org/details/beatricedesteduc25622gut (accessed 3 January 2017).

Caruso St John Architects (2013), Available at: www.carusostjohn.com/projects/ nagelhaus-venice-bienna (accessed 22 May 2017).

Castellucci, R. (2011), *Box No. 7, Persona*. Available at: http://www.intersection.cz/umelci2/soc-etas-raffaello-sanzio/ (accessed 4 November 2016).

Castillo, G. (2008), 'Marshall Plan Modernism in Divided Germany', in Pavitt, J. and Crowley, D. (eds), *Cold War Modern: Design 1945–1970*, 66–93, London: V & A Publications.

Castillo, G. (2010), *Cold War on the Home Front: The Soft Power of Midcentury Design*. Minneapolis: University of Minnesota Press.

Cicero, *De Oratore*. Available at: ttps://archive.org/stream/cicerodeoratore01ciceuoft/cicerodeoratore01ciceuoft_djvu.txt (accessed 4 January 2017).

Collins, J. and Nisbet, A., eds. (2010), *Theatre and Performance Design: A Reader in Scenography*, Milton Park: Routledge.

Coulton, J. J. (1983), *'Greek Architects and the Transmission of Design'*, Actes du Colloque international organisé par le Centre National de la Recherche Scientifique et l'École Française de Rome (Rome 2–4 Décembre 1980). Available at: Publication de l'Ecole Francaise de Rome, Année 1983 Volume 66 Numéro 1, 453–470 (accessed 4 January 2017).

Craig, E. G. (1903), 'On Stage Scenery', *The Morning Post*, 13 October 1903.

Craig, E. G. (1908), 'The Actor and the Uber-Marionette', *The Mask* 1 (2): 3–15.

Craig, E. G. (1923), *Scene*, London: Humphrey Milford & Oxford University Press.

Craig, E. G. (1957), *Index to the Story of My Days: Some Memoirs of Edward Gordon Craig, 1872–1907*, Cambridge, New York: Cambridge University Press (1981 printing).

Craig, E. G. (1980), *On the Art of Theatre*, London: Heinemann.

Craig, E. G. and Wijdeveld, H. T. (1921), *Wendingen No. 7 and 8*, Amsterdam: De Hooge Brug.

Cunningham, P. (1842), *Extracts from the Accounts of the Revels at Court, in the Reigns of Elizabeth and King James I, from the Original Office Books of the Masters and Yeomen*, London: Shakespeare Society.

Davies, C. (2013), *The Volksbühne Movement: A History*, London: Routledge.

De Certeau, M. (1984), *The Practice of Everyday Life*, Berkeley: The University of California Press.

De la Gorce, J. (1983), 'Twenty Set Models for the Paris Opéra in the Time of Rameau', *Early Music* 11 (4): 429–440.

Dezzi-Bardeschi, M. (1980), 'Venezia Spazio Scenico', *Domus* (602): 13.

Di Benedetto, S. (2012), 'Camillo's 4-D Theme Park Attractions', *Performance Research* 17 (3): 57–62.

Drama Queens: The Soap Opera in Experimental and Independent Cinema. MoMA, New York, 4–19 June 2011.

Dreissigacker, T. (2015), 'Modellieren', in Badura, Jens et al. (eds), *Künstlerische Forschung – Ein Handbuch*, 181–185, Zürich/Berlin: Diaphanes Verlag.

Dunn, N. (2010), *Architectural Modelmaking* (Portfolio Skills), London: Laurence King Publishers.

Eaton, R. (2002), *Ideal Cities: Utopianism and the (Un)built Environment*, London: Thames & Hudson.

Eliasson, O. (2007), 'Models Are Real', in Abruzzo, E., Ellingsen, E. and Solomon, J. D. (eds), *Models: 306090 Books*, Volume 11, 18–25, New York.

Elser, O. and Schmal, P. C., eds. (2012), *Das Architekturmodell: Werkzeug, Fetisch, Kleine Utopie*, Zürich: Scheidegger & Spies.

Eversmann, P. (2007), 'The International Theatre Exhibition of 1922 and the Critics', in Beckmann, Klaus and de Vries, Jan (eds), *Avantgarde and Criticism*, 67–90, Amsterdam/New York: Rodopi.

Findlen, P. (1994), *Possessing Nature: Museums, Collecting and Scientific Culture in Early Modern Italy*, Berkeley/Los Angeles/London: University of California Press.

Fischer, L., ed. (1991), *Imitation of Life: Douglas Sirk, Director*, New Brunswick: Rutgers University Press.

Fischer-Lichte, E. (2008), *The Transformative Power of Performance*, London: Routledge.

Floré, F. and Devos, R. (2014), 'Model Interiors and Model Homes at the Expo 58', in *Dash 10 – Interiors on Display*, 32–47, Rotterdam: nai010 uitgevers.

Forster, K. (1977), 'Stagecraft and Statecraft: The Architectural Integration of Public Life and Theatrical Spectacle in Scamozzi's Theatre at Sabbioneta', *Oppositions 9*: 63–87.

Foucault, M. (1984 [1967]), '*Of Other Spaces*: Utopias and Heterotopias', trans. Jay Miskowiec, *Diacritics* 16 (Spring 1986): 22–27.

Frascari, M. (2011), *Eleven Exercises in the Art of Architectural Drawing: Slow-Food for the Architect's Imagination*, Milton Park/New York: Routledge.

Furttenbach, J. (1628), *Architectura Civilis*, Ulm. Available at: http://digi.ub.uni-heidelberg.de/diglit/furttenbach1628a (accessed 4 January 2017).

Furttenbach, J. (1641), *Architectura Privata*, Ulm. Available at: http://digital.slub-dresden.de/werkansicht/dlf/1289/1/ (accessed 4 January 2017).

Furttenbach, J. (1663), *Mann-hafter Kunst-Spiegel*, Augsburg: Schultes.

Gallanti, F. (2010), 'The Teatro del Mondo as a Singular Building. A Tribute to Aldo Rossi'. Available at: http://www.abitare.it/en/events/2010/02/08/il-teatro-del-mondo-edificio-singolare-omaggio-a-aldo-rossi-2/ (accessed 19 December 2016).

Gameren, D. van and Andel, F. van. (2013), *Woningbouwtentoonstellingen = Housing Exhibitions*, Rotterdam: nai010 uitgevers.

Geddes, N.B. (1977), *Horizons*, Freeport, New York: Books for Libraries Press.

Gennep, A. van. (1960), *The Rites of Passage*, Chicago: University of Chicago Press.

Gerstner, M. (2007a), *Zu Bösen Häusern Gehen. Number Nine Barnsbury Road Soho*, Bern: Christian Merian Verlag.

Gerstner, M. (2007b), *B's Complex - THE HELPER'S CABIN*, Bern: Federal Office of Culture.

Gioni, M. (2013), 'Encyclopedic Palace Highlights Biennale', Available at: http://www.artkabinett.com/ak-file/encyclopediac-palace-highlights-biennale (accessed 12 December 2016).

Goodman, N. (1976), *Languages of Art: An Approach to a Theory of Symbols*, 2nd edition, Indianapolis: Hackett Publishing Company.

Grajetzki, W. (2013), *Tomb Treasures of the Late Middle Kingdom: The Archaeology of Female Burials*, Philadelphia: University of Pennsylvania Press.

Grau, O. (2003), *Virtual Art: From Illusion to Immersion*, trans. G. Custance, Cambridge, MA: The MIT Press.

Gregotti, V. (1996), *Rethinking Architecture*, Cambridge, MA: The MIT Press.

Groys, B. (2007), 'Der Idiot', Available at: https://www.volksbuehne-berlin.de /praxis/der_idiot/?langtext=1 (accessed 4 January 2017).

Groys, B. (2009), *The Politics of Installation*. Available at: http://www.e-flux.com /journal/02/68504/politics-of-installation/ (accessed 6 December 2016).

Grund, U. (2002), *Zwischen den Künsten. Edward Gordon Craig und das Bildertheater um 1900*, Berlin: Akademie-Verlag.

Halbwachs, M. (1992), *On Collective Memory*, ed. and trans. L.A. Coser, Chicago: University of Chicago Press.

Hannah, D. and Harsløf, O., eds. (2008), *Performance Design*, Copenhagen: Museum Tusculanum Press.

Hauss-Fitton, B. (1996), 'Futurama, New York World's Fair 1939–40', *Rassegna* XVI (6).

Hayes, M.K. (1998), *Architecture Theory since 1968*, Cambridge, MA: The MIT Press.

Healy, P. (2008), *The Model and Its Architecture*, Rotterdam: 010 Publishers.

Herbert, S. (2000), *A History of Pre-Cinema*, Volume 2, London: Routledge.

Herkomer, H. von. (1892a), 'On Scenic Art I', *The Magazine of Art*, 259–264.

Herkomer, H. von. (1892b), 'On Scenic Art', *London Daily Telegraph*, 6 February.

Herkomer, H. von (1908), *My School and My Gospel*, London: Archibald Constable and Company Unlimited.

Hewitt, B., ed. (1958), *The Renaissance Stage: Documents of Serlio, Sabbattini and Furttenbach*, trans. A. Nicoll, J. H. McDowell and G. R. Kernodle, Coral Gables, FL: University of Miami Press.

Hick, T. (2013), *1:1 model Golfclubhaus Mies van der Rohe*. Available at: http:// www.robbrechtendaem.com/projects/rural/1-1-model-golfclubhaus-mies-van-der-rohe (accessed 3 January 2017).

Highfill, P. H., ed. (1991), *A Biographical Dictionary of Actors, Actresses, Musicians, Dancers, Managers & Other Stage Personnel in London, 1660–1800*, Carbondale and Edwardsville: Southern Illinois University Press.

Huhtamo, E. (2013), *Illusions in Motion: Media Archaeology of the Moving Panorama and Related Spectacles*, Cambridge, MA: The MIT Press.

Hurtzig, H., ed. (2001), *Imitation of Life: Bert Neumann Bühnenbilder*, Berlin: Theater der Welt.

Innes, Christopher (1998), *Edward Gordon Craig: A Vision of Theatre*, Milton Park: Taylor & Francis.

Izenour, G. C., Knudson, V. O. and Newman, R. (1996), *Theater Design*, 2nd ed., New Haven, CT: Yale University Press.

Jones, M. W. (2003), *Principles of Roman Architecture*, 2nd ed., New Haven, CT: Yale University Press.

Karssen, A. and Otte, B.(2014), *Model Making: Conceive, Create and Convince*, Amsterdam: Frame Publishers.

Kiesler, F. J. (1924), *Als ich das Raumtheater erfand (When I invented the Space Theatre)*, Wien: Oesterreichische Friedrich und Lillian Kiesler Privatstiftung.

Kiesler, F. J. (1939), 'On Correalism and Biotechnique. Definition and Test of a New Approach to Building Design', *Architectural Record* 86 (3) (September): 60–75.

Kirkbride, R. (2008), *Architecture and Memory*, New York: Columbia University Press.

Kleinman, K. and van Duzer, L. (2005), *Mies van der Rohe: The Krefeld Villas*. New York: Princeton Press.

Koolhaas, R. (2014), 'Fundamentals'. Available at: http://www.labiennale.org/en /architecture/archive/14th-exhibition/14iae/ (accessed 4 January 2017).

Krasnoff, L. (2008), *Hegel's Phenomenology of Spirit: An Introduction*, Cambridge: Cambridge University Press.

Krier, L. (2013), *Albert Speer Architecture 1932–1942*, Danvers, MA: The Monacelli Press.

Lange, C., ed. (2014), *Mies 1:1. Ludwig Mies van der Rohe: The Golf Club Project. Das Golfclub Projekt*, Köln: Verlag der Buchhandlung Walther Koenig.

Laube, S. (2009), *Giulio Camillo: L'idea del Theatro*. Available at: http://diglib.hab .de/content.php?dir=edoc/ed000188&distype=optional&xml=tei- introduction.xml&xsl=http://diglib.hab.de/rules/styles/projekte/theatra/tei- introduction2 .xsl&metsID=edoc_ed000188_introduction (accessed 9 January 2017).

Le Corbusier (1986 [1931]), *Towards a New Architecture*, trans. F. Etchells, Mineola, NY: Dover Publications.

Lefebvre, H. (1991), *The Production of Space* [1974], trans. David Nicholson-Smith, Malden, MA: Blackwell.

Lepik, A. (1994), *Das Architekturmodell in Italien 1335–1550*, Worms: Wagner'sche Verlagsgesellschaft.

Lévi-Strauss, C. (1962), *The Savage Mind*, trans. G. Weidenfield, Chicago: University of Chicago Press.

Lotker, S. (2011), *Intersection. Intimacy and Spectacle*. Available at: http://www. intersection.cz/prague/boxes/ (accessed 6 December 2016).

Lotz, W. (1931), *Die Form*, Heft 6, 15. 6. 1931, Available at: http://www. deutscherwerkbund-nw.de/index.php?id=371 (accessed 12 August 2014).

Maeterlinck, M. (1890), 'Menus propos - le théâtre', *La Jeune Belgique* 9 (September): 331.

Mahr, B. (2008), 'Cargo. Zum Verhältnis von Bild und Modell', in Reichle, I., Siegel, S. and Spelten, A. (eds), *Visuelle Modelle*, **17–40**, München: Wilhelm Fink Verlag.

Matussek, P. (2001), 'The Renaissance of the Theatre of Memory Giulio Camillo', *Janus* 8: 4–8.

Matussek, P. (2012), 'Memory Theatre in the Digital Age', *Performance Research* 17 (3): 8–15.

Mayor, H. A., ed. (1964), *Giuseppe Galli Bibiena, Architectural and Perspective Designs*, New York: Dover.

McCaughan, S. (2016), 'The *Full-Size Architectural Mock Ups* of *Miami's Latest Starchitect-Designed Buildings*', Available at: https://www.gridics.com/news /full-size-architectural-mockups-miamis-latest-starchitect-designed-buildings (accessed 4 January 2017).

McKinney, J. and Palmer, S. (2017), 'Expanded Scenography. An Introduction', in McKinney, Joslin and Palmer, Scott (eds), *Expanded Scenography*, London: Bloomsbury Methuen Drama.

McQuaid, M., Bee, H. S. and Droste, M. (1996), *Lilly Reich, Designer and Architect: [exhibition... Museum of Modern Art, New York, February 7–May 7, 1996]*, New York: Museum of Modern Art.

Meadow, M. A. and Robertson, B., ed. and trans. (2003), *The First Treatise on Museums: Samuel Quicchelberg's Inscriptiones 1565*, Los Angeles, CA: Getty Research Institute.

Meiningen, H. von (1874–1890). Available at: http://www.wikiwand.com/de /Theatermuseum_Meiningen (accessed 10 September 2016).

Millon, H. A. (1994), *The Renaissance from Brunelleschi to Michelangelo: The Representation of Architecture*, Milano: Rizzoli.

Molnár, V. (2013), *Building the State: Architecture, Politics, and State Formation in Post-War Central Europe*, London: Routledge.

Moon, K. (2005), *Modelling Messages: The Architect and the Model*, New York: The Monacelli Press.

Morris, M. (2006), *Models: Architecture and the Miniature*, Chichester: Wiley Academy.

Mueller-Tischler, U. (2010), 'Der Raum muss ein Geheimnis haben. Der Bühnenbildner Bert Neumann über den Reiz des Flüchtigen, künstlerische Freiheit, und die Rückeroberung des öffentlichen Raumes im Gespräch mit Ute Mueller-Tischler', *Theater der Zeit*, November Heft 11, 8–11.

Newman, L. M., ed. (1995), *The Correspondence of Edward Gordon Craig and Count Harry Kessler*, London: W.S. Maney & Son.

Nietzsche, F. (1998 [1962]), *Philosophy in the Tragic Age of the Greeks*, trans. with an introduction by Marianne Cowan. Washington, DC: Regnery Publishing Inc.

Norberg-Schulz, C. ([1958] 1991), 'A Talk with Mies van der Rohe', trans. and reprinted in Fritz Neumeyer, *The Artless World. Mies van der Rohe on the Building Art*, 338–339, Cambridge, MA: The MIT Press.

O'Doherty, B. (1976), *Inside the White Cube: The Ideology of the Gallery Space*, Berkeley and Los Angeles: University of California Press.

Oldenziel, R. and Zachmann, K. (2009), 'Kitchens as Technology and Politics: An Introduction', in Oldenziel, R. and Zachmann, K. (eds), *Cold War Kitchen: Americanization, Technology, and European Users*, 1–29, Cambridge, MA: The MIT Press.

Olivier, M. (2005), 'Jean-Nicolas Servandoni's Spectacles of Nature and Technology', *French Forum* 30 (2): 31–47.

Orton, K. (2004), *Model Making for the Stage: A Practical Guide*, Ramsbury: The Crowood Press.

O'Toole, S. (2013), *Mies 1:1 Golf Club Project by Robbrecht & Daem*. Available at: http://www.bdonline.co.uk/mies-11-golf-club-project-by-robbrecht-and -daem/5057873.article (accessed 3 January 2017).

Paduan, U. L. (1966), 'Teatri e "Teatri del Mondo" nella Venezia del Cinquecento', *Arte Veneta, Rivista di Storia Dellarte* 1: 37–46.

Palmer, S.D. (2013), *Light: Readings in Theatre Practice*, Basingstoke: Palgrave Macmillan.

Peacock, J. (1995), *The Stage Designs of Inigo Jones: The European Context*, Cambridge: Cambridge University Press.

Pelletier, L. (2006), *Architecture in Words. Theatre, Language and the Sensuous Space of Architecture*, London and New York: Routledge.

Perren, C. and Breen Lovett, S., eds. (2013), *Reverse Projections: Expanded Architecture at The Rocks*, Sydney: Broken Dimanche Press.

Perren, C. and Breen Lovett, S., eds. (2016), *Expanded Architecture: Temporal Formal Practices*, Leipzig: AADR Art Architecture Design Research Bauhaus Edition 47.

Plato. (2000), *The Republic*, ed. G.R.F. Ferrari, trans. Tom Griffith, Cambridge: Cambridge University Press.

Plato. (2008), *Timaeus and Critias*, trans. Robin Waterfield, Oxford: Oxford University Press.

Pollesch, R. (2015), 'Jeder Raum, den du gebaut hast, erzählt diese Autonomie, lieber Bert. Und lässt einen an der eigenen Autonomie bauen'. Available at: http://www.nachtkritik.de/index.php?option=com_content&view=article&id=11355:laudatio-fuer-bert-neumann-von-rene-pollesch-zur-verleihung-des-hein-heckroth-buehnenbildpreises-im-2015&catid=53:portraet-a-profil&Itemid=83 (accessed 4 January 2017).

Pommer, R., Herbert, C., Frampton, K. and Kolbowski, S., eds. (1981), *Idea As Model: (22 Architects 1976/1908)*, New York: Institute for Architecture and Urban Studies.

Pormale, M. (2011), *Exhibit No. 17*. Available at: http://www.intersection.cz/umelci2/monika-pormale-2/ (accessed 4 November 2016).

Portoghesi, P. (1980), *Prima Mostra Internazionale di Architettura: La Presenza del Passato/First International Architecture Exhibition: The Presence of the Past*, Venice: Corderie dell'Arsenale, Edizioni La Biennale di Venezia.

Quatremère De Quincy, A. C. (1830), *Histoire de la Vie et des Ouvrages des Plus Célèbres Architectes...*, Volume 2, Paris: Paul Renouard.

Quiccheberg, S. (1565), *Inscriptiones vel tituli Theatri Amplissimi, complectentis rerum vniuersitatis singulas materias et imagines eximias*, Munich: Ex officina Adami Berg typographi, anno 1565.

Reid, P. (1976), *Theory and Craft of the Scenographic Model*, Carbondale: Southern Illinois University Press.

Reid, S. E. (2008), 'Our Kitchen Is Just as Good: Soviet Responses to the American National Exhibition in Moscow, 1959', in Pavitt, J. and Crowley, D. (eds), *Cold War Modern: Design 1945–1970*, 154–161, London: V & A Publications.

Rendell, J. (2009), *The Re-Assertion of Time into) Critical Spatial Practice*, Massey: Massey University.

Rossi, A. (1981), *A Scientific Autobiography*, Cambridge, MA and London: The MIT Press.

Rossi, A. (1982), *The Architecture of the City*, trans. D. Ghirardo and J. Ockman (revised for the American Edition by Aldo Rossi, and Peter Eisenman), Cambridge, MA and London: The MIT Press.

Sabbatini, N. (1638), *Pratica di fabrica scene e machine ne' teatri*, Ravenna: Per Pietro de' Paoli e Gio. Battista Giouannelli stampatori.

Sass, L. (2014), *Project Summary Digital Design Fabrication Group*. Available at: https://ddf.mit.edu/news/2014/project-summary (accessed 29 May 2017).

Schmidt, H. (1927), *Die Wohnungsausstellung*, Stuttgart: Das Werk.

Schwartz, F. J. (1996), *The Werkbund: Design Theory and Mass Culture before the First World War*, New Haven, CT: Yale University Press.

Sejima, K. (2010), 'Introduction'. Available at: http://www.labiennale.org/en/architecture/archive/exhibition/sejima (accessed 4 January 2017).

Semper, M. (1904), *Theater Handbuch der Architektur*. Part 4, 6th Semi-Volume, Booklet 5, Stuttgart: Arnold Bergstraesser.

Senelick, L. (1982), *Gordon Craig's Moscow Hamlet. A Reconstruction*, Westport and London: Greenwood Press.

Sirk, D. (1971), *Sirk on Sirk. Interviews with Jon Halliday*, London: Secker & Warburg in association with the British Film Institute.

Smith, A. P. C. (2004), *Architectural Model as Machine: A New View of Models from Antiquity to the Present Day*, Boston: Architectural Press.

Smits-Veldt, M. B and Spies, M. (2012), 'Vondel's Life', in Bloemendal, Jan (ed), *Joost van den Vondel (1587–1679): Dutch Playwright in the Golden Age*, 51–84, Volume 1, Leiden: Koninklijke Brill.

Speck, L. (2012), 'Futurama', in Albrecht, D. (ed) *Norman Bel Geddes Designs America*, 289–303, New York: Abrams.

Stachowiak, H. (1973), *Allgemeine Modelltheorie*, Wien: Springer Verlag.

'Stage Scenery: Mr Craig's Inventions' (1911), *The Times* (London, England), 23 September: 8; Issue 39698.

Streitberger, W. R. (2016), *The Masters of the Revels and Elizabeth I's Court Theatre*, Cambridge: Cambridge University Press.

Sudjic, D. (2010), *Norman Foster: A life in Architecture*, New York: The Overlook Press.

Szacka, L-C. (2012), 'The 1980 Architecture Biennale: The Street as a Spatial and Representational Curating Device', in *Exhibitions Showing and Producing Architecture*, 14–25, OASE 88, Rotterdam: The Netherlands Architecture Fund.

Tafuri, M. (1980), 'L'Éphémère est Eternel: Aldo Rossi a Venezia', *Domus* 602: 7–11.

Tarn, J. N. (1974), *Five Per Cent Philanthropy: An Account of Housing in Urban Areas Between 1840 and 1914*, Cambridge: Cambridge University Press, London.

Taussig, M. (1993), *Mimesis and Alterity: A Particular History of the Senses*, New York and London: Routledge.

Tegethoff, W. (1981), *Die Villen und Landhausprojekte von Mies van der Rohe*, Volume 1, Essen.

Tesch, S. (2016), *Hitler's Architekten. Albert Speer (1905–1981)*, Wien, Weimar, Köln: Boehlau Verlag.

Turner, H. S. (2006), *The English Renaissance Stage: Geometry, Poetics and the Practical Spatial Arts 1580–1630*, Oxford: Oxford University Press.

Uricchio, W. (2012), 'A Palimpsest of Place and Past', *Performance Research: On Technology & Memory* 17: 45–49.

Vicentini, Andrea (1593), *Il 'teatro del mondo' galleggiante, progettato da Vincenzo Scamozzi per l'incoronazione della dogaressa Morosina Grimani*.

Viebrock, A. (2011), *Box No. 12, THE THINGS/DIE DINGE. Scenographic Installation*. Available at: http://www.intersection.cz/umelci2/anna-viebrock (accessed 4 November 2016).

Virilio, P. (1994), *The Vision Machine*, trans. J. Rose, Bloomington and Indianapolis: Indiana University Press.

Vitruvius (1999), *Ten Books on Architecture*, ed. and trans. I. D. Rowland and T. Howe, Cambridge: Cambridge University Press.

Wartofsky, M. W. (1979), *Models: Representation and the Scientific Understanding*, Dordrecht, Holland, Boston: D. Reidel Publishing Company.

Weihsmann, H. (1998), *Bauen Unterm Hakenkreuz. Architektur des Untergangs*, Wien: Promedia-Verlag.

West, W. N. (2002), *Theatres and Encyclopedias in Early Modern Europe*, Cambridge: Cambridge University Press.

Wolters, R. (1941), 'Neue Deutsche Baukunst', in Speer, Albert (ed), *Neue Deutsche Baukunst*, Berlin: Volk und Reich Verlag.

Yates, F. (1996), *The Art of Memory*, London: Routledge.

Yeats, W. B. ([1911] 2007), Preface to 'Plays for an Irish Theatre, Variorum Plays 1301', in Fleischer, M., *Embodied Texts: Symbolist Playwright–Dancer Collaborations*, Amsterdam/New York: Rodopi.

Zedelmaier, H. (2008), 'Navigieren im Textuniversum. Theodor Zwingers Theatrum Vitae Humanae'. Available at: http://www.metaphorik.de/sites/www.metaphorik.de/files/journal-pdf/14_2008_zedelmaier.pdf,113–135 (accessed 16 December 2016).

Zimmerman, C. (2014), *Photographic Architecture in the Twentieth Century*, Minneapolis: University of Minnesota Press.

Zucker, P. (1917), 'Zur Geschichte des Klassizistischen Buehnenbildes', *Monatsheft fuer Kunstwissenschaft* 2/3: 65–96.

About the Authors

Thea Brejzek is Professor for Spatial Theory at the University of Technology Sydney, Director of the Interior and Spatial Design Program in the School of Design at UTS, and Co-Director of the Joint PhD program 'Critical Spatial Thinking: Performative Practices and Narrative Spaces in Design' in collaboration with TU Berlin. She has a background in opera stage directing and theatre studies. From 2007 to 2012 she was a Professor at Zurich University of the Arts (ZHdK), Switzerland. In her research, she publishes and lectures widely on the history and theory of scenography and performative environments with a particular interest in transdisciplinary practices and the politics of space in performance. In 2011, Thea Brejzek was the Founding Curator for Theory at the Prague Quadrennial for Performance Design and Space (PQ). She is a member of the scientific advisory board of the Bauhaus Dessau and Associate Editor of the Routledge journal, *Theatre and Performance Design* and has been Visiting Professor at Bartlett School of Architecture.

Lawrence Wallen is Professor and Head of the School of Design at the University of Technology Sydney, Director of the spatial prototyping lab and Co-Director of the Joint PhD program 'Critical Spatial Thinking: Performative Practices and Narrative Spaces in Design' in collaboration with TU Berlin. He has a background in architecture, visual arts and design. From 2002 to 2012 he was Professor of Scenography at the Zurich University of the Arts (ZHdK). His spatial practice ranges from stage design and installation to immersive and ambient media with recent projects realised in Italy, Australia and Cyprus, combined with a body of scholarly research focused on scenography, material thinking, spatial practices and landscape theory. He has been a guest artist at the Centre for Art and Media (ZKM) in Germany and is Head of Applied Media at the Salzburg Urstein Institute.

Long-term collaborators Thea Brejzek and Lawrence Wallen are Research Fellows at TU Berlin and have been awarded Bogliasco Fellowships in 2017.

Index

Note: Locators with the letter 'n' refer to notes.